Industrial Policy American Style

Industrial Policy American Style

From
Hamilton
to HDTV

Richard D. Bingham

M. E. Sharpe
Armonk, New York
London, England

Copyright © 1998 by M. E. Sharpe, Inc.

Library of Congress Cataloging-in-Publication Data

Bingham, Richard D.
Industrial policy American-style: from Hamilton to HDTV
by Richard D. Bingham.
p. cm.
Includes bibliographical references and index.
ISBN 1–56324–596–5 (cloth: alk. paper). —
ISBN 1–56324–597–3 (pbk. : alk. paper)
1. Industrial policy—United States. I. Title.
HD3616.U47B564 1997
338.973—dc21
97–20514
CIP

Printed in the United States of America

The paper used in this publication meets the minimum requirements of
American National Standard for Information Sciences—
Permanence of Paper for Printed Library Materials,
ANSI Z 39.48-1984.

BM (c)   10   9   8   7   6   5   4   3   2   1
BM (p)   10   9   8   7   6   5   4   3   2   1

Dedicated
to
Helen Donnelly Bingham

Contents

Preface

Interest in industrial policy in the United States is always in a state of flux—its ebb and flow being related to the state of the economy. During good times the American people show little interest in it; during bad times it moves to the top of the political agenda. What may seem like an obscure concern today will not be so tomorrow.

While the topic of industrial policy may rise and fall in the marketplace of ideas, opinions about American industrial policy among economists, political scientists, academics in general, and journalists of most of the nation's influential media are pretty fixed. For all of them America's industrial policy is a disaster. Those on the right see almost any aid to American industries as an inefficient distortion of a pretty efficient market system. For those from the left, efficiency is also a concern. But they see American industrial policy as a bunch of inefficient, uncoordinated, sector-specific programs, often operating at odds with each other. For them, an industrial policy modeled after Japan's would be far more appealing.

Industrial policy is by its very nature political. And as with most things political, there is no one correct answer, but there are a lot of different perspectives. This is one of those perspectives, though I hope it is both a unique one and one that makes some sense.

Purpose of the Book

After studying and teaching about the American economy and industrial policy, and founding and editing the journal *Economic Develop-*

ment Quarterly, I began to see industrial policy in a different way. I began to see that it was much more deeply ingrained into the fabric of American policy than most conservatives would care to admit. I also saw that, over the years, there were more regularities to the policy than liberals would suggest. This book puts forth a position that is clearly centrist and, as such, presents some new ideas. Centrist positions are not always heard.

Another major observation comes from my studies. That is, to understand what industrial policy is really all about at any given point in time, it is better to watch what politicians *do* rather than to listen to what they *say*. In fact, it is probably better not to listen to them at all, for like most people with deeply held beliefs, they often let their ideology interfere with their perception of reality.

The final thing I have noticed about industrial policy is that it is constantly evolving. It is always there but it is always changing. For a while the government will focus on one type of industry, say real estate. But ten years later one might look again and find that real estate is out of vogue and that the major focus of industrial policy is on something entirely new and different.

Organization of the Book

Books like this one do not have the suspense of an Elmore Leonard novel. But that does not mean that they need be uninteresting and fail to hold the reader's attention. Unfortunately, many are written that way. Part of the problem is that they resemble instruction manuals. The author outlines at the beginning what the book is going to tell us. Then he tells us what he wants to tell us. Then he tells us what he told us. Reading such a book is about as much fun as reading an economics text. (My apologies to Paul Samuelson.)

By avoiding this process I hope to hold your attention. I will start by talking about industrial policy and the politics of industrial policy in general. I next briefly look at some examples of industry policies over the past hundred years. This is only to show that industrial policy is hardly a new idea for the United States. But the focus of the book is on the last twenty years—Jimmy Carter's presidency through Bill Clinton's first term.

The book exposes the basic elements of contemporary industrial policy—elements that conservatives cannot see and liberals will not see.

If the book works, the conclusion follows logically. A few of the conclusions I have already mentioned briefly—but most I have not.

There is also a curious appendix to the book entitled "Japanese Industrial Policy: Does It Work?" This was originally one of the chapters, but my editor convinced me that including it in the front of the book "takes away momentum." She was right. But this is not to trivialize the material in the appendix. To really understand America's industrial policy, one needs to understand Japan's. The appendix provides this opportunity. Readers not intimately familiar with Japan's industrial policy might want to start with this little diversion.

Acknowledgments

Professor Koji Sato of Kanagawa University was kind enough to review the appendix for historical and technical accuracy. (The conclusions, however, are mine alone.) My friends and colleagues, John Blair of Wright State University and David Morgan of the University of Oklahoma, provided early support for the project. An extremely thoughtful external reviewer of the initial manuscript convinced me to make major changes in the ways in which some of the arguments were framed and presented. My editor at M.E. Sharpe, Patricia Kolb, successfully mediated the differences between the reviewer and myself and made some great suggestions herself. My copyeditor, Susanna Sharpe, was terrific.

My thanks also go to my administrative assistant at Cleveland State University, Muriel Robinson. I never did make sense of the publisher's formatting and word-processing requirements, but Muriel did.

I am indebted to Cleveland State University's faculty leave (sabbatical) program. The university provided me with the support to spend a year in Washington, D.C., researching and writing this book. My Thai and Thai-American friends provided a needed respite—Jiab, Rose, Tom, and little Kristy, to name a few. And Claire, as always, was there when I needed her.

Richard D. Bingham
Cleveland, Ohio

Abbreviations and Acronyms

ACRS	accelerated cost recovery system
ADC	acquisition, development, and construction
AFDC	Aid to Families with Dependent Children
AMLCD	active-matrix display
ARM	adjustable rate mortgage
ARPA	Advanced Research Projects Agency
ATP	Advanced Technology Program
BRIE	Berkeley Roundtable on the International Economy
CAB	Civil Aeronautics Board
CCC	Commodity Credit Corporation
CMI	civil-military integration
COLA	cost-of-living allowance
CRADA	cooperative R&D projects
CRT	cathode ray tube
CVD	countervailing duty
DARPA	Defense Advanced Research Projects Agency
DDI	Daini Denden (Japanese communications company)
DIDC	Depository Institutions Deregulation Committee
DIDMCA	Depository Institutions Deregulation and Monetary Control Act
DoD	Department of Defense

DoE	Department of Energy
DSB	Defense Science Board
DSU	Dispute Settlement Understanding (of World Trade Organization)
EHFA	Electric Home and Farm Authority
ELD	electroluminescent display
EPG	Economic Policy Group
ERTA	Economic Recovery Tax Act of 1981
Fannie Mae	Federal National Mortgage Association
FCC	Federal Communications Commission
FDIC	Federal Deposit Insurance Corporation
FEDs	field-emission displays
FHA	Federal Housing Administration
FHL	Federal Home Loan banks
FHLBB	Federal Home Loan Bank Board
FIRREA	Financial Institutions Reform, Recovery and Enforcement Act
FMS	flexible manufacturing system
FPDs	flat panel displays
FSLIC	Federal Savings and Loan Insurance Corporation
GAAP	generally accepted accounting principles
GATS	General Agreement on Trade in Services
GATT	General Agreement on Tariffs and Trade
GDP	gross domestic product
GM	General Motors
HDS	high-definition systems
HDTV	high-definition television
HTS	high-temperature superconductivity
HUD	Department of Housing and Urban Development
ICBMs	intercontinental ballistic missiles
ICC	Interstate Commerce Commission
IP	industrial policy
ISIS	International Superconductivity Industry Summit
JAST	joint advanced strike aircraft
KSP	Kanagawa Science Park
LCD	liquid-crystal display
LDP	Liberal Democratic Party (Japan)
MAFF	Ministry of Agriculture, Forestry, and Fisheries (Japan)
MFA	Multi-fiber Agreement

MITI	Ministry of International Trade and Industry (Japan)
MOF	Ministry of Finance (Japan)
MOSS	market-oriented, sector-specific trade agreement
mpg	miles per gallon
MPT	Ministry of Posts and Telecommunications
NAFTA	North American Free Trade Agreement
NASA	National Aeronautics and Space Administration
NCAICM	National Center for Advanced Information Components Manufacturing
NCRA	National Cooperative Research Act of 1984
NFPDI	National Flat Panel Display Initiative
NIST	National Institute of Science and Technology
NOI	net operating income
NRA	National Recovery Administration
NTT	Nippon Telegraph and Telephone
OECD	Organization for Economic Cooperation and Development
OMB	Office of Management and Budget
OSTP	Office of Science and Technology Policy
OTS	Office of Thrift Supervision
PDP	plasma-display panel
PIPS	pattern information processing system
PMLCD	passive-matrix display
PNGV	Partnership for a New Generation of Vehicles
R&D	research and development
RAP	regulatory accounting principles
RFC	Reconstruction Finance Corporation
RTC	Resolution Trust Corporation
S&Ls	savings and loans
Sematech	semiconductor manufacturing technology
SIA	Semiconductor Industry Association
SME	semiconductor materials and equipment suppliers
SMES	superconductivity magnetic energy storage systems
SPI	Superconductivity Partnership Initiative
STR	Special Representative for Trade Negotiations
TPM	trigger price mechanism
TRA	Tax Reform Act of 1986
UAW	United Auto Workers
UDAG	Urban Development Action Grant

USABC	United States Advanced Battery Consortium
USCAR	United States Council for Automotive Research
USITC	United States International Trade Commission
USTR	United States Trade Representative
VER	voluntary export restraint
VLSI	very large-scale integrated circuit
WFC	War Finance Corporation
WTO	World Trade Organization
Zenno	National Federation of Farmers (Japan)
zoku	LDP Farm Policy Group (Japan)

Industrial Policy American Style

1

What's in a Name?

Since the early 1970s, Americans have generally been concerned about the economy, and with some justification. The nation experienced a period of incredible inflation coupled with high interest rates. It went through a depression like nothing that had been seen in recent times. But that was some time ago. Most Americans have done pretty well over the past fifteen years. In his economic report to the Congress in 1992, President Bush told us that the U.S. economy is the largest and strongest in the world; that the American people enjoy the highest standard of living on earth; that American productivity is second to none; and that, with less than 5 percent of the world's population, America produces one-fourth of the world's output.[1]

And President Clinton, in his 1995 economic report, reminded the American people that the performance of the economy in 1994 was outstanding; that nonfarm employment grew by 3.5 million jobs; that the unemployment rate was only 5.4 percent; and that the core rate of consumer price inflation registered its smallest increase in 28 years.[2] So why the concern?

Because things are not always what they seem. For example, median family income in 1993, adjusted for inflation, was virtually unchanged from what it was twenty years earlier, in spite of the fact that real output had increased by 57 percent. Also, in 1993, the number of Americans living in poverty reached a thirty-year high of 39.3 million. In part as a result of rapid changes in technology and the global economy, the real average earnings of male high school graduates declined by 15 percent between 1979 and 1992. Almost one-fourth of all women who ever received Aid to Families with Dependent Children (AFDC) ended up receiving AFDC for more than ten years during their lifetimes. Personal savings also declined—from about 5.5 percent in the 1970s to only 3.5 percent today. And, in recent years, about 2 million American workers each year have lost their jobs through no fault of their own when plants closed or massive layoffs occurred.

On the international front, America's merchandise trade deficit rose by 2.7 percent of gross domestic product (GDP) in 1994, reaching a total of $169 billion. The value of U.S. assets owned by foreigners is larger than the value of foreign assets owned by Americans, and that gap continues to grow. Also, in 1994, the value of the dollar declined about 8 percent against the currencies of the nine major foreign industrial countries.[3]

We have entered a new world order, one in which we are no longer the undisputed economic leader. Significant economic problems arise every day: stock prices decline, the economy "overheats," the value of the dollar falls against international currencies, or the Japanese fail to import "enough" American-made cars. And each of these economic events causes the government to take action. That action might affect the entire economy in general, as when the Federal Reserve raises the discount rate. Or it may be sector-specific action, like the legislation enacted in 1994 essentially to complete the deregulation of the trucking industry.

These two examples illustrate the two ways in which the national government attempts to influence the nation's economy, either with economywide policies like Federal Reserve actions, or with sector-specific policies like the deregulation of the trucking industry. The latter is a sectoral industry policy. The nation's overall industrial policy is made up of the sum total of its sectoral policies.

Ideally, these sectoral industrial policies are *coordinated* and *rational*. Otis Graham, Jr., a professor of history at the University of California at Santa Barbara, defines a nation's comprehensive industrial policy as "a nation's declared, official, total effort to influence sectoral development and thus, national industrial portfolio."[4] This would indeed be ideal—a declared, official industrial policy. But in the United States this has never been.

In spite of the sustained efforts of a strong and popular president in

Franklin D. Roosevelt, a planned economic system in the United States never came about. Instead, from the Great Depression emerged a "broker state" political economy.[5]

> In that system . . . the government did not look ahead, aiming at coherent strategic objectives. Instead, the Broker State orchestrated the conflict of organized interest groups. Washington was not the site of a government with its own purposes, but of a sort of modified marketplace, a "parallelogram of pressures," or place of political exchange where groups within the economy and society brought their special problems and bargained for state-conferred benefits. The economy aimed itself; the government's role was to ensure that it did not slow down, too much, for too long. The style of policymaking was incremental and piecemeal, the government's time horizon close in, timed to the electoral cycle. It displayed a weak sense of an overriding public interest and a deferential reliance upon the electorate's, and in particular large corporations' private agendas. It was a reactive system, flexible and responsive to its admirers, aimless and without vision to its detractors.[6]

A broker state, of course, could not have a declared, official industrial policy. It could have only a de facto industrial policy. And that is what the United States has—"an unacknowledged mélange of all federal, state, and local government policies affecting goods producing sectors."[7]

But this book is hardly the first to raise the specter of a de facto industrial policy. Graham's book on the industrial policy debate is replete with quotes from academics and government officials about this policy. Commerce Department aide Jerry Jasinowski raised the issue during the Carter administration: "It seems increasingly clear that the government has always pursued industrial policies. . . ."[8] Carter's domestic chief of staff, Stuart Eizenstat, called the U.S. policy "a crazy-quilt—a makeshift industrial policy of often contradictory individual decisions."[9] Graham quotes automaker Lee Iacocca: "'We have an industrial policy,' it began far back in the colonial era, and today 'it's a bad one.'"[10] Harvard law professor Julian Gresser: "We already have an industrial policy—it is just an ineffective one."[11] MIT economist Lester Thurow: "America now has an industrial policy. It just happens to be an industrial policy to shoot ourselves in the economic foot."[12] And economist and former Secretary of Labor Robert Reich: "Thus evolved the haphazard pattern of industrial policies—the state responding to industrial crisis. . . ."[13]

It would thus not be an understatement to say that America's industrial policy is not perceived in positive terms by those who think about it. Graham puts it pretty succinctly: "The existence of a de facto IP, once discovered, had no defenders. A nation should have either no IP, or an effective one; it should not have a de facto IP that no one would defend."[14]

But what upsets the industrial policy critics is not that the IP is de facto, in reality or fact, or is a mélange, a mixture of policies, but more that it is a hodgepodge, a mixture of dissimilar ingredients. In fact, it is such a hodgepodge that it has remained largely undefined. But can it be defined? As is the case of most public policies, there are regularities to be found in our sectoral policies. And there are enough regularities so that if one looks hard enough, certain dimensions appear. And if one analyzes those dimensions it may turn out that U.S. industrial policy is not such a hodgepodge after all. And, it may not even be that dissimilar from Japan's industrial policy, which is very structured indeed.

Industrial Policy Defined

Graham's definition of industrial policy, raised several paragraphs ago, is a good one—"a nation's declared, official, total effort to influence sectoral development and thus, national industrial portfolio"—although it is probably a little strict. Among the industrialized nations, Japan probably comes closest to having a "declared, official" effort to influence sectoral development with its extraordinary laws on various industrial sectors (e.g., semiconductors). But even in Japan, industrial policy is not always declared or official. Japanese bureaucrats have enormous discretionary power and make industrial policy through interpretation and administrative guidance (see the appendix for a thorough discussion). So for our purposes, we will loosen Graham's definition a little and define industrial policy as *a nation's official total effort to influence sectoral development and thus, the national industrial portfolio.*

It is also useful at this point to distinguish between national industrial policy and industrial policies as they apply to specific industries. A policy for a specific industry is not really an industrial policy. Instead it is an *industry policy,* because it pertains to one specific industry. Thus, a nation's industrial policy is the sum total of its specific industry policies.

Industrial Policy and Economic Policy

Economic policy and industrial policy are terms that are often used interchangeably, but they are not the same thing. The term *economic policy* is both much broader and more confusing. It is more confusing in that it is in widespread general usage but is seldom defined. For example, the *MIT Dictionary of Modern Economics*[15] doesn't mention it at all. In the *McGraw-Hill Encyclopedia of Economics,*[16] economic policy is not a subject in the text but is found in the index with the following subheadings: agricultural, antidumping, antitrust, contestable market theory, economic planning and economic policy, externalities, macroeconomic and economic policy, and poverty. The *Fortune Encyclopedia of Economics*[17] devotes Chapter 4 to "Economic Policy" without ever saying what it means. Chapter 4 has short articles by leading economists on the following topics: Federal Budget, Federal Debt, Fiscal Policy, Government Spending, Industrial Policy, Monetary Policy, Phillips Curve, Privatization, Reaganomics, Redistribution of Income, Social Security, and Unemployment Insurance.

In discussing economic policy in his text, economist William Shepard comes close to a definition when he says, "The basic results of good economic performance have long been recognized to include efficiency, progress, equity, and certain wider benefits."[18] For us, this is good enough.

The relationship between industrial policy and economic policy is shown in Figure 1.1. As can be seen, industrial policy (and subsequently all the specific industry policies) is totally subsumed under the broader economic policy as are fiscal and monetary policy. But other policy areas are only partially subsumed under economic policy. Take education policy as an example. The part of national education policy that deals with increasing the number of college graduate engineers in our society so that American industries remain internationally competitive, for example, would also be a part of the nation's economic policy. On the other hand, the part of education policy that provides Head Start classes to economically deprived children in order that they may enter kindergarten with the same cognitive skills as the economically more fortunate, is not. It is part of a broader social policy.

Is it possible for education policy or manpower policy to also be industrial policy? It is conceivable although unlikely. If, for example, the U.S. government began a grant program that would pay the tuition

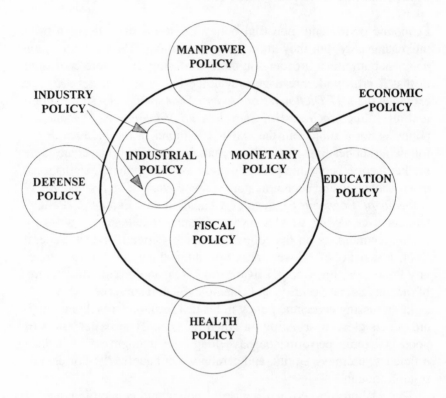

Figure 1.1. **Relationship of American National Industrial Policy to Economic Policy**

for biotechnology engineers to obtain graduate school training in some exotic form of biotechnology *to keep the United States in "first place" in the biotechnology field*, that would be industrial policy because the effort was aimed at a specific industry. Pell grants, on the other hand, are not industrial policy.

The Pros and Cons of Industrial Policy

There are good reasons why a nation should have an industrial policy, and there are good reasons why a nation should not. The principal goal of a nation's economic policy is to produce a high and rising standard of living for its citizens. The ability of a country to do so depends on the productivity[19] with which its resources are deployed. Productivity depends on both the quality and the features of the nation's products and services (which determine price) and the efficiency with which they are produced.[20] And given that a nation's industrial policy is part of its economic policy, these are also the industrial policy's goals— making the country's industries more efficient and productive.

Industrial policies are sometimes developed to provide a nation with the presence of an industry it deems vital to its economic future. This was the case with Japan's development of the semiconductor industry (see the Appendix), and it is now the case with U.S. attempts to develop a commercially viable flat panel display industry (see Chapter 6).

Market failure is a common reason for nations to adopt industrial policies. In the United States most utilities are publicly licensed monopolies. There is thus little incentive for them to be innovative or particularly efficient. An industrial policy might be adopted to move a protected industry in a direction it ultimately would have taken itself had it been in a competitive environment. This is indeed the direction suggested for the development of high-temperature superconductivity in Chapter 7.

Sometimes industrial policies are adopted to promote the national interest or to correct an industry's negative externalities. This was most likely the government's motive in initiating the Partnership for a New Generation of Vehicles (also discussed in Chapter 7). It is in the nation's best interests to have a fuel-efficient, nonpolluting automobile, but it is not necessarily in the auto companies' best interests.

There is a belief among some that technology-intensive industries make special contributions to the long-term health of the American economy. As economist Laura Tyson points out:

> A dollar's worth of shoes may have the same effect on the trade balance as a dollar's worth of computers. But . . . the two do not have the same effect on employment, wages, labor skills, productivity, and research— all major determinants of our long-term economic health. In addition, because technology-intensive industries finance a disproportionate share of the nation's R&D spending, there is a strong presumption . . . that they generate positive externalities for the rest of the economy.[21]

If this is indeed the case, a serious argument can be made for an industrial policy that promotes high-technology industries.

Some components of trade policy are also part of industrial policy. Those components push nations with restrictive trade practices into opening up their markets. The Section 301 regulation discussed in Chapter 4 is an example. Section 301 is used to deter or compensate for foreign practices not adequately covered by multilateral rules. A portion of Chapter 4 discusses President Clinton's efforts to open up the Japanese market to U.S. autos and auto parts—an example of a 301 action.

But, in truth, industrial policies do not always make a nation's industries more efficient and productive. Sometimes they backfire and actually promote a misallocation of resources as some of the cases in this book show. One of the most egregious of these involved the Economic Recovery Tax Act (ERTA) of 1981, discussed at length in Chapter 5. The act caused a frenzy of overbuilding of commercial structures and multifamily dwelling units, which in turn contributed to the savings and loan debacle (Chapter 3). Thus many economists are wary of industrial policies. For example, most economists subscribe to the theory of comparative advantage. And most have serious doubts about a government's ability to identify general criteria that will allow one to predict the industries in which a country will be particularly successful.

Charles Schultze, the chair of President Carter's Council of Economic Advisers, like others, feared that the United States would most likely end up supporting older and troubled industries that other governments are heavily subsidizing. This would lead to a systematic reallocation of investment away from other American industries and toward those that would lower the growth of national output and thus real wages.

Schultze also contends that the American political system is incapable of making choices among particular firms or industries, determining which ones will prosper and which will not. Yet such choices are exactly those that have to be made for industrial policy to be anything more than a political pork barrel.[22]

Many analysts hold that the competitive marketplace would be replaced by a new coordinating mechanism that would create more distortions than those it would seek to remedy. If business planners cannot see beyond next quarter's profit-and-loss statement, how can one expect government decision makers to behave any differently?

Then there is the issue of other people's money. Those in govern-

ment can hardly be expected to bet other people's money more care-
fully than those who bet their own.[23]

The Public Debate over Industrial Policy

The public discussion of an industrial policy for the United States, in
any modern sense, began in the Carter administration with events that
were even then considered obscure. Graham has said that "Industrial
Policy was part of Carter's vanished legacy. . . . Carter's involvement
with the IP idea went virtually unnoticed."[24]

It began in 1977 over steel. It was the old, now-familiar story.
American steel could no longer compete with European, Asian, and
South American facilities. In August and September of 1977 alone,
fourteen mills closed, costing 20,000 workers their jobs. A steel caucus
in Congress became active, crying for presidential action. President
Carter was forced to establish a "trigger price mechanism" (TPM)—a
price floor for foreign steel. The TPM was to give the steel companies
some time to modernize. Instead, they chose to diversify (e.g., U.S.
Steel became USX, reflecting its diversification). This was hardly an
auspicious beginning for sectoral management.

The second cloud on the industrial horizon was the near failure of the
Chrysler Corporation and an estimated potential loss of half a million
jobs. Chrysler was the last in a decade of bailouts that included the Penn
Central and Lockheed. But it was Chrysler that grabbed the public's
attention. Railroads were always viewed by the public as a sort of
utility, and Lockheed was unique because of its national defense implications. But Chrysler was different. Arranging the Chrysler bailout
was an exhaustive process that preoccupied President Carter and cost
the White House and the federal bureaucracy thousands of hours in staff
time.[25] Much more will be said about Chrysler in Chapter 3.

But President Carter's flirtation with industrial policy encompassed
more than bailouts. In the later years of the administration, an Economic Policy Group (EPG) of cabinet-level officials was formed to
conduct a review of industrial policy. (A report on industrial problems
was required by the Trade Agreement Act of 1979.) A wide variety of
industrial policy ideas were kicked around by the group, including
discussions of America's "de facto" industrial policy, of "creating winners" and "restructuring less efficient industries," and of a revived
Reconstruction Finance Corporation. But the group was widely split

over the issues, and nothing definitive came from the discussions. Even the papers that emerged from the group's staff were inconclusive.[26]

Nothing regarding industrial policy ever formally emerged from the White House until August 28, 1980, when, in a campaign speech, President Carter announced an "Economic Revitalization Program." In it, the president proposed an industrial policy. Graham reports:

> The president had proposed: (1) a new institution, the Economic Revitalization Board, to institutionalize "cooperation" throughout the economy and to advise the president on the creation of (2) an "industrial development authority" (read "bank"). Along the way, he had proudly listed and stressed the great importance of sectoral interventions under way—building a new synfuels industry, doubling the size of coal output—and plans to "retool the automobile industry to . . . meet any competition from overseas," to modernize steel, and "to create a whole new industry to produce solar and other renewable energy systems." These were, by any definition, targeted industrial policies, and new policy-shaping institutions would guide them: an Economic Revitalization Board, a national development bank, and tripartite committees such as those set up in the steel and auto industries.[27]

But the proposal died as quickly as it was born. The Economic Revitalization Board never met, and Jimmy Carter lost the election and moved back to Georgia. In fact, the administration's parting shot was an apparent repudiation of his industrial policy ideas, declaring that the strategies of "picking winners," "supporting older industries," and "supplanting the private sector in allocating capital" were "industrial policy" and beyond the scope of federal activities.[28] And that was that.

When Ronald Reagan replaced Jimmy Carter, it was clear from the outset that he would have nothing to do with industrial policy—at least not publicly. But the public suddenly became interested in the idea. A series of books and articles appeared in the 1980s beginning with Pat Choate and Gail Schwartz's *Being Number One,*[29] Lester Thurow's *The Zero-Sum Society,*[30] and a special issue of *Business Week* magazine.[31]

The discourse raised by Thurow and *Business Week* was described by economist R.D. Norton[32] as a debate between the "preservationists" and the "modernizers." While neither Thurow nor *Business Week* raised the issue of targeted industrial policy, both urged a "reindustrialization" of America. Thurow called for a modern version of the Reconstruction Finance Corporation (RFC) to redirect investment from "sunset" to "sunrise" industries. For Thurow, the bank was needed because market forces failed to shift capital to growing industries fast enough. Thurow, of course, was one of the first modernizers.

In contrast, *Business Week* called for targeted industrial policies to counter market forces. In the second of *Business Week*'s special issues on the subject,[33] the authors suggested targeting industries to counter the market trends shifting funds to the energy and high-tech sectors in the South and West and away from traditional manufacturing in the Northeast and Midwest—a preservationist strategy.

Felix Rohatyn, an investment banker who ran New York's Municipal Assistance Corporation during the city's fiscal bailout, echoed the *Business Week* position. He suggested using an RFC-type organization to force modernization through capital investment by requiring concessions from management and labor.[34]

At about the same time, sociologist Amitai Etzioni published a compilation of essays he had written on the same subject.[35] He also saw market failure in the delivery of capital. He suggested channeling funds away from consumption and into investment in infrastructure and the capital goods sectors.

Also, at the same time, Robert Reich's *Next American Frontier*[36] appeared. Reich, a modernizer, became the spokesperson for the industrial policy cause by virtue of the support his ideas received from Walter Mondale, the Democratic candidate for president. Reich argued that America's economic competitors—specifically Japan, Germany, and France—recognized that the key to the economic future was in activities requiring skilled labor, such as custom-designed and/or technology-intensive products. The United States, on the other hand, was still mired in the old "Fordist" scheme left over from the past era of mass production. Reich thus advocated policies to move capital and labor into high value-added activities.

These proposals were hardly met with universal acceptance, particularly among economists.[37] The common criticisms fell into three camps. First was the question of whether the United States was actually experiencing a decline in competitiveness.[38] Second was a challenge to the assumption that market failure calls for government action.[39] And third was the charge that industrial policy proposals would result in more bureaucracy.[40]

This apparently intense public interest in industrial policy did not go unnoticed by the Democrats. Searching for an answer to Reagan's supply-side economics, industrial policy emerged as *the* Democratic alternative. Congressman John La Falce called it "the leading issue for 1984."[41] And the Democrats in Congress were quick to react. A count by the Library of Congress in November 1983 found seventeen bills proposing development boards, commissions on competitiveness, and so forth, with nine proposing a new RFC in some form or other.

The Reagan administration responded to the activity of the Democrats with a delaying action. In June 1983, the president appointed a Commission on Industrial Competitiveness "to identify sectoral problems and recommend changes in governmental policies to improve the private sector's competitive ability in international markets. . . ."[42] In a clear effort to diffuse the issue, the president called for the report after the 1984 election.

But the Democrats were not to be outdone and were ready to provide a legislative banner for the Democratic candidate for president to carry into the fall election. On February 8, 1984, House Resolution 4360 cleared Congressman La Falce's Subcommittee on Economic Stabilization (of the House Banking Committee). The resolution was then endorsed by the Banking Committee on April 10. The bill proposed (1) a sixteen-member tripartite Council on Industrial Competitiveness to conduct sectoral analyses, to form subcouncils for industries, and to provide advice to (2) a Bank for Industrial Competitiveness. The Bank was to provide government financial assistance to upgrade the nation's industrial structure.

Democrats being Democrats, the main impact of the bill was to split the party along regional and ideological lines. The bill split the high-technology Sunbelters from the mature industry Frostbelters. The major debate, of course, was over the Bank. The Sunbelt Congressmen were afraid that the ultimate purpose of the Bank would be to save the smokestack industries of the Northeast and Midwest.

All this did not go unnoticed by Walter Mondale and his staff. (Earlier Mondale had remarked "this'll do it for the Democrats," in response to reading Robert Reich's industrial policy book *The Next American Frontier*.) Mondale decided to distance himself from the legislation.

In fact, Mondale decided to distance himself from industrial policy in general. Neither Mondale nor President Reagan ever mentioned the words industrial policy in their debates or speeches. The only industrial policy issue mentioned in the campaign were the two candidates' plans to revitalize the steel industry. Reagan favored an agreement reducing steel imports while Mondale wanted a restructuring agreement from the industry in exchange for a five-year period of import restrictions.[43]

But why did Mondale back off? Mondale was "for" an industrial policy, but his concept of industrial policy was strictly limited. He thought of industrial policy essentially as a way to bail out industries (like steel) and companies (like Chrysler). The only difference between Mondale and a good many Republicans was that Mondale believed tough concessions had to be extracted from the "bailee" in exchange for government assistance. Besides, Mondale thought that attacking Reagan's macroeconomic policies was much more fertile ground.[44]

The last shot from the industrial policy cannon was the report from the president's Commission on Industrial Competitiveness. It proposed a cabinet-level Department of Science and Technology and a Department of Trade. But the president would have none of it. In response to a reporter's question, Reagan said that it was not the time for a government reorganization.[45] And that was that—at least for the moment.

But industrial policy was not quite dead. The caterpillar was back in its cocoon awaiting a new metamorphosis. And it came in 1988 under the guise of international competitiveness.

Competitiveness emerged from the Democrats' newfound interest in foreign trade. And trade policy was about all the Democrats had in order to mount a political assault on the president. After two years of work, the Congress passed a massive trade reform bill that was termed "protectionist" by the president and vetoed. Adjustments were made and the Omnibus Trade and Competitiveness Act of 1988 again passed Congress. This time it was signed by President Reagan in August, and with it came industrial policy. The act established a Competitiveness Policy Council of twelve members charged with identifying sectoral problems and developing and recommending corrective strategies. The Democrats' 1984 proposal became a reality (but without the Bank).

The competitiveness theme really changed the focus of the debate from micro to macro, at least for the next few years. Three broad themes emerged, drawing virtually no opposition: defects in fiscal policy, education, and research and development. Meanwhile, sector interventions broadened, but they were not discussed. The White House seemed to think that if it wasn't discussed it didn't exist.

As George Bush replaced Ronald Reagan, sectoral interventions became more pronounced and, for a moment, there was dissension in

the Republican ranks. Commerce Secretary Robert Mosbacher and Defense Advanced Research Projects Agency (DARPA) director Craig
Fields were both outspoken advocates of a comprehensive industrial
policy, particularly with regard to high-definition television (HDTV).
But their positions drew the wrath of the White House chief of staff.
Mosbacher was reprimanded and Fields was forced out of his job. As
far as George Bush was concerned, George Bush did not have an
industrial policy.[46]

But the public debate continued and even intensified, as the competitiveness issue swung back from macro to micro. (The accepted definition of competitiveness is the nation's ability to produce goods and
services that meet the test of international markets while the citizens
enjoy a rising and sustainable standard of living.)[47] The reason for the
debate is that technology-intensive industries (the subject of the competitiveness debate) violate the assumptions of free trade theory. The
characteristics of high-technology industries—imperfect competition,
strategic behavior, dynamic economies of scale, and technological externalities—make them fertile ground for industrial policy. A study by
the Organization for Economic Cooperation and Development
(OECD) holds that "Oligopolistic competition and strategic interaction
among firms and governments rather than the invisible hand of market
forces condition today's competitive advantage and international division of labor in high-technology industries."[48] Thus, competitiveness
and industrial policy have become like brother and sister.

One of the intellectual leaders of the competitiveness movement
was Michael Porter of the Harvard Business School. Porter's *The
Competitive Advantage of Nations* provided the intellectual framework
for the movement. Porter sought to replace traditional trade theory with a
new paradigm. He believes that the "assumptions underlying factor comparative advantage theories of trade are unrealistic in many industries,"[49]
that these assumptions are outdated, and that they "were more persuasive
in the eighteenth and nineteenth centuries, when many industries were
fragmented, production was more labor- and less skill-intensive, and
much trade reflected differences in growing conditions, natural resources, and capital."[50] Porter's theory concentrates on firms and industries:

> Theory begins from individual industries and competitors and builds up
> to the economy as a whole. The particular industry—passenger cars,

facsimile machines, accounting services, ball bearings—is where competitive advantage is either won or lost. The home nation influences the ability of its firms to succeed in particular industries. The outcome of thousands of struggles in individual industries determines the state of a nation's economy and its ability to progress.[51]

Porter's massive book (more than 850 pages) was music to the ears of the industrial policy community, for Porter saw government as an important influence on the four determinants of national competitive advantage. And those influences were the tools of industrial policy.[52]

At about the same time, a new movement appeared. Berkeley economist Laura D'Andrea Tyson and her colleagues at the Berkeley Roundtable on the International Economy (BRIE) became the leading proponents of a "managed trade" (some call it "strategic trade") policy for international competitiveness. Managed trade is commonly understood to encompass any trade agreements that establish quantitative targets on trade flows.[53] Tyson advocated that the United States should continue unilateral sector-specific negotiations with trading partners to obtain improved trading and investment opportunities for American companies. She advocated "aggressive unilateralism" through Section 301 and Super 301 (discussed in Chapter 4).

Then the Clinton administration came to power. At last, the industrial policy advocates had one of their own in the White House. But best of all, Bill Clinton looked like a free trader. He was a strong defender of the North American Free Trade Agreement (NAFTA) and continued to push for open markets in the Uruguay Round of the General Agreements on Tariffs and Trade (GATT). Thus, his political opponents painted him with this free trade brush (remember Ross Perot and his "giant sucking sound" of jobs moving to Mexico).

And the industrial policy proponents/managed traders/strategic traders, or whatever one wants to call them, came to Washington. Robert Reich, author of a recent book, *The Work of Nations*,[54] became secretary of labor; Ira Magaziner, the entrepreneurial consultant and author of the Rhode Island Compact, became the czar of health care reform (along with Hillary Rodham Clinton); and Laura D'Andrea Tyson was appointed chair of the prestigious Council of Economic Advisers.

All of the influential books knocking the theory of comparative advantage, calling for new paradigms, and promoting managed trade infuriated traditional economists—both liberal and conservative. But it especially infuriated liberal economists who had seen themselves as the new Keynesians and the heirs apparent to the Reagan/Bush supply-siders (more about this in Chapter 8).

Thus ends the short history of the politics of industrial policy. And, as we have seen, while the term is no longer in vogue (the term "industrial policy" had been associated with government planning and thus liberalism, and had to be abandoned), industrial policy is alive and well in the guise of competitiveness policy and/or managed trade. Industrial policy/competitiveness policy/managed trade are all variations on the same theme—our national industrial portfolio. A rose by any other name. . . .

Goals of the Book

It is time now to move beyond politics and rhetoric to policy itself. The primary purpose of this book is to identify the regularities in the hodgepodge of sectoral policies that make up the U.S. industrial policy and to group them in a way that makes sense. Only in this way can we see that there are identifiable dimensions to the policy and that these dimensions are actually somewhat reasonable.

There is also a secondary purpose, however. That is to examine how these policies play out under different administrations and different political parties. One would expect that they would be very different due to the very different philosophies of governing held by the Republicans and Democrats.

Harvard Business School professor George Lodge identifies two ideological paradigms concerning the role of government in society: individualistic and communitarian. In an individualistic society the role of government is limited. Its primary economic purposes are to protect property, enforce contracts, and keep the marketplace open for business. Government intervenes only if health and safety or a crisis is involved. Government is typically viewed with suspicion and citizens are anxious about government power. Long-range government planning is anathema to the society.

In a communitarian society government is authoritative and sometimes authoritarian. Government's role is to define the needs of the society and to see that those needs are met. Government plays a central role in defining the direction in which society will move.

Individualism tends to produce a "regulatory" state where government regulates business only to achieve ends that the market cannot meet. Communitarianism, on the other hand, produces a "developmental" state in which it is government's responsibility to define national priorities and see to it that they are met.[55]

Lodge, of course, was talking about nations and governments, but his typology is really based upon the attitudes of the people. Japan can be seen as communitarian because its assessments of national priorities are well standardized. Consensus on major policies is important to the Japanese. A Japanese is primarily a member of a group, and the success of the group is dominant over the success of the individual.[56]

Although Lodge's typology was about nations and government, it also fits the political parties of the United States. Republicans can be seen as individualistic and Democrats as communitarian. This being the case, one would expect to see an ebb and flow of industrial policy activity depending on the political party in the White House. Again, we are not talking about rhetoric, but actual practice. If Republicans practice what they preach, sector-specific policy activity should shrink during Republican years and expand with a Democrat in the White House.

The period 1976 through 1996 provides an ample time span for policy contractions and expansions to occur. If the individualistic/communitarian paradigm holds, sector-specific policies should have contracted when Ronald Reagan succeeded Jimmy Carter and remained at a relatively low level through the two Reagan terms and the four years of the George Bush presidency. When Bill Clinton took over the reins of government, industrial policy initiatives should have blossomed. This is particularly true given the influential positions Laura Tyson and Robert Reich held in the Clinton administration. Thus the chapters dealing with the specific dimensions of industrial policy will all cover the Carter through Clinton presidencies.

Before delving into the U.S. industrial policy initiatives of the modern era, it is useful to develop some industrial policy background. This diversion will take place in Chapter 2, which will put U.S. industrial policy in historical context. Popular discussion of national industrial policy really only goes back to about 1980. This could lead one to believe that, at least for the United States, industrial policy is a contemporary phenomenon. Nothing could be further from the truth. Sector-specific government policies have a long history in the United States. Chapter 2 presents examples of some of these policies and illustrates how pervasive industrial policy has been in the history of the United States.

It might also be illuminating for some readers to spend a little time viewing industrial policy in a country where the role of government is very different from ours. Japan is a useful example in this regard because it is so different from the United States in terms of its underlying cultural and societal values. Among developed societies, the United States is one of the most individualistic while Japan is among the most communitarian.[57] Interested readers should refer to the appendix entitled "Japanese Industrial Policy: Does It Work?"

2

In the Beginning: America's Long History of Industrial Policy

In 1791 Secretary of the Treasury Alexander Hamilton submitted a remarkable document to Congress—his "Report on the Subject of Manufactures."[1] Hamilton proposed a specific industrial policy for the United States designed to encourage the development and growth of manufacturing. It was, among other things, probably the first formal proposal for an industrial policy for the United States. The "Report on Manufactures" consists of eleven principles including protective tariffs, export restrictions, direct government subsidies to targeted industries, tax exemptions for manufacturing inputs, and support for infrastructure improvements. Hamilton concluded his report by detailing sector-specific policies for major manufacturing sectors in the United States including iron, copper, coal, grain, cotton, glass, gunpowder, and books.

This is a classic work made even more significant by the fact that manufacturing in the United States was very much in its infancy. The interesting thing about reading the "Report" is the realization that industrial policy ideas have not moved much beyond Hamilton's proposals in 200 years. Here are some of his specifics:

- Protective tariffs set at high enough levels to enable the nation's manufacturers to undersell foreign competitors;
- Outright prohibition of foreign goods once a competitive number of producers exists locally in a given industry;
- Providing a direct government subsidy (or bounty) to infant industries. Hamilton suggests that funds for the bounty could be generated by duties on imports of the protected good. "One per cent duty on the foreign article, converted into a bounty on the domestic, will have an equal effect with a duty of two per cent, exclusive of such bounty. . . ."[2] At the same time he recognizes that the subsidy should be granted only in the very early stages of manufacturing, lest the subsidy discourage production efficiencies. "The continuance of bounties on manufactures long established, must almost always be of questionable policy: because a presumption would arise, in every such case, that there were natural and inherent impediments to success. But, in new undertakings, they are as justifiable as they are oftentimes necessary."[3]
- Exempting inputs to infant manufacturing industries from duties;
- Prohibiting the export of innovative implements and machinery (to prevent their use by foreign competition); and
- Improving the nation's network of roads and canals (thus lowering the transportation costs of goods).

Hamilton was adamant in his belief that the promotion of manufacturing served a national purpose: "There is no purpose to which public money can be more beneficially applied, than to the acquisition of a new and useful branch of industry; no consideration more valuable, than a permanent addition to the general stock of productive labor."[4]

While industrial policy does go back to the founding of the nation, the purpose of this chapter is not to provide a complete history of industrial policy in the United States but to recount "snippets" of that history. Before looking at today's "three peas in a pod"—industrial policy, competitiveness policy, managed trade, or whatever one wants to call it—it is useful to skim through the first three-quarters of the twentieth century and see how industrial policy was part of the fabric of the development of the modern U.S. economy. This is best accomplished by looking at government policies toward specific industries. Those selected are the railroads, trucking, the maritime industry, air carriers, agriculture, oil, and banking.

Government Assistance to Business

While some may abhor the idea of a national policy and government promotion of individual industries, it is simply wrongheaded to believe that the government in modern American economic history has been laissez faire in this regard. During the first three-fourths of the twentieth century, the U.S. government provided significant support to a large number of industries and was massively involved with many of the most important ones. Government assistance came in two forms—through direct or indirect promotion and through regulation.

Direct Assistance

There are six main types of government promotional activities relevant to the twentieth century: subsidy, tax exemption, direct loans, insurance, government contracts for construction, and the promotion of research.[5] A government subsidy simply directs resources to preferred industries. The examples we all know about from high school history class are the federal land grants made to the railroads. Land grant subsidies were the principal form of aid to the railroads given by the federal government. Railroads were given public lands to construct rights-of-way as well as additional acreage along each side of the rights-of-way. The total federal grants to railroads have been estimated at more than 127 million acres. This is on top of state land grants of more than 48 million acres. The net value of these grants to the railroads was more than $516 million.[6]

Tax exemption is a similar method of subsidizing the firms in an industry. A familiar example of this form of tax favoritism is the depletion allowance on minerals. At one point in our recent history the depletion allowance on oil was as high as 27.5 percent of gross income. The tariff is a similar form of tax when it is used for the protection and promotion of a domestic industry.

A third form of promotion is direct loans to private firms. An example is the system of Federal Land Banks set up in 1916 to make direct loans to farmers. While direct loans to agriculture were the most common form of direct loans, they were by no means unique. At one time or another the federal government has made loans to firms in many other industries.

Government insurance, or government-sponsored insurance, is another form of subsidy. To this day, the government is directly involved in crop insurance to farmers. And, of course, the example closest to all of us is the insurance on bank deposits. While it is our deposits that are insured, one of the major reasons for the federal insurance program in the first place was to provide stability to banks (to prevent runs on the banks).

The fifth method of industrial promotion involves government contracts for construction. Government-paid construction of industrial facilities was extremely common in World War II. Thousands of industrial plants were built by the Reconstruction Finance Corporation (RFC) as part of the war effort and were leased and later sold to private companies.

The War Assets Administration spent $770 million on steel plants during World War II. Four large new integrated mills were built with government financing—one in California, one in Utah, and two in Texas. These plants were used chiefly to produce plates and structural steel for shipbuilding.[7]

Finally, there is government support for research and development (R&D). The history of military-industrial relations is replete with examples of R&D support for product development. The Air Force has historically been the leader in relying on industry for research and development. In the aerospace revolution of the 1950s, the Air Force relied entirely on private industry for the research and development of intercontinental ballistic missiles (ICBMs). The Army, on the other hand, preferred to develop their missiles in-house at the Army's Redstone Arsenal and contract with the auto industry for fabrication. In the end, the Army found that it could not produce such complex equipment without a more specialized industry and ended up going with the same contractors the Air Force used. Private-sector, for-profit R&D is a mainstay of the defense industry.[8]

Regulation

There are four types of regulatory action with respect to specific industries, which, in comprehensive form,[9] are considered industrial policy: prescription of standards, licensing, price control, and limitations on production.[10] An example of the prescription of standards is the service requirements once imposed on airlines mandating service to small cities; these ultimately proved unprofitable.

Licensing is another regulatory tool of industrial policy. Essentially, licensing requires government approval before an action can be taken. Thus, a permit is required in Texas to drill for oil. In the past, government permission was required for an airline to begin service to a new city.

Price control is the third type of regulatory action. In the early part of the twentieth century, price control was regarded as an exceptional procedure and was essentially allowed by the courts only in industries with a public interest, like the railroads and utilities. But in 1939 the Supreme Court rejected this limitation and held that price control was within the discretion of legislative bodies.[11] Legislative bodies have initiated price controls to protect both buyers (e.g., utilities, banking, insurance) and sellers (milk industry, coal industry). In addition to directly dictating price, governments use indirect measures such as agricultural price supports to support prices.

The final regulatory type, limitation on production, includes actions to restrict entry, restrict expansion, or allocate production. Production controls were established for many industries during the Depression (1933–35). For most of the latter part of the century, however, production control has applied mainly to agriculture and crude oil.

Selected Industry Policies

Economic historians often characterize the three decades from 1900 to 1930 as an era of sweeping developments in overall business–government relations. But it was not. Overall government policy did not change; what did change were government's policies toward particular industries.[12]

Factory workers, farmers, and small businessmen were not pleased with the changes taking place in the United States. They often felt threatened by what they saw as a centralization of power in America's large corporations. They joined forces in appealing for a new brand of political economy. And government responded with three industrial policy innovations. These were the independent regulatory commission, antitrust laws, and the establishment of the Federal Reserve Bank.[13]

The Railroads

One of the first industries to be subject to regulation was the railroads. The railroads were among the largest and most highly organized industries of the 1800s. Shippers dependent on the railroads complained that the rates were too high and too unpredictable. In truth, rates were unstable and often discriminatory. Where competition did not exist, rates were frequently extremely high—even for short hauls. Small shippers, including farmers, were typically forced to pay the top rates while larger shippers received huge discounts. Mounting pressures finally forced Congress to do something about the situation.

Federal railroad regulation essentially began with the Interstate Commerce Act of 1887 and the founding of the Interstate Commerce Commission. This act and others strengthening it were primarily designed to prevent abuses, particularly discriminatory and excessive rates. However, with the passage of the Transportation Act of 1920, a major shift in public policy came about. The objective now became consistent with the definition of industrial policy. Congress imposed upon the Commission the duty to maintain adequate railway service for the nation. To this end, the Commission's power was extended over every important aspect of railroad management except labor relations.

Some features of the 1920 act were found to be unworkable and were abandoned or later modified, yet the 1920 act formed the nation's industrial policy toward railroads for well over forty years. One of the major powers of the ICC under the act was comprehensive rate making. In theory (although not in practice), by adjusting rates the ICC could ensure the survival of the railroads in good times and in bad. The act also contained a provision requiring the Commission to develop a plan for rationalizing the railroads. This they did, and in 1929 the ICC issued its plan for railway consolidation that would result in a nineteen-carrier railway system. The plan was never implemented, and in 1940 Congress repealed the provisions for a consolidation plan and allowed the railroads to combine as they saw fit, subject only to the approval of the Commission.[14]

The 1920 act was the most ambitious piece of industrial policy in the history of the country up until that time. According to political scientist Emmett Redford, writing back in 1965, "It showed great faith in the ability of men to order an industry according to a plan."[15] While history gives the ICC's policy and managerial decisions on railroad matters a mixed review, it was the nation's first significant industrial policy effort.

Motor Carriers

Federal regulation of the trucking industry began when Congress passed the Motor Carrier Act of 1935. The basic goals of the act were to hold competition to reasonable limits and to ensure a coordinated transportation system for the nation. With certain exceptions (e.g., agricultural products), the ICC was given jurisdiction over the interstate trucking industry in addition to the railroads. Its major function under the act was the management of competition. It exercised this function through its power of "control over entry," granting permits restricting the movement of specific commodities, routes, or classes of service. Thus routes granted could be limited to certain named cities; and carriers could even be limited to hauling in one direction. The result was that motor carrier operating rights were chopped up into thousands of little pieces.

Prospective new carriers needed to show that the added service was for "public convenience and necessity." This meant that the applicant had to show that present service was inadequate—not always an easy task, even with the support of shippers.

The second instrument in the management of competition was control over minimum rates. The purpose of minimum rates was to avoid destructive rate competition and thus to avoid the financial failure of motor carriers.

This control over rates set the tone for a government-operated, micromanaged system. Rate controls extended government's authority to each specific rate to be charged and led to ICC consideration of thousands of cases each year.[16]

The Merchant Marine

For years, it was the official maritime policy of the United States to foster the development and maintenance of a merchant marine, which was owned and operated as a private enterprise under the flag of the United States by citizens of the United States.[17] Congress justified this policy on the grounds that the national interest required a shipping fleet capable of sustaining a substantial portion of foreign commerce with the United States, and also capable of serving as a naval auxiliary in times of war or national emergency.

However, as far back as the last half of the nineteenth century this goal was illusive. Foreign competition provided service that was too low in cost for the American maritime industry to match. The United States experimented with postal subsidies to aid the industry, but these did little more than support established operators.

World War I, however, led to a new kind of subsidy. The shortage of American ships caused the government to build ships and operate its own merchant fleet. A total of over $3 billion was spent on this new construction. Huge profits were made by the shipbuilders, suppliers, and contractors. Shipyards were built at government expense and mushroomed all over the country.

With the end of the war the question then arose as to what should be done with the government's fleet. Congress decided that the proper course of action was to dispose of the ships. A government Shipping Board was established to carry out this policy. Ships costing $200 to $250 per deadweight ton were sold for $12 to $18 per deadweight ton. This sale constituted a huge grant to the shipping industry tantamount to a construction subsidy. The Shipping Board also leased many of the vessels to private steamship companies at extremely low rates. The contracts were so favorable as to virtually guarantee a substantial profit to lessees. But there was also a downside to this action. The disposal of the government fleet wiped out demand for new construction in American shipyards.

The government responded by creating a construction-loan fund and deepening the postal subsidies. But competition from foreign maritime nations was becoming increasingly severe and the industry continued to decline. By 1928 the government decided that direct subsidies were required to save the industry.

After several years of experimentation, the government settled on a dual subsidy system for both construction and operation. Subsidies were granted for the construction of vessels in American shipyards for American firms, the amount being determined by the difference in the cost of building a ship in an American shipyard versus the cost of building it in a foreign shipyard. In addition, national defense requirements were built into subsidized ships. For example, a ship had to be capable of taking on armor, requiring stronger decks. Also, defense-required ships had to have a speed in excess of normal merchant marine requirements—an expensive proposition. As a result, construction subsidies consisted of two parts—the parity subsidy and the national defense subsidy. In addition, the shipper was often able to obtain a government mortgage for the purchase.

Operating subsidies were given to American firms applying for and proving the need for subsidization. The amount of the subsidy was the difference in the costs of operating American steamships and the costs of using competing foreign lines.

Both subsidy systems bore enormous regulatory costs, in the form of numerous government regulations and much government oversight. As a result, many American companies preferred to ignore the subsidies and choose foreign registry.

When the United States entered World War II the subsidy system was replace by a huge government shipbuilding program. By the end of the war the government owned about 5,000 ships and Congress again required disposal of the fleet. By 1951 about 850 ships had been sold while others were scrapped or mothballed. Of course this again depressed the construction industry.

The above describes American merchant marine industrial policy in the international arena. The coastal fleet, however, had protection from foreign competition dating back to 1789. Only American companies were permitted to own and operate vessels in the coastwide trade. The lack of foreign competition negated the need for subsidies and there were none. Up until World War II this portion of the industry thrived under America's protectionist policies. But during the war, when the coastwide industry was activated for war-related shipping, the railroads and truckers took over most of its freight business. The coastwide industry never recovered. For the most part, it lost its competitive edge.[18]

Air Carriers

The airline industry essentially owes its birth to the U.S. Post Office through the development and support of air mail service. Initially the Post Office had its own fleet of aircraft and directly provided air mail service. But in 1925 Congress authorized the postmaster general to contract with private carriers for air mail service. By 1928 the privatization of air mail carriage was complete, and, with a short exception, private delivery was the case with routine air mail service throughout the century. But what the privatization of air mail carriage did was lead to the development of air transport in the United States as a private industry; this was unlike most other countries, where air transport was a public enterprise. One of the main reasons that the system developed this way was a requirement by the Post Office Department that carriers transport passengers. Thus, commercial aviation was born.

One of the most interesting developments in government subsidization of industry occurred with the airlines. The first subsidies (1925) paid private carriers based on the amount of postal revenues their routes produced. In the next year a change was made and the government decided to pay the airlines by the pounds per mile of mail carried and not in proportion to the postage revenue generated.

In essence, under these early plans the government was simply paying for services rendered. But 1930 brought in a revolutionary subsidy. Congress substituted an available-space per mile formula for the old pounds per mile payment system. It no longer mattered how much mail an airline actually carried; airlines were now paid based on how large their planes were. The larger the planes the higher the payment. The specific objective of the subsidy was the promotion of aviation by stimulating the airlines to develop passenger business. It worked. The attitude of the industry changed from an overriding concern with carrying the mail to the development of passenger traffic. Airlines were induced to buy larger planes and put passenger seats in the space not needed for mail. Furthermore, the Post Office mail contracts favored the airlines with the biggest and fastest planes.

The net result was not only the development of the airline industry but the development of the aircraft industry. Airline demands for larger and faster planes produced an aircraft industry interested in research and innovation.[19]

In 1938 Congress enacted a comprehensive aviation policy (industry policy) in the Civil Aeronautics Act (replaced in 1958 by the Federal Aviation Act, which did not substantially change the system). The act put in place a system of economic regulation under the Civil Aeronautics Board (CAB). The board was composed of five members appointed by the president with the Senate's approval. The objectives of economic regulation under the act were twofold: the promotion of air transportation "to meet the needs of the foreign and domestic commerce of the United States, of the Postal Service, and of the national defense," and the maintenance of sound economic conditions in the industry.

The objectives of economic regulation were met through a certificate system set in place by the CAB. The legal features of the regulatory system were patterned after rail and motor transportation. In administering the certificate system the CAB accepted the philosophy of "regulated competition" to protect against wasteful duplication of services and destructive competition. The two major types of certificates were for trunk lines and local service operations. Trunkline service is scheduled service between major traffic centers. Local service airlines (service began in 1946) provided service between smaller cities, and between smaller cities and trunkline cities. It was the board's policy to keep local service companies out of trunkline business and vice versa. Initially, 19 airline companies provided trunkline service and 22 provided local services. By 1965 these numbers had declined to 11 and 13 respectively.

The board exercised two functions in its rate-setting capacity—setting (or approving) rates charged to the public and determining the subsidy through mail pay. (In the mid-1960s mail subsidies accounted for over 30 percent of local service airline revenues.) In setting mail rates, the board considered two factors: mail pay sufficient to ensure air mail service, and providing the carrier with additional revenues to continue the development of airline passenger service throughout the United States. In other words, mail pay gave the government the opportunity to provide a direct subsidy for unprofitable passenger service. In the early 1940s it became apparent that some of the trunklines were self-sufficient and no longer needed the subsidy, so the CAB began figuring some mail rates on a compensatory basis for services rendered. By the mid-1950s the trunklines no longer required a subsidy. But the subsidy remained for local service carriers.

In setting rates charged to the public the board used a traditional rate of return based on the cost of capital. This meant a determination of the proportions of debt and equity capital, and the rate of each one that would be necessary to attract capital to the industry.

The result of America's industry policy for airline development was threefold: A "higher than normal" amount of resources were attracted to the airline industry; service was provided to more city-pair markets than could be sustained commercially; and there was a faster rate of development of commercial aircraft than market forces alone would have produced.[20]

Agriculture

In the United States, agriculture policy was historically the granddaddy of industry policies. Pressure for governmental aid to farmers began in the 1920s with wheat producers in the Midwest. By the end of the decade, cotton producers in the South had joined in the struggle and a coalition of southern and midwestern congressmen was able to pass an agriculture assistance program as early as 1928.

But it was the new Roosevelt administration's actions in 1933 that set the industry policy for agriculture that has existed up to the present. The goal was "parity" for farmers. Parity income sets as a goal the principle that the income of farmers should bear the same relationship to the income of nonfarmers as it did in some base years (with base years being those in which farmers did particularly well). The Agricultural Adjustment Act of 1933 set the policy of the United States to "give agricultural commodities a purchasing power with respect to articles farmers buy, equivalent to the purchasing power of agricultural commodities in the base period 1909–1914"[21] (for tobacco, the base period was 1919–29).

Parity prices were set by the Department of Agriculture and were maintained in two ways—by reducing production, or by withholding commodities from the market. New Deal legislation from 1933 to 1935 provided for the control of acreage in basic commodities (corn, cotton, peanuts, rice, tobacco, and wheat). This legislation was found unconstitutional but was "corrected" in subsequent years. Controls on production were accomplished in a multistep process, first by setting a national acreage allotment for each crop. The secretary of Agriculture did this by estimating national need (domestic consumption, exports, and reserve supplies minus carryover from the previous year). He thus determined the national acreage allotment, which was the number of acres required to produce the annual need. The national acreage allotment was then apportioned among the states based on past proportions of the national acreage. The state acreage was then subdivided among counties and allocated to farmers based on past production. If a reduction in acreage was necessary, the secretary would announce payments for soil conservation practices (thus acreage restrictions). The farmers who complied were paid for withdrawing their acreage from production and were also entitled to price supports for the crop produced on the allotted acreage.

During the Eisenhower administration this program was expanded into the soil bank program. Under it, farmers were paid for taking crop land out of production and rotating it into soil-building crops.

Under certain circumstances (large projected surplus, approval of farmers) quotas were sometimes imposed on each commercial grower. Farmers who complied with the quota were rewarded with price supports.

In 1938, with a major expansion in 1949, Congress required that the Commodity Credit Corporation (CCC) make loans on storable agricultural commodities. The loans were to be made at a certain percentage of parity and the commodities served as security for the loans.[22] The CCC was the federal agency the Department of Agriculture used to maintain agricultural prices. This was accomplished in two ways:

> In the one case the farmer will go to his bank and borrow on his commodity as security. The amount of the loan will be related to the support price. Later, the farmer may repay the loan and regain the commodity. Presumably, he will do this if the market price of the commodity increases, and in this situation the CCC is not involved. However, if the market price remains below the support price, the farmer will take the debt to the CCC, which will pay off the loan at the bank and take title to the commodity that served as security. . . .
>
> The second means of price support by the CCC is through purchase from cooperating farmers at the prices specified in the program. The farmer is not obligated to sell to the CCC, but the CCC is obligated to purchase from the cooperating farmer the amount he wishes to deliver. The CCC's action may have the consequence of bolstering the price of the commodity so that the support price and the market price are identical. If the market price is higher than the support price, the farmer will obviously sell at the market price. However, if the market price is lower, the cooperating farmer will deliver his commodity to the CCC and receive the support price.[23]

The heyday of agricultural policy is now almost in the past. In the spring of 1996 the Congress approved, and President Clinton signed, a farm bill that virtually abandons price supports. The growers of corn and other feed grains, cotton, rice, and wheat will receive guaranteed, but declining, "market transition payments" over seven years. The bill also phases down government support prices for butter, powdered milk, and cheese over four years.[24]

Oil

The history of government's industrial policy for the oil industry is unusual because of the heavy involvement of the states. Much of this involvement rested on the peculiar nature of oil as a property. This deals with the right of ownership by the owners of the land over mineral deposits, and with the right of capture allowing an owner to drill wells on the land and take ownership of all of the oil and gas captured by those wells (including that of neighbors). But what of an adjoining owner who wants to conserve her oil? Is there anything she can do to protect her oil? A judge has held: "Nothing; only go and do likewise."[25] The obvious consequence was a race in drilling and a rapid withdrawal of oil and gas. And this is what brought about an industry policy for oil and gas.

On October 3, 1930, Texas wildcatter "Dad" Joiner brought in a well in East Texas. Unbeknownst to him at the time, he had discovered the largest oil deposit the world had seen—a field eight miles wide and forty-two miles long. By June there were more than 700 wells in the field, at times producing more than a million barrels of oil per day (in a nation whose total daily oil production the year before was only about 2 million barrels). And, of course, the price of crude oil dropped from over one dollar per barrel to about ten cents. The reason for all this production was that the field was divided among many small farmers and village lot owners having rights of capture. These owners followed the judge's directive and did likewise. "I want mine and I want it now" was the rule of the day.

Oil and gas production was under state, not federal, jurisdiction as the production itself did not involve interstate commerce. In Texas, the office governing oil and gas production was the Railroad Commission. And while the Railroad Commission had administrative authority to issue rules regulating oil production, including waste, it was specifically prohibited from regulating "economic waste."

The Commission proved itself incapable of handling the chaos that developed in the East Texas fields; Governor Ross Sterling, a multi-millionaire and former president of Humble Oil, declared martial law. He ruled East Texas with state troops until his action was declared unconstitutional by the U.S. Supreme Court.[26]

Sterling was a conservative and a strong believer in a laissez faire approach to government. Yet he was a practical man who had just witnessed a plunge of 90 percent in the price of oil. He and the legislative leaders recognized that they had to do something to strengthen the Commission. In the end, the legislature amended the statute and allowed the Commission to restrict oil production for economic reasons. Proration to reasonable market demand became state policy.

Proration to market demand eventually became the policy of the majority of oil producing states. And while this was still state policy, the federal government was very much involved. The U.S. Bureau of

Mines issued monthly estimates of the market demand for oil and broke them down for the producing states. The federal government was also involved in solving the problem of "hot oil"—that is oil produced in excess of that allowed by state regulators. Reaching back to 1935, the federal government has prohibited the interstate shipment of oil produced in violation of state law.

The petroleum industry has also received special treatment in the income tax laws. Because in mineral production the asset itself (the mineral) is used up, a depletion allowance is accepted on the income obtained from the production of minerals. For oil, it was a whopping 27.5 percent.[27]

Banking

Banking has always been a sort of sacred industry, and for very good reason. But it was not until after the crash of 1929 and the near-total collapse of the banking system that strong national policies were enacted, designed to protect the banks and the banking system. The Banking Acts of 1933 and 1935 made significant changes in the banking industry.

The Federal Deposit Insurance Corporation (FDIC) was created in 1933 to protect small depositors. Commercial and investment banking functions were separated. Interstate branch banking was forbidden. "Regulation Q" gave the Federal Reserve the power to set ceilings on interest rates on time and savings deposits.

One of the lessons of the Depression was that the Federal Reserve system was incapable of overcoming the fundamental weakness of a mostly unfettered capitalistic system. There were several reasons for this. First, economic theory was not sufficiently developed as to help bankers really know what to do. And second, the structure of the Federal Reserve system would have made remedial action difficult in any case. In the course of the Depression a Utah banker, Marriner Eccles, became the savior of the Federal Reserve System. A Keynesian before Keynes, Eccles personally designed the legislation that reformed the Fed—stripping the twelve Federal Reserve Banks of their veto power and their autonomy and vesting the control of monetary policy in the Board of Governors.

Other reforms gave the Board of Governors bureaucratic authority over the reserve banks—on everything from building plans to salaries to changes in the discount rate. The control of monetary policy was vested in a new institution—the Federal Open Market Committee—composed of the seven governors and five of the reserve bank presidents.[28]

One of the clearest examples of industry policy in the 1933–35 bank reforms was the prohibition against commercial banks paying interest on checking accounts. In exchange for this permanent subsidy, "banks were expected to be more prudent in lending and also more tolerant when recessions made it harder for borrowers to keep up the payments."[29]

The Reconstruction Finance Corporation (RFC)

The RFC has a unique although not very well understood place in America's history. It was a national development bank—something common to other nations but very, very foreign to Americans. The RFC was created by Herbert Hoover in 1932, established for the purpose of targeting government loans to businesses and industries in need of capital. Between 1932 and 1935 it distributed approximately $2 billion in loans to businesses unable to obtain credit in the private sector.

In the larger scheme of things, the RFC does not seem very important—almost a footnote to history. But in the industrial policy literature this little known and poorly understood institution is pivotal. The RFC, or more accurately an RFC-like structure, was central to much of the industrial policy debate of the 1980s. As was shown in Chapter 1, many IP proponents backed an RFC-like institution for the Untied States while IP foes were adamantly opposed. This is why it is worth a second look.

While the RFC is commonly associated with Franklin Roosevelt and the New Deal, it was actually a product of the Hoover administration. But its roots go back even further than that—to 1918, when President Woodrow Wilson as part of the World War I campaign established the War Finance Corporation (WFC) to augment capital investment markets and make loans to war industries. William McAdoo was put in charge of the WFC. The agency was extremely successful, loaning millions of dollars to public utilities, railroads, banks, and building and loan associations. Congress continued to find the WFC useful after the war, authorizing the agency to make export loans as a means of increasing domestic manufacturing and loans to farmers needing intermediate credit. The government began liquidating the WFC in 1924 and closed its doors six years later.

By 1931, in the depths of the Depression, Hoover's aids urged him to revive the War Finance Corporation. He did just that, proposing the Reconstruction Finance Corporation to Congress in December 1931. The Congress responded quickly and authorized the RFC in January 1932.

President Hoover saw the Depression as a crisis in confidence. He did not believe that the economy would revive until private bankers increased business lending. He saw thousands of frustrated business owners lining up for credit but with timid bankers unwilling to make loans (more than 5,000 banks had failed during the 1920s).

The RFC was to make low-interest loans to commercial banks, savings and loans, insurance companies, mortgage companies, and railroads. Like the WFC, the RFC was to be a temporary institution and was expected to go out of business with the revival of normal credit channels.

The RFC was an independent agency. It was independent of Congress, the executive branch, and the public. It could sell notes and obligations privately with loan repayments providing a revolving fund for future activities. By the end of 1932 (and after Hoover had lost the election), the RFC had authorized loans totaling $1.6 billion to thousands of financial institutions and the railroads. But the economy did not improve and the railroads were in terrible shape. The banks held millions of dollars in railroad bonds, which the railroads could not pay. The bonds were unmarketable assets for thousands of banks. But the worst was yet to come.

During the first two months of 1932 (when Herbert Hoover was a lame-duck president), thousands of banks failed, including many of the nation's largest. Bank holidays were declared by many states. By inauguration day, March 4, 1933, the economy had ground to a halt. The RFC had failed to save the financial market.

On March 6, two days after his inauguration, President Roosevelt declared a national banking holiday. He also replaced Atlee Pomerene as chairman of the RFC with the flamboyant Texas entrepreneur Jesse Jones. Jones completely dominated the RFC and was the central figure in the New Deal's state capitalism of the 1930s. Jones ran the RFC from 1933 to 1939. He then became head of a new agency, the Federal Loan Agency, which was given oversight of the RFC. He essentially ran the RFC through the following five phases of New Deal public policy:

1. Bank reconstruction and cooperative planning (1933–34);
2. The direct loan phase (1934–35);
3. Budget balancing (1936–37);
4. Recessionary spending (1938–39);
5. War phase (1940+).

Bank Reconstruction and Cooperative Planning

Because of its revolving credit fund and loan-making experience, the RFC became the capital bank of the New Deal. It financed a host of new deal agencies like the Home Owners' Loan Corporation, Farm Credit Administration, Federal Home Loan banks, Federal Housing Administration, and the Rural Electrification Administration. But in the early years of the New Deal it was rescuing banks that the agency was all about. After the bank holidays were over the RFC was instrumental in reorganizing and saving thousands of banks through loans and by purchasing shares of preferred stock in the banks (thus providing new capital). By June 1935, when the preferred stock program ended, the RFC had purchased $1.3 billion in stock from 6,800 banks. The RFC owned more than one-third of all outstanding capital in the banking system. In addition it had loaned more than $1.4 billion to 10,576 banks and trust companies. The RFC had indeed helped stabilize the money markets. Success was affirmed in 1934 and 1935 when only 61 and then 32 licensed commercial banks failed.

The RFC was a major player in the government's attempt to save the railroads. In 1934 the RFC estimated that thirty-two of the nation's forty-six largest railroads were in serious danger of bankruptcy. By the end of 1935, in spite of $500 million in RFC loans, the problem was just as bad. The railroads were suffering from multiple problems: heavy debt structure, overbuilding, declining freight revenues, and competition from trucks. In addition to loans, RFC rescue attempts included the direct purchases of railroad obligations such as equipment trust certificates and the provision of capital through the purchase of railroad stock. But this merely postponed the inevitable. If the stabilization of the money markets can be considered an RFC success, the attempts to save the railroads must be considered an RFC failure.

While the RFC and Federal Reserve had helped the nation overcome the banking crises, the banks refused to loan or invest, instead accumulating huge excess reserves. The Roosevelt administration saw this as a major impediment to the recovery and decided to initiate a program of direct business loans as part of the National Recovery Administration (NRA) program.[30] Two existing RFC credit agencies—the Electric Home and Farm Authority (EHFA) and the Commodity Credit Corporation (CCC)—reinforced the administration's conviction that a significant demand for business credit existed. (The EHFA program stimulated farmers to purchase appliances and consume more electricity and the CCC ran the agricultural price support program. Both were highly successful.)[31]

Direct Loan Phase

The RFC began its direct business loan program in 1934. The program was limited to NRA "Blue Eagle" members, which were financially solvent and able to supply adequate security. Loans were for working capital only. Applicants had to prove failure to secure credit from a commercial bank. The program was unsuccessful. There were very few qualified applicants. In 1935 the RFC liberalized the loan requirements (e.g., it could make industrial loans of up to $1 million for ten years, allow the loans to be used for a variety of business purposes), but the program still never got off the ground. There was less demand than expected and the borrowers were generally marginal.

Budget Balancing

By 1936 the country had entered a modest expansion. Treasury Secretary Henry Morgenthau, Jr., convinced the president that a balanced budget was in the country's best interest. This led to a significant scaling back in RFC activity. In October 1937 President Roosevelt informed Jesse Jones that the RFC was finished; it should make no new loans and should work toward dissolution.

But the cuts in government spending brought the recovery to a grinding halt. The result was the recession of 1937–38. The only answer was more spending, and the RFC was back in business.

Recessionary Spending

One of the major RFC initiatives during the period was the establishment of the Federal National Mortgage Association (Fannie Mae) within the RFC to provide a secondary mortgage market for Federal Housing Administration (FHA) loans. A second was the resumption of railroad loans, and a third was the revival of direct commercial lending. Fannie Mae was a clear success, but the railroad loans and the direct loans to business were no more successful than in the earlier period. The problem of the recession was never a problem with the supply of capital, it was a demand problem—a problem with consumer demand.

War Phase

World War II was the RFC's finest hour. Suddenly there was a shortage of capital and an unprecedented demand for credit. For the first time the RFC found itself facing a huge demand for loans from sound companies. In 1940 Jones established the Defense Plant Corporation to take over some of the work of the Business Loan Division and finance new plant construction for war industries. He also established the Defense Supplies Corporation to acquire critical industrial materials. In 1942 he set up the Smaller War Plants Corporation to finance plant construction of small industries.

By 1945 the Defense Plant Corporation had invested $9.2 billion, the Supplies Corporation $9.3 billion, the Smaller Plants Corporation invested $200 million, and the RFC business loan program $4.4 billion. The Defense Plant Corporation constructed 2,300 factories and equipped them with tools and machinery. Most were leased to private corporations including the nation's largest—companies like General Motors, Dow Chemical, General Electric, Sperry, B.F. Goodrich, Chrysler, and Ford. After the war most of the plants were sold to the companies leasing them.[32]

Historian James Olson summarizes the RFC's place in history:

> Conservative but not ideological, pragmatic but not experimental, the RFC avoided political extremes while wholeheartedly accepting its responsibility for saving capitalism. It was, quintessentially, a product of the American mainstream. Along with the National Recovery Administration and the Agricultural Adjustment Administration, the Reconstruction Finance Corporation was a major recovery agency and, as the only one to survive intact throughout the 1930s and World War II, the most symbolic of the New Deal and the state capitalism it fostered.[33]

Conclusion

There is no point in beating a dead horse here. The purpose of this chapter was modest—to show that the United States, throughout its modern history, has selected industries for targeted assistance. Some analysts, like Louis Galambos and Joseph Pratt, have concluded that these policies were, overall, highly successful:

> Under the guidance of the CAB after the second World War, a modern American airline industry emerged whose service and prices were the envy of the industrial world. In the same era AT&T, a technologically oriented monopoly regulated by state utility commissions and the FCC, promoted the work of a system of laboratories generally acknowledged to be the best in the world. Working within the framework of regulatory policies, the Bell System spread telephone service to the masses throughout the nation. The FCC also supervised the extension of television to a mass audience. Under rules enforced by several regulatory agencies, most notably the Texas Railroad Commission, the petroleum industry fueled the nation's growth with cheap, abundant energy. At the same time, utility companies throughout the nation not only kept pace with dramatic increases in the demand for electricity but also steadily lowered their unit costs. Finally, the banking industry (which is now remembered as "stodgy and conservative") facilitated in these years the flow of credit needed to sustain investments while making financial services such as checking accounts available to much broader segments of the population. Taken as a whole, the performances of these regulated businesses were excellent.[34]

Consider again the airlines. The Civil Aeronautics Act of 1938 established the Civil Aeronautics Board (CAB) with a mandate to regulate the airlines and foster their development. World War II brought about tremendous technological improvements in aircraft (a different form of industrial policy) and demonstrated the potential promise of commercial aviation. With this beginning, and very little guidance from Congress, the CAB sought to create a modern, rationalized airline industry. What resulted was a government-sponsored cartel that emphasized the protection of the economic health of the existing airline companies and the extension of airline service to virtually all cities of moderate size.

The CAB ran this system in a number of ways to achieve its goals.

It strictly regulated the number of airlines flying interstate routes. New airlines (or those flying intrastate) could not enter the interstate airline business without CAB approval. This resulted in a national airline system made up of only eleven carriers by the 1960s.

The CAB also strictly regulated airline routes. An airline could neither establish nor abandon a route without CAB approval. In order to assure the broadest possible extension of air service, the CAB allowed the airlines to charge higher rates on their profitable routes between major cities and directed them to use these "excess profits" to subsidize traffic on the less profitable (or unprofitable) feeder routes.[35]

It is hard to see how anyone could argue that industrial policy is not a part of America's industrial heritage unless, of course, they can say that there is nothing "regularized" about the nation's policy toward individual industries. Or that the various policies toward individual industries are ad hoc (recall from Chapter 1 that this is exactly what both liberals and conservatives have done); that there is actually no policy, just a bunch of reactions. Or they might argue that there might have been industry policies toward a few specific industries in the past but that "deregulation" has done away with the most "offensive."

But this is not the case, as the following chapters will show. The United States does have a definable industrial policy with specific components that can be identified. The first of these has been termed "functional problem solving" by Kenan Jarboe.[36] Functional problem solving is the first of the five IP strategies of the United States and is the subject of the next chapter.

3

Functional
Problem Solving

Functional problem solving is the simplest and traditionally most common approach to industrial policy. With functional problem solving, a problem facing a specific firm or industry is identified and government actions are taken to alleviate it. Thus, each industry is treated as an individual case, in isolation from the problems of other industries. The main feature of this approach is its isolated focus. Each firm or industry is viewed in isolation from all others. The only concerns are with the problems of a specific industry or company.

The obvious consequence of this is that industrial policy becomes discrete and multiple. Rather than a single unitary policy, functional problem solving leads to multiple policies. And, while the actions taken under the problem solving approach may, in fact, solve the problem, there is always the danger that the symptoms are treated while missing the disease.[1]

Over the past twenty years there have been two major examples of functional problem solving as an approach to industrial policy. These are the Chrysler bailout and the savings and loan bailout, both of which this chapter will examine in some detail. But while it is these large cases that catch the public's eye, functional problem solving has been used over the years in a number of cases that are seldom reported to the public. Several of these cases will be discussed briefly.

Chrysler

In 1979 the Chrysler Corporation, the nation's fourteenth-largest firm, was facing impending bankruptcy. Chrysler appealed to the government to help it by guaranteeing its loans. Washington did so. The Corporation sustained enormous losses through 1980 and 1981, but then, thanks to the fresh money that made it possible for Chrysler to retool, Chrysler broke even in 1982 and then made record profits in 1983 and paid back its guaranteed loans. By 1984 the company had completely revived, earning $2.4 billion and bringing thousands of workers back to their jobs.[2]

The Chrysler bailout made history and attracted national and international attention—but it was not the first such bailout. Chapter 2 documented the role of the RFC in providing loans to failing corporations during the 1930s. But Chrysler was not even the first of the modern corporate bailouts; the cases of the Penn Central Railroad and the Lockheed Corporation preceded it.

The Precedents

In 1968 two of the nation's largest troubled railroads, the Pennsylvania Railroad and the New York Central, merged, forming the largest corporate merger in history. The new Penn Central became the sixth-largest corporation in the country with more than 100,000 employees. But the merger did nothing for the new firm's financial condition and by June 1970 it was bankrupt. The company had less than $7 million in cash and its liabilities of $750 million were offset by only $280 million in current assets. The failing company sought a government loan guarantee of up to $200 million but the Nixon administration rejected this proposal.

Instead, Congress created the National Railroad Passenger Corporation (Amtrak), which took over the nation's entire intercity rail passenger service, including the routes being operated by Penn Central at huge losses. Then in 1976 Congress created the Consolidated Rail Corporation (Conrail), a quasi-governmental corporation, to take over and operate the unprofitable freight operations of the Penn Central and five other bankrupt eastern railroads.

Relieved of its losing railroad operations by the public, Penn Central soon emerged from bankruptcy. By 1980 it was making substantial profits and was able to pay off its $2 billion in debt. Its stock prices climbed and Penn Central became a leading American firm.

The Lockheed Corporation was one of the Pentagon's chief defense suppliers. Its products included the Trident ballistic missile and the Agena spacecraft. By the end of the 1960s it had suffered losses of $500 million due to cost overruns on four defense contracts. It was also having problems with potential overruns on its L-1011 Tristar commercial passenger aircraft. By 1971, U.S. banks refused to loan Lockheed additional funds unless the federal government guaranteed the loans. Supporters of Lockheed warned that failure of the firm would lead to devastating job losses with a study at the University of California at Los Angeles predicting an overall loss of 65,000 jobs in the economy if Lockheed were allowed to fail.

After much debate, Congress passed the Nixon administration's bailout plan. The plan placed a number of conditions on Lockheed in agreeing to guarantee $250 million in loans (outstanding at any one time). With the guarantee in place, Lockheed's lenders agreed to a restructuring of $400 million in unguaranteed credits and temporarily cut their interest rate to 4 percent while extending loan maturities by two years. The banks also converted $75 million in debt to preferred stocks and warrants. Finally, Lockheed's customers advanced payments of $100 million toward the purchase of the L-1011s.

The bailout saved Lockheed and the firm survived and prospered. The company abandoned the civilian aircraft business altogether and concentrated on military contracts. In 1977 it paid off the last of its government guaranteed loans. By 1983 Lockheed was ranked number five among the Fortune 500 in terms of total returns to investors over the previous ten years.[3]

During the 1980s and early 1990s it purchased electronics maker Sanders Associates and General Dynamics' fighter aircraft division. In 1985 it merged with Martin Marietta Corporation to become the Lockheed Martin Corporation, the nation's largest defense contractor with 165,000 employees. In 1996 it agreed to buy most of the Loral Corporation, another huge defense contractor, for $9.1 billion. Loral employed another 37,000 workers.

The Chrysler Bailout

So, in 1978, when Chrysler first ran into trouble, there was an adequate precedent for Chrysler to approach the federal government for assistance. Not only had Chrysler lost money in 1978 ($205 million), but it was facing enormous capital requirements, which it blamed on retooling made necessary by government regulations requiring fuel-efficient and less-polluting cars. By early 1979 the bond services downgraded Chrysler's bond ratings and made it impossible to increase its debt. The company was losing money every day but could not cut its capital improvement program for fear of losing out in the race for the market in compact cars. The company proceeded to sell off major portions of its worldwide assets in order to continue its capital program. Chrysler employment in the United States fell from 130,000 to around 100,000.

Early in 1979 Chrysler recognized that it was going to need some kind of government help in order to survive. It then hired the firm of "Tommy" Hale Boggs, Jr., son of the late Congressman Hale Boggs of Louisiana, as its Washington lobbyist. Later the company added more firepower with Republican lobbyist William Timmons and former Michigan Congressmen Garry Brown and James O'Hara and ex-Senator William Hathaway of Maine.

After an ill-fated attempt to obtain a tax credit, Chrysler settled on the loan guarantee, but much of Congress was skeptical. It wanted a scapegoat and an admission of mismanagement by Chrysler. Chrysler Chairman John Riccardo became that scapegoat and was forced to resign. He was replaced by Lee Iacocca.

Treasury Secretary William Miller became the Carter administration's point man in its negotiations with Chrysler. Miller insisted that the company cut its costs and obtain sacrifices from its constituents before it reached any deal with the government. The first sacrifice was to come from Chrysler's workers. Recognizing the seriousness of the situation, United Auto Workers (UAW) President Douglas Fraser reopened its contract with Chrysler in October of 1979. After several weeks of negotiation the UAW and Chrysler reached a deal. Kick-in dates for scheduled wage increases throughout the three-year contract would each be delayed by a few months. Chrysler workers would get twenty paid personal holidays as opposed to the twenty-six days workers would receive at Ford and General Motors (GM). Pension increases for Chrysler retirees would be less than those for the other automakers. And finally, benefit improvements for Chrysler workers would be slower than for Ford and GM workers. These concessions would save Chrysler $203 million over the course of the contract. However, Chrysler workers would still maintain their cost of living allowances

(COLAs), so that wages and benefits would keep pace with inflation. Finally, Douglas Fraser would be given a seat on Chrysler's board of directors.

Also in October, the company submitted its final revised financial plan to the Treasury. The plan asked for a loan guarantee of $750 million (down from the $1.2 billion in earlier versions). President Carter approved the guarantees contingent on a matching sacrifice from Chrysler's constituents. But when the administration's proposal was submitted to Congress on November 1, it was for a $1.5 billion package of loan guarantees conditioned on matching concessions from the company's banks, suppliers, dealers, employees, and state and local governments (the figure was raised from $750 million to $1.5 billion based on government-commissioned reports from Booz, Allen & Hamilton and accountants Ernst & Whinney). The proposal required private money to match the government's contribution dollar for dollar, but it did not specify how much each group would have to give.

The House and Senate Banking Committees each drafted and approved their own versions of legislation and sent them to both houses of Congress on December 6. Chrysler's lobbying campaign kicked into high gear. With pressure from Chrysler dealers throughout the nation, the UAW, mayors, and governors, the bills passed both the House and Senate and went on to the conference committee. The bill that emerged from conference required that Chrysler get binding commitments from its constituents before the government would issue any guarantees. The guarantee would be authorized by a Loan Guarantee Board consisting of the secretary of the Treasury, the chairman of the Federal Reserve, and the comptroller general. The secretaries of Labor and Transportation would be nonvoting members. The Loan Board was authorized to guarantee interest as well as principal at its discretion—potentially adding an additional $225 million to the package. The conference bill passed both houses of Congress in late December and the Chrysler Loan Guarantee Act of 1979 was signed into law by President Jimmy Carter two weeks later.[4]

The act was very specific in terms of the concessions it required of all parties:

1. Unionized workers were required to provide concessions worth $462.5 million (includes the $203 million in concessions in the October 1979 contract);

2. Nonunion workers would contribute $125 million;
3. Chrysler's U.S. banks would have to contribute $500 million—80 percent in new loans and 20 percent in concessions on already outstanding debt;
4. Foreign banks were required to contribute $150 million in new loans;
5. The company would be required to sell off another $300 million in assets;
6. State and local governments would have to provide $250 million in aid;
7. Suppliers and dealers would provide $180 million; and
8. Chrysler would be required to sell $50 million in new stock. (Chrysler was also forbidden to pay any dividends as long as any of the guaranteed loans were outstanding.)

Nevertheless, the Loan Board did have some flexibility. It could modify the amount of assistance provided by any one of the Chrysler constituents, except labor, as long as the total amount of concessions equaled the amount of the guarantees.

Chrysler and government negotiators labored long and hard with Chrysler's constituents to reach an agreement. Finally, in May 1980 the Loan Guarantee Board accepted Chrysler's plan. The terms of the plan were:

> Lenders would extend the maturity dates on $154 million in loans, forgive $181 million in interest, and defer $345 million in interest (this totals $680 million—a figure Chrysler had been using—but the government valued the package at $642 million). After 1983 Chrysler would have the option—if its cash flow improved and the K-car sold well—of giving the banks an equivalent value of preferred stock instead of paying deferred interest. Union employees would sacrifice $462.5 million, and nonunion benefits would be cut by $125 million. In addition, $418 million in pension fund deferrals would be valued at $342 million (given Pension Benefit Guarantee Corporation claims). The board counted $628 million in asset sales, based on "reasonable assurances" of $171 million from real estate sales, $250 million for a chunk of Chrysler Financial, and $100 million as an asset sale for the stock-secured loan from Peugeot, plus $106 million from subsidiaries in Brazil, Argentina, and Australia. Michigan lent Chrysler $150 million, and Delaware and Indiana were listed for loans of $5 million and $32 million. Canada would

contribute $170 million in loan guarantees after 1982. Finally, the $78 million in convertible debentures to dealers and suppliers counted as $63 million, for a total private aid package of $2.6 billion.[5]

In return for guaranteeing the new debt, the government would collect a fee of 1 percent per year on outstanding guaranteed loans, would hold claim to Chrysler assets of at least $2.4 billion at liquidation, and would hold 14 million warrants to buy Chrysler stock at $13 a share anytime up to the end of 1990.

The deal was ratified in June 1980, and the first $500 million in guaranteed bonds were sold carrying an interest rate of 10.35 percent. The bonds sold out the first day.

But this was not the end of the story. Chrysler was still in bad shape. It had lost $1.1 billion in 1979—more than any other company had ever lost in any one year. In order to break even Chrysler needed to sell 2.6 million vehicles in 1980 and it was not even going to come close. The Loan Board estimated that Chrysler would lose $1.2 billion in 1980.

On July 31, 1980, an additional $300 million in guaranteed notes were put on the market. The interest rate on these notes was 11.4 percent. The next day Chrysler announced that it was cutting another 5,400 of its white collar workers, this in addition to the 10,000 who had already lost their jobs since 1978. By September 1980, 9 of Chrysler's plants had been closed and another 23 were targeted for sale or shutdown. Chrysler's third quarter loss was $490 million.

Enter Ronald Reagan. In November 1980 Ronald Reagan defeated Jimmy Carter's bid for reelection. And while Reagan had declared his support for Chrysler during the campaign, many of his aids were categorically opposed. Treasury Secretary Miller thus warned Lee Iacocca that he had better hurry if he was going to ask for any of the $700 million in loan guarantees still available. Miller would recommend approval of only another $400 million but was requiring more concessions. With high interest rates stifling the demand for cars and with it clear to Lee Iacocca that Chrysler was not going to have the profitable fourth quarter predicted earlier, Chrysler had to go for it.

Miller told Iacocca that only a wage freeze could yield the cash necessary for a recovery. Again the UAW acceded.

> The deal required, first, that Chrysler's workers must ratify a concession package that would cut wages by $1.15 hourly on March 1 and

freeze them until September 1982, as well as freeze certain pension and other benefits. Second, Chrysler's lenders must convert half of their holdings of Chrysler debt into preferred stock and accept repayment on the other half at a rate of thirty cents on the dollar. Third, suppliers must lock themselves into price breaks of $36 million and promise a further 36 million. Fourth, Canada must agree to a smaller investment package—by 40 percent—than it had previously negotiated with Chrysler. Fifth, a largely symbolic but nonetheless irksome sacrifice: Chrysler must sell its company airplanes.[6]

The parties reluctantly approved the deal and on February 27, 1981, the Loan Board approved the issuance of another $400 million in guaranteed notes. These notes paid an interest rate of 15.13 percent and could be paid off ahead of schedule after three years. The day after the money arrived Chrysler announced its 1980 results—it had lost $1.71 billion.[7]

Through all of 1981 the company barely stayed alive. At one point in November its cash balance reached a low of $1 million—this against an average daily expenditure of $50 million. Chrysler needed more cash. Iacocca knew that the odds of getting the remaining $300 million in guaranteed loans were slim—Reagan's Treasury secretary, Donald Regan, had already told him that. Chrysler had only one option and that was to sell the profitable tank division. In February 1982 General Dynamics took over the tank division paying $340 million for the operation. Chrysler was in business again, and this time it was on the road to recovery.

Curiously, it was two economic initiatives of the Reagan administration that aided immeasurably in the recovery. The first was a part of the bundle of tax cuts in the Economic Recovery Tax Act of 1981. It was called safe-harbor leasing. Under safe-harbor, money-losing companies, like Chrysler, could sell and lease back their plant and equipment to profitable companies and the profitable companies could use the depreciation allowances and investment tax credits associated with the leased plant and equipment to reduce their tax burdens. Thus a great deal of money could be made by both parties to such transactions.

Chrysler worked out a deal with the General Electric Credit Corporation that transferred tax benefits on $100 million of Chrysler equipment to GE. Chrysler received $26 million. It would also gain some $38.4 million from safe-harbor leased transactions in 1981, $10.1 million in 1982, and $19.8 million in 1983.

The second benefit Chrysler received from the Reagan administration was an agreement with Japan whereby the Japanese agreed to limit export of automobiles to the United States. (See the appendix to this chapter for details.) In any event, these export restraints protected the American automakers and allowed them to raise prices without losing sales.

Chrysler sustained an operating loss of $70 million in 1982, one of the deepest recessionary years in modern times. But the money from the sale of the tank division yielded a net profit of $170 million. And Chrysler's cost-cutting campaign was showing dividends. A Chrysler assembly worker now earned $9.07 an hour compared to Ford and GM's $11.70.

In the summer of 1983 Chrysler pulled the unexpected—it paid back all $1.2 billion in federally guaranteed loans. But it still had one more obligation to the government—the 14.4 million warrants. By 1984 Chrysler's stock was selling at almost $30 per share (recall that the value of the warrant was $13 a share). Chrysler wanted the warrants retired and appealed to the government to sell it the warrants. It offered $218 million. The Treasury Department, however, decided to sell off the warrants at public auction to the highest bidder. With Chrysler stock selling for $29 a share it was easy to calculate the minimum value of the warrant at about $16. Chrysler entered the bidding and added a $5.10 premium to the value of the warrant. The strategy was successful—it won. Its bid was 93.4 cents per share over its nearest competitor. Chrysler wrote a check for $311.1 million to the Treasury.

The rest of the story is familiar. Chrysler returned to profitability and Lee Iacocca became something of a folk hero. The bailout worked.[8]

One could argue with some justification that the Chrysler bailout was a Democratic deal and that Ronald Reagan and the Republicans had very little to do with it. President Reagan simply held his nose and saw his predecessor's policy through to its conclusion.

This being the case, Republicans might hold that functional problem solving was a leg in the Democrats' industrial policy stool and that the GOP, and certainly a conservative president like Ronald Reagan, was not about to milk any cows from that stool. But, as it turned out, Ronald Reagan liked functional problem solving. He embraced it as an industrial policy approach more often than did his Democratic predecessor. One example is the rescue of the Continental Illinois National Bank.

Continental Illinois

By the end of the 1970s, Continental Illinois of Chicago had become one of the darlings of the banking industry. Under the direction of its chair, Roger Anderson, Continental had initiated an aggressive loan policy and had become one of the industry's high flyers with its stock selling around $40 a share. But all was not well in the Windy City. It turns out that Continental had picked up more than $1 billion in risky "upstream" oil loans from Penn Square Bank in Oklahoma before the latter folded. In addition, Continental had its own losers in its portfolio. In early May 1983, rumors held that something was obviously wrong with the Chicago bank and investors began dumping the bank's CDs as if they were radioactive. In a matter of days the nation's seventh-largest bank was brought to its knees.

The Federal Reserve Bank, the FDIC, and other government agencies agreed that Continental Illinois could not be allowed to fail because this might literally lead to hundreds of other failures of banks that were in fairly precarious positions themselves and with large deposits with Continental. These included First Chicago and Manufacturers Hanover as well as hundreds of small banks.

On May 16, Chairman of the Federal Reserve Paul Volker, FDIC head William Isaac, and Comptroller of the Currency Todd Conover met with the leading bankers in New York to work out a deal. The following morning they announced the largest bailout in banking history.

The FDIC put up new capital in the amount of $4.5 billion and assumed liability for the bulk of Continental's bad loans. The Federal Reserve agreed to lend whatever short-term funds were necessary to keep the bank afloat while the FDIC searched for a buyer. The Fed eventually provided Continental with emergency loans in the amount of $8 billion. But the most striking element of the bailout was the government's agreement to protect *all* depositors—insured and uninsured, and even the bank's bondholders.

What actually happened was that the federal government ended up owning and operating Continental Illinois, not as a central bank but as a regular commercial bank. The FDIC paid some $5.5 billion for 160 million shares of Continental's stock. It fired the management and hired new executives to run the bank. The federal government ended up in the banking business for about eight years until the bank was healthy enough for the FDIC to sell its stock on the open market.

But the bailout created a precedent far greater than the Chrysler bailout. And that precedent was that the largest banks would never be allowed to fail, no matter what the cost to the government, and ultimately, to the people. In hearings before the House of Representatives, the comptroller of the currency admitted that the country's largest banks would never be allowed to fail. This meant that probably some 50 or even 100 banks would always be safe because the banking system could not tolerate their failures.[9]

This doctrine, known literally as "too big to fail," was a policy that William Seidman tried to end in his term as chair of the FDIC (he replaced William Isaac). He was not successful. Large banks still have the upper hand. Regulators and policymakers believe that if a major money center bank (like Continental Illinois) failed, confidence in the entire American financial system would be shaken.[10]

This policy has created a dual banking system in the United States in which smaller banks will suffer competitively and the larger banks will benefit. Why would large depositors (those with deposits above the $100,000 insurance guarantee) ever put money in smaller banks when they know that their deposits will be perfectly safe in the largest (no matter how poor their management)? The federal government has created a system in which acquisitions and mergers are the only sensible thing to do as size becomes synonymous with invulnerability.[11]

The Savings and Loan Bailout (or, Other People's Money)

The savings and loan bailout is the second of the "mega" functional problem solving industrial policy events of the past twenty years. Between the latter years of the Carter administration and the early years of the Clinton presidency, about one in every three savings and loans (S&Ls) went bellyup. This was a failure of enormous proportion. The total cost of the bailout is likely to be over $200 billion in taxpayer money[12]—an amount equal to about 3 percent of gross domestic product. (The term "likely to be" is used because the bailout is still not complete.) The savings and loan crisis did not appear overnight nor was the ultimate resolution to the problem as worked out by the Bush administration the only attempt to save the industry. The Carter administration took several halting steps to correct the problems in the industry. And the Reagan administration made several misguided attempts to save the industry but ended up seriously compounding the problem. It was finally up to George Bush, the president who said that he did not have an industrial policy, to affect the bailout. But before examining the Carter/Reagan/Bush industrial policy for the savings and loan industry, some background is in order.

Background

In the early years of the nation, savings and loans concentrated on home loans and were regulated by the states. In only two periods during their first 150 years of existence did the S&Ls suffer a significant number of failures—the downturn of the 1890s and the Great Depression. Because they did not offer demand deposits, savings and loans historically held very few assets; in fact, many state laws discouraged the accumulation of reserves.

But during the Great Depression, savings and loans experienced record failures as members withdrew their savings in an attempt to maintain consumption and as the assets of the S&Ls (relatively non-liquid home mortgages) declined in value due to the number of real estate delinquencies and defaults. This forced the federal government to step in. In 1932 it established the Federal Home Loan Bank Board system consisting of twelve regional Federal Home Loan (FHL) banks and the Federal Home Loan Bank Board (FHLBB), the supervising agency. The system was designed so that the FHL banks could issue notes in the capital markets and advance these funds to member banks as needed to stabilize (not "bail out") these institutions. In 1933 the FHLBB was given the power to charter and regulate federal savings and loans. The Federal Savings and Loan Insurance Corporation (FSLIC) was created to provide federal insurance for deposits at federally chartered savings and loans and state-chartered S&Ls electing to join. The FSLIC insured deposits up to $40,000.

For the next four decades the S&Ls grew like weeds, although their functions were limited to lending for home mortgage loans and liabilities restricted almost entirely to savings deposits.

Precipitating Events

Through the mid-1960s the S&Ls were in an enviable position. Interest income from home mortgages exceeded the cost of deposits by a comfortable margin. Passbook savings accounts were a stable and low-cost source of funds. During this lengthy period it was profitable to "borrow short and lend long." That is, to use short-term savings accounts to fund long-term, fixed interest rate mortgage loans. But as it turned out, "borrow short and lend long" was a formula for disaster. Several events brought this about.

The first was a new form of competition. During the late 1960s and through the 1970s, new nondepository institutions (e.g., Sears) developed money market funds and other competitive investments that were able to successfully compete for the savers' dollars by offering interest rates higher than those offered by the S&Ls—competition S&L executives were not accustomed to. In some cases this competition led to panic and unsound business decisions as savers moved their deposits out of their passbook accounts and into more attractive investments.

The second precipitating event was a period of high and volatile interest rates. The late 1970s and early 1980s was an era characterized by superinflation. To combat this inflation, the Federal Reserve forced interest rates to unprecedented levels, severely affecting the financial condition of the savings and loan industry. When interest rates skyrocketed, S&L net operating income plummeted. It was here that "borrow short and lend long" came unglued as the S&Ls found that the short-term interest that they were forced to pay depositors was more than the income they were receiving from their long-term mortgage holdings. Thus, by 1981, 85 percent of all savings and loans were unprofitable, and virtually all would have been insolvent if they had been forced to market their mortgage portfolios.

While these two "events of history" "caused" many of the industry's problems, the structure of the industry itself made it nearly impossible for the industry to react. Laws and regulations significantly restricted the activities the S&Ls were allowed to engage in. For example, they were restricted in terms of the types of real estate loans they were allowed to offer (e.g., severe limits on commercial property mortgages) and even the types of home mortgages offered (no adjustable rate mortgages, or ARMs). Thus, their profits were largely determined

by the amount the interest rate earned on home mortgages exceeded
the interest rate paid on passbook deposits.[13]

The Government Responds

The government's initial response came toward the end of the Carter
administration. The Depository Institutions Deregulation and Monetary
Control Act (DIDMCA) of 1980 was a Carter administration initiative
designed to remove interest rate ceilings on deposit accounts and eliminate many of the distinctions among different types of depository
institutions. The specific provisions of the act were:

- All depository institutions could issue interest-bearing checking
  accounts and had to hold reserves at the Federal Reserve.
- S&Ls could have up to 20 percent of assets in a combination of
  consumer loans, commercial paper, and corporate debt instruments.
- Federal S&Ls could offer credit card services and engage in trust
  activities.
- A statutory capital requirement of 5 percent of deposits was re-
  placed with a range of 3 to 6 percent to be set by the Home Loan
  Bank Board.
- Deposit interest rate ceilings were to be phased out over a six-
  year period and the interest rate differential for S&Ls with it.
  Interest rate deregulation was to be administered by the Deposi-
  tory Institutions Deregulation Committee (DIDC) with the secre-
  tary of the Treasury as chair and the heads of the Federal
  Reserve, the FDIC, the Bank Board, and the National Credit
  Union Administration as voting members.
- Deposit insurance limit was raised to $100,000.
- There was federal preemption for state usury laws for mortgages
  and certain other loans.
- Statewide branching was permitted for federal S&Ls.
- Geographic limits for lending or service company operations
  were ended.
- Authority of federal S&Ls to make acquisition, development, and
  construction (ADC) loans was expanded.[14]

Thus, the federal government tried to cope with the situation by
giving the S&Ls new powers. The Carter administration began, and the

Reagan administration accelerated, reductions in regulations in the industry patterned after reductions in government regulation of the airlines, trucking, railroads, communications, and finance. The savings and loan industry became part of this movement. But S&L deregulation differed from deregulation in the other industries because S&Ls were never subjected to the discipline of the marketplace. The industry obtained substantial new investment powers and was subjected to less supervision, while government-backed deposit insurance was retained and even increased. "Shielded from the market discipline of depositors at risk, and with strong incentives to enter risky new areas, the industry was doomed and the insurance system set on a course that would involve huge claims on it."[15]

The Results

Inflation proved to be a tough nut to crack and interest rates remained in the double digits. Besides, the Carter reforms were too little, too late. By the end of 1981, 85 percent of all S&Ls were unprofitable with $29 billion in assets in insolvent S&Ls. One hundred twelve S&Ls were insolvent (but this constituted only 3 percent of all S&Ls).[16]

The Reagan Initiatives

The Reagan administration responded with a two-pronged attack. It completed the legislative deregulation started by Jimmy Carter and, through the Bank Board, it substantially loosened regulatory restrictions on the S&Ls. The Garn–St. Germain Depository Institutions Act of 1982 was the Reagan initiative that completed the process of giving the S&Ls powers to diversify their activities. The major provisions of the act were:

- Effectively eliminated deposit interest-rate ceilings.
- Expanded substantially the asset powers of federal S&Ls by permitting:
    Up to 40 percent of assets in commercial mortgage loans.
    Up to 30 percent of assets in consumer loans.
    Up to 10 percent of assets in commercial loans.
    Up to 10 percent of assets in commercial leases.

- Eliminated the previous statutory limit on the loan-to-value ratio, i.e., what an S&L could lend to a developer compared to the appraised value of the project for which the funds were lent.
- Authorized the FDIC and the FSLIC to issue "net worth certificates."
- Expanded the powers of the FSLIC to deal with troubled institutions.
- Restricted the ability of bank holding companies to acquire failed S&Ls.[17]

From 1980 through 1982 the Federal Home Loan Bank Board substantially loosened regulatory restrictions on the industry. The process began under Chairman Jay Jannis in 1980 but accelerated markedly under Richard Pratt, who served as chairman from March 1981 through May 1983.

First, the Bank Board dealt with the problem of the declining net worth of the industry by lowering the net worth requirement from 5 percent of total deposits to 4 percent, then to 3 percent. Thus, with the 3 percent standard an S&L could support every $1 million in assets with as little as $30,000 in net worth.

On top of that, the Bank Board retained a twenty–year phase-in and five–year averaging rule. Under the twenty–year phase-in, an S&L had twenty years to meet the net worth requirement from the date it was established. Thus, a five–year-old S&L only had to meet 5/20ths of the net worth requirement (or 0.75 percent). This made it very profitable to establish new S&Ls because very high leverage could be achieved for a small initial capital investment by the owners.

Under the five-year averaging for existing S&Ls, the net worth requirement was applied not to existing deposits, but to an average of the deposits over the previous five years. This policy rewarded rapid deposit growth as a method of reducing the net worth requirement and increasing leveraging.

The Bank Board also eliminated restrictions on the required number of S&L stockholders. Previously, 400 stockholders were required with no individual owning more than 10 percent of the stock and no controlling group owning more than 25 percent. With the new regulation there could be a single owner. In addition, takeovers were made easy by allowing acquirers to put up real estate in lieu of cash (often at inflated appraisal values).

These changes allowed developers, others with conflicts of interest, and outright crooks to take over S&Ls. It also allowed them to milk their institutions and rob them blind.

The Bank Board was able to avoid dealing with the net worth problem and the other problems to be discussed below by simply changing accounting standards. They moved from what is called "generally accepted accounting principles" (GAAP), which were themselves abused by many S&Ls, to far looser "regulatory accounting principles" (RAP). Under the Bank Board's RAP there were far fewer S&Ls in trouble than under GAAP, as is shown by the following figures for 1983.

	Number of S&Ls Insolvent	Assets in Insolvent S&Ls
Under RAP	48	$12 billion
Under GAAP	293	$79 billion

Accounting trickery was the reason. In addition to changing net worth standards, RAP allowed numerous other shenanigans. The Bank Board introduced "loss deferral" as a component of RAP accounting. With loss deferral an S&L could sell loans at a loss, take the loss for tax purposes, but amortize the loss over the contractual life of the asset. In a classic maneuver, the Bank Board under GAAP allowed "goodwill mergers." Goodwill mergers permitted and encouraged assets of an acquired savings and loan to be marked down to market value, and the difference between its liabilities and the market value of assets (substantially lower than liabilities) was "goodwill," which the acquirer carried on its books both as an asset and as a contribution to net worth. Thus goodwill was a sham method of increasing the net worth of an acquirer while making it look like the problem of the insolvent S&L had been solved.

To top it all off, any appreciation in the value of the discounted assets received at time of sale was treated as income and could be paid out rather than used to reduce goodwill. So acquisition of insolvent S&Ls was tempting to other S&Ls facing insolvency because they could show fictitious income and still pay high dividends, executive bonuses, and megabucks salaries. The acquirer received the added bonus of regulatory forbearance as a reward for taking over an insolvent S&L.

Several other events occurred that made matters even worse. Beginning in 1982 and running through 1985 (when supervisory responsibility was shifted to the Home Loan Banks), reductions in the number of Bank Board examiners decreased the board's ability to police the industry. In addition, the loosening of federal regulations "set off a competition in laxity in state regulation."[18] California, Florida, and Texas opened up virtually any activity to their state-chartered S&Ls.

Finally, the Reagan administration's 1981 Tax Act, its major tax-reduction initiative, reduced the depreciation life of real estate to fifteen years (from up to sixty years). It also made depreciation available to passive investors. These moves led to a frenzy in real estate development and speculation, which, when the bubble burst in 1986, caused enormous losses in many S&Ls.[19]

The Results

Throughout most of the 1980s, S&L problems were like the proverbial hot potato—no one wanted to touch it; not the Bank Board, not the Reagan administration, not Congress. The Bank Board went through two other chairmen, Edwin Gray and Danny Wall, but neither was effective in dealing with the debacle. The National Commission on Financial Institution Reform, Recovery, and Enforcement estimated that had the Bank Board moved in 1983 to close insolvent institutions, the total cost probably would not have exceeded $25 billion,[20] as opposed to the $200 plus billion it will eventually cost. But instead, the Bank Board and the whole federal government tried to cope with the situation by engaging in extended forbearance for insolvent institutions. They hoped that by buying time the problem would go away. They were counting on deregulation, lower interest rates, and an improved economy to solve the problem. The Reagan administration stuck its head in the sand and refused to recognize or deal with the extent of the problem. Its only concern was to keep any potential solution off-budget.

The end result was that by the end of the 1980s hundreds of savings and loans had failed and had to be "resolved" by the FSLIC. Over the decade of the 1980s the FSLIC took actions against 917 thrifts. The extent of this activity was about $50 billion. But to no avail. The debacle continued and even got worse. A thoroughly politicized and industry-dominated Bank Board was unwilling to take action and the FSLIC was essentially bankrupt. And the S&L debacle became George Bush's problem.

But before discussing the final resolution of the crisis it is useful to digress a bit to look at other causes of the debacle. Extended forbearance, deregulation, and loosened regulatory restrictions have already been discussed. But there are other contributing causes.

Deteriorating Asset Quality

Plunging oil prices in the early 1980s were followed by plunging real estate prices as Texas entered a regional recession. As a result, the S&Ls that had financed much of the Texas real estate boom were stuck with overvalued assets as mortgages defaulted. As a result, industry losses became increasingly concentrated in Texas after 1984, with most of the losses being due to asset write-downs.

Federal and State Deregulation

Savings and loans had been heavily regulated for years and were in serious trouble by the early 1980s as they found themselves vulnerable to competition from new types of financial institutions. Congress (for federally chartered institutions) and many states (for state-chartered institutions) responded by giving the S&Ls new and expanded powers. As a result, competition among the S&Ls, and between them and other financial service firms, increased. As a result, some institutions failed. Further, deregulation allowed inadequately capitalized institutions the freedom to adopt highly risky strategies. In hindsight, it is clear that the deregulation was too late. The industry was already in trouble and deregulation gave some already-troubled S&Ls the opportunity to do themselves in.

Fraudulent Practices

Many Americans can still recall the "adventures" of Charles Keating and the Lincoln Savings and Loan in Southern California. Keating, however, was only an icon. There is no question but that fraudulent practices played a significant part in the savings and loan debacle. Some scholars have suggested that fraudulent activities were found in roughly half of the savings and loans resolved. Further, the Resolution

Trust Corporation found fraudulent activities in over half of the insolvent savings and loans that came under its control during the first year of operation.

Moral Hazard

Most analysts agree that the system of deposit insurance for S&L savings deposits set up by the federal government made failure inevitable in a go-for-broke market. The government FSLIC insurance program (first $40,000, then $100,000) took the risk away from S&L investments as far as savers were concerned. Depositors could seek out the institution paying the highest interest rate without having to worry about the financial health of the S&L. The same attitude was prevalent among those who ran the institutions. S&L executives never had to worry about the safety of depositors' money.

Inaction by the Executive Branch

Officials in the Reagan administration and those appointed by President Reagan to oversight agencies consistently took action to cover up as opposed to solve the debacle. There are literally hundreds of examples, but two of the most egregious were the change in accounting standards to aid in the cover-up, and removal of the 5 percent minimum statutory capital requirement then in effect in the industry.[21]

Politics

The iron triangle of interest group politics was certainly a root cause of the federal government's inaction. Savings and loan money was spread far, wide, and deep to assure a cozy relationship between the industry, Congress, and administrative overseers. Influential congressmen were bought and paid for by the industry and played a huge part in the cover-up. The history of congressional abuse and influence peddling went far beyond the Keating five.[22]

The Final Resolution

The election of George Bush to the presidency in November 1988 brought about a change in policy toward the S&Ls and with it a recognition that the problem would not go away. Early on, the Bush team estimated that between 300 and 400 institutions with $200 billion in assets were still in trouble. After George Bush was elected president, but before he took office, the FDIC and the Treasury staff worked feverishly to design a rescue plan that President Bush could implement after his inauguration in January.[23] That rescue plan, the Financial Institutions Reform, Recovery and Enforcement Act (FIRREA), was signed into law on February 6, 1989 (showing that Congress can act quickly if it wants to). The major provisions

- Gave $50 billion of new borrowing authority with most financed from general revenues and the rest from industry;
- Abolished the Federal Home Loan Bank Board and the FSLIC; regulation was shifted to the newly established Office of Thrift Supervision (OTS) within the U.S. Treasury, and deposit insurance was shifted to the FDIC for the newly designated thrift institutions;
- Imposed meaningful net worth requirements[24] and regulations by the OTS and the FDIC, entities that were not captives of the industry they were to regulate;
- Allocated funds to the Justice Department to help finance prosecution of the wrongdoers who had for too long ranged within the industry.[25]

FIRREA also created the Resolution Trust Corporation (RTC), which would "take over, dissect, bury, and dispense with the sick and dying S&Ls."[26] The RTC took its name from the financial term "resolve," which means to dispose of a firm's assets and reach a final solution for the firm. The RTC's initial organizational structure was a compromise between management efficiency and bureaucratic politics. Three separate decision-making bodies were involved: the RTC Oversight Board, the FDIC, and the RTC itself. The Oversight Board's responsibilities were to set strategy and manage funds, the RTC was to take over and dispose of the failed thrifts, while the FDIC became the operating manager of the RTC. Thus, the chair of the FDIC, William Seidman, became the operating head of the RTC. The governing board of the FDIC became the governing board for operations (but not planning or finance) of the RTC. There was also another agency involved—the OTS. When the OTS through its regulatory and inspection functions found a thrift to be insolvent, it was turned over to the RTC for liquidation.

Having an Oversight Board clearly defied organizational logic, but not political logic. A majority of the seats on the Oversight Board were to be filled by Bush administration appointees: the secretary of the Treasury, the secretary of the Department of Housing and Urban Development, and two public members to be named by the president. The fifth member was the "independent" chair of the Federal Reserve Board. The reason for the Oversight Board was the administration's belief that since the RTC was going to be responsible for billions in spending to clean up the S&L mess, it was only logical that oversight be provided by people who would be accountable to the administration.[27]

The RTC was not long into its mission when it became clear that the original estimate of 350 to 400 insolvent institutions worth $200 billion in assets was much too low. In less than a year the estimate had grown to 700 to 800 insolvent S&Ls with assets over $400 billion and potential losses to the taxpayers of more than $100 billion.

The bailout required an enormous amount of up-front cash. Seidman describes the need for cash and how the system worked:

> If the institution [the failed S&L] had $6 billion in loans on the books and $6 billion in deposits, we [RTC] would have to pay off the depositors. That would demand $6 billion of our cash up front, but as we sold the $6 billion in assets—loans on empty office buildings, desert land, or whatever harebrained schemes in which the S&L had invested its depositors' money, we would probably realize only about $4 billion. Thus, even though the loss might be only $2 billion, we would still need $6 billion in cash—working capital of $4 billion, plus the additional $2 billion to meet losses, in order to close and dispose of the institution. The funds we needed to do the job were far larger than the final cost, and they had to be borrowed from the government.[28]

It was not long before the RTC became a large bureaucratic organization. Within a year it had some 8,000 employees and had hired thousands of independent contractors. It employed more than 1,500 people in its Legal Division alone, hired more than 1,000 outside law firms, and its legal bill was almost $1 billion (yes, billion) a year. It was prosecuting more than 150,000 lawsuits. A major task of the RTC was collecting the hundreds of thousands of loans made by defunct S&Ls. Most of the lawsuits were taken against individuals who were in no rush to make good on loans obtained from institutions that no longer existed.

The assets the RTC had to dispose of were primarily mortgages of one-to-four-family homes. Most of these were easy to dispose of through sales to Fannie Mae. Other assets were not so marketable. These included golf courses, marinas, condominiums, uranium mines, resorts, ranches, farms, works of art, coin collections, and office buildings—almost anything a borrower wanted to put up as collateral.

By March 1990 the RTC had an inventory of about $40 billion in "difficult assets." Bill Seidman concluded that if it were to sell $1 million in assets every day, it would have taken more than 120 years to clear out its inventory. (But the RTC was mandated to close down on or before December 31, 1996.) The RTC's strategy therefore was to sell in bulk. It packaged a large pool of assets, which it sold to one buyer in a single portfolio. In order to sell small properties not suitable for pooled sales, it developed a graduated pricing system—much like Filene's basement in Boston. The longer the holding period, the lower the price, down to 50 percent of the original sales price.[29]

Over its lifetime, the RTC resolved all 747 institutions for which it was appointed conservator or receiver. From its inception in August 1989 through the end of 1995, it disposed of assets with a book value of more than $455 billion, or approximately 98 percent of the assets under its control.[30] Its work essentially complete, the RTC went out of business on January 1, 1996. Its affairs have been taken over by the FDIC.[31]

Perhaps the best way to close this discussion of the S&L debacle is with a quote from William Seidman, first head of the RTC:

> The S&L crisis was born in the economic climate of the times. It was nurtured, however, in the fertile ground of politics as usual and the political mentality of "not on my watch." The system may have given rise to the crisis, but human beings, with all their faults, ultimately determined the scope of the debacle. The S&L mistakes resulted in the closing down of one-third of the industry, destroying the agency charged with promoting and insuring it, and costing the American taxpayers around $200 billion, plus interest on that amount, probably forever! No larger financial error appears to be recorded in history. And all because the use of the full faith and credit of the U.S. government was not treated with the respect and fear that must be accorded it.[32]

Too Big to Fail

In his opposition to the Chrysler bailout, Senator William Proxmire of Wisconsin is reported to have said:

> If we provide loan guarantees to Chrysler, we will be saying, in effect, to every business in the country that it doesn't matter if you make bad management decisions, it doesn't matter if you no longer make products that enough people want to buy, it doesn't matter if the federal government has no direct stake in your continued existence. None of this matters so long as you are big enough and can muster enough interest groups to fight your case in Washington.[33]

And, of course, Proxmire is right. "Too big to fail" is the major criterion for the use of the functional problem solving approach. It is not the approach itself but the reason for functional problem solving that is in question—the company is too big, the bank is too big, or the industry is too important, both politically and economically.

The problem, too big to fail, causes the government to devise policies to avert the failure. Much of the time the policies are successful, but occasionally they are not. Witness the Reagan administration's actions (and inactions) with regard to the savings and loan crisis. So functional problem solving is one of our industrial policy strategies. But it is not ours alone. Functional problem solving is a policy approach common to most industrialized nations. The Japanese have used it to "rationalize" their machine tool and shipbuilding industries, for example.

The next chapter looks at a derivative of functional problem solving as it plays out in the arena of international trade—"aggressive unilateralism." Aggressive unilateralism is a trade-specific functional problem solving approach that supports (or has supported) a number of specific American industries, quite often those in the high-technology sector, like semiconductors, computers, and communications equipment.

Appendix: Reagan's Restriction on Japanese Autos

For a number of years under the Carter presidency, the U.S. auto industry had been lobbying for protection from Japanese imports. The Ford Motor Company had proposed a cap on Japanese imports of a million cars a year. Ford was supported by powerful allies—General Motors, Chrysler, and the United Auto Workers.

Shortly after Ronald Reagan took office, Republican Senator John Danforth of Missouri and Democratic Senator Lloyd Bentsen of Texas introduced legislation limiting Japanese imports to 1.6 million cars a year. The administration wanted to support the American automobile industry, but administration supply-siders opposed limiting legislation on philosophical grounds. But White House Counselor Edwin Meese and Chief of Staff James Baker III worked out a compromise. "The restraints would be imposed by the Japanese themselves. There would be no formal trade action, no demands, no bilateral negotiations, and no technical violation of international trade law. The White House simply would signal to the Japanese that they must restrain their auto shipments."[34]

That spring, U.S. Trade Representative William E. Brock was sent to Tokyo to signal to the Japanese the acceptability of various Japanese proposals. On April 30, 1981, Japan's Ministry of International Trade and Industry (MITI) announced that it was imposing a limit of 1.68 million autos to be shipped to the United States. Also, growth of Japanese exports to the United States would be limited to 16.5 percent of any expansion of the U.S. automobile market.

For U.S. consumers, the end result was a situation where U.S. automakers could raise prices without having to fear a loss in sales. This amounted to a significant price increase on both imported and domestic cars to the benefit of U.S. auto manufacturers. By the third year of the restraint it was estimated that American consumers were paying about $5 billion a year in higher auto prices than they would have paid without the voluntary export restraint (VER).[35] (VERs are now banned under the Uruguay round of the GATT.)

4

Aggressive Unilateralism in a Free Trade Environment

In 1985 the United States adopted a more aggressive position with its trading partners—a position that has been given the unwieldy label of "aggressive unilateralism." A more appealing title to this chapter would have been "Managed Trade in a Free Trade Environment." But unfortunately both the terms "managed trade" and "aggressive unilateralism" have been given limited and technical meanings,[1] now generally accepted by economists studying trade issues. So "aggressive unilateralism" will have to do.

Aggressive unilateralism represents a more assertive trade stance for the United States in demanding that trading partners reduce barriers to U.S. exports and investments. The trade stance is aggressive because it is often backed by threats of retaliation under provisions of U.S. trade law. It is unilateral because (1) the United States unilaterally decides that the actions of a trading partner are unfair, and (2) it requires that its partner unilaterally liberalize without any reciprocal concessions from the United States.[2] And, although aggressive unilateralism has been defined as export policy, there is no reason why the term cannot be used with regard to unfair trading practices with imports as well.

"Managed trade" refers to trade agreements between trading partners that have fixed quantitative trade outcomes. This is distinguished from "trade management," whereby trade agreements are established through a system of agreed-upon rules.[3]

The two terms—aggressive unilateralism and managed trade—are not necessarily unrelated. For example, a managed trade agreement may result from aggressive unilateralism. In fact, this is exactly what happened in one of the cases discussed in this chapter—the case of U.S. demands that Japan open its auto and auto parts markets.

Aggressive unilateralism is a relatively new approach. The traditional U.S. approach to trade has been to encourage multilateral solutions to trade problems whereby countries exchange reciprocal commitments to lower trade barriers under the auspices of the General Agreement on Tariffs and Trade (GATT). The driving force behind the U.S. commitment to GATT has been a long-term commitment to free(er) trade.

However, in recent years some U.S. policymakers reached the conclusion that the traditions of free trade so widely held needed to be modified. This belief came as case after case has come to light illustrating how subsidies and protective devices have skewed markets for U.S.-produced products both at home and abroad. And this has been particularly true in what is commonly referred to as the high-technology sector.[4]

These technology-intensive industries violate the assumptions of free trade theory. A nation's competitive position in these industries is often a function of that nation's interactions between its firms and government and the firms and governments of other nations. Most now agree that competitive advantage in high-tech industries is created and that governments the world over have earmarked them for special support. This, of course, is industrial policy. Furthermore, it violates the tenants of free trade. The most dogmatic of the free trade arguments holds

> that foreign promotional policies usually worsen the terms of trade for the country initiating them and benefit its trading partners. According to this logic, when the Japanese subsidize semiconductors or the Europeans subsidize aircraft, the United States enjoys the benefits of cheaper foreign products. A note of thanks is more appropriate than a threat of retaliation.
>
> Similarly, traditional free traders contend that if the Japanese restrict access to their market, whether intentionally through overt trade barriers or unintentionally through regulatory policies, they will pay higher prices and reduce their own economic welfare. True, the United States' and Japan's other trading partners will suffer some loss of efficiency,

because the gains from trade will be reduced. And standard economic logic assumes that the composition of trade does not matter—a dollar's worth of exports or imports of shoes has the same effect on national economic welfare as a dollar's worth of exports or imports of computers. . . . Many traditional free traders recognize that . . . barriers are likely to fan protectionist sentiments at home and retaliation abroad. . . . But traditional free traders believe that the appropriate response to such dangers is the development of new multilateral rules, not unilateral actions, particularly if those actions transgress existing rules.[5]

The tenor of U.S. trade relations for most of this century has favored free trade. But within this free trade protocol there have always been exceptions—ways of protecting American industries from the unfair practices of other nations through trade remedies. These remedies are "designed to offer recourse to interests seriously injured by imports and to those up against what were considered 'unfair' foreign practices."[6] They are in essence a series of rules. They are also a specialized form of the instrument-specific approach to functional problem solving. They are decision rules for industrial policy and, because they are targeted at remedying problems of specific industries, the sum of their outputs is industrial policy. Free trade, of course, is not industrial policy. It is macroeconomic policy. It is aggressive unilateralism that produces industrial policy.

Background

The Tariff Act of 1930, commonly known as "Smoot–Hawley," established the highest general tariff rate structure the United States had ever seen. By one estimate, the tariff on dutiable imports, on average, reached 60 percent. Country after country raised barriers in retaliation. Imports dropped from $4.4 billion in 1929 to $1.5 in 1933, and exports dropped from $5.2 billion to $1.7 billion. The Great Depression deepened and became global. Today, virtually everyone except perennial Republican presidential hopeful Pat Buchanan concedes that Smoot–Hawley was one of the major causes of the Depression. And even though Congress has the primary responsibility under the Constitution to regulate "commerce with foreign nations," Smoot–Hawley was the last general tariff law to be enacted by the Congress of the United States.

Four years after Smoot–Hawley, Congress began tearing down the trade barriers it had created by authorizing the president to enter into bilateral negotiations to reduce U.S. tariffs by up to 50 percent. By 1945, the United States had entered into some 32 such agreements with 27 countries. And under American leadership the GATT was negotiated, providing the framework for multilateral tariff negotiations. Since that time there have been eight "rounds" to further reduce barriers to international trade. For most of this era, free trade was the dominant paradigm.

The United States was in an enviable economic position immediately following World War II. Europe and Japan were devastated. The United States was in a position to sell far more abroad than the rest of the world could sell her in return. Liberal trade policy (freer trade) made practical sense. And trade policy could be subordinated to the broader American foreign policy of reconstructing the free world.

But in the early 1960s, after the formation of the new European Economic Community, the Congress began having doubts about the wisdom of subordinating trade to foreign policy within the State Department and established (with some opposition from President Kennedy) a Special Representative for Trade Negotiations (STR) in the Executive Office of the president. The STR has evolved into the present-day Office of the United States Trade Representative (USTR), which is still located in the Executive Office of the president.

One of the principal functions of the USTR is to administer the American system of trade remedies to those industries and companies seriously injured by imports or unfair foreign trade practices. Many of today's remedies go well back in history. For example, a law dating from 1897 required that the secretary of the Treasury impose an offsetting duty if he found that a foreign government was subsidizing exports with a bounty. Similarly, the Anti-Dumping Act of 1921 also called for duties if foreign manufacturers were selling goods on our market at prices below their home market prices. And while trade remedies have been subject to some changes in criteria and eligibility, they have remained remarkably stable.[7] Today's major remedies are succinctly defined by trade policy expert I.M. Destler:

Antidumping Investigation. Any investigation instituted by an importing country in response to a claim that a foreign supplier is selling merchandise at "less than fair value." (See "dumping.") In the United States, if the Department of Commerce finds dumping has occurred, and the US International Trade Commission finds that US firms have been materially injured, the law provides that customs officials levy an additional import duty equal to the calculated price discrepancy. GATT Article VI authorizes such measures. The Uruguay Round antidumping code, signed in 1994, aims to standardize and discipline national government practices. . . .

Dumping [is t]he sale of a commodity in a foreign market at "less than fair value." Fair value is usually considered to be the price at which the same product is sold in the exporting country or to third countries, but under US law dumping can also be established by comparing the export price to the estimated costs of production of the merchandise in question. When dumping occurs, the legal remedy is imposition of a special duty equal to the "margin" of dumping, the difference between fair value and the actual sales price. . . .

Countervailing Duty Investigation. An investigation instituted by an importing country when given evidence that foreign goods sold within its borders are subsidized by the government in the country of its production. If a subsidy is found by the US Department of Commerce, and the US International Trade Commission finds that US firms have been materially injured, US law generally requires imposition of a duty to offset the subsidy. The Uruguay Round code on subsidies and countervailing measures, signed in 1994, aims to standardize and discipline national practices on subsidies and offsetting duties. . . .

Escape Clause (Section 201, Article XIX). A provision of the GATT articles, and of US law, authorizing import relief as a temporary "safeguard" for domestic producers injured by import competition. Originally limited to those whose losses resulted from prior US trade concessions, escape clause eligibility was extended in Section 201 of the Trade Act of 1974 to all who could establish that imports were "a substantial cause of serious injury, or the threat thereof." The Omnibus Trade and Competitiveness Act of 1988 stipulated that the goal of any relief must be "positive adjustment." If the US International Trade Commission finds injury and recommends relief, the president must grant it or report to Congress why, after reviewing the "national economic interest of the United States," he has decided there is "no appropriate and feasible action to take." Congress may then override his decision through enactment of a joint resolution, imposing thereby the remedy recommended by the USITC. . . .

Section 301. Under this provision of the Trade Act of 1974, as amended by the Omnibus Trade and Competitiveness Act of 1988, the USTR is required to take all appropriate action, including retaliation, to obtain the removal of any act, policy, or practice of a foreign government that violates an international agreement or is unjustifiable, unreasonable, or discriminatory, and burdens or restricts US commerce. In practice, it has been employed increasingly on behalf of American exporters fighting foreign import barriers or subsidized competition in third-country markets. . . .

Special 301. This clause in the 1988 Omnibus Trade Act requires the USTR to investigate countries determined to have a history of violating existing laws and agreements dealing with intellectual property rights. Such countries must have their current practices reviewed each year, and, if they are not found to be improving, are subject to mandated retaliation under Section 301. . . .

Super 301. Under this amendment to Section 301 of the 1988 Trade Act, the USTR was required in 1989 and 1990 to designate "priority foreign countries," chosen for the "number and pervasiveness" of their "acts, policies, or practices" impeding US exports, and for the US export gains that might come from the removal of these practices. The law called for retaliation if foreign action was insufficient or not forthcoming. In March 1994, President Clinton issued a so-called "Super 301" executive order targeting "priority foreign country *practices.*" Its provisions, carrying through 1995, were codified in the Uruguay Round implementing legislation.[8]

The "super" and "special" variants of Section 301 of the 1988 Trade Act are what led Jagdish Bhagwati to come up with the term "aggressive unilateralism." Thomas Bayard and Kimberly Elliott, however, date aggressive unilateralism to September 1985 when President Reagan called for "free but fair" trade and instructed USTR Clayton Yeutter to launch an aggressive export promotion policy using Section 301.[9] But with Super 301, Congress was looking for a "results oriented," low-tolerance approach to trade—particularly trade with Japan.

These congressional trade revisionists complained of three elements of the "Japanese problem." First, the revisionists argued that given the structural nature of Japanese obstacles to trade (see the appendix), Japanese markets were not likely to be opened through changes in trade rules. Second, they argued that Japan has historically opened her markets only when confronted with threats. And third, they complained that Japanese trade impediments are particularly unfair given the openness of the U.S. market to Japanese companies. Section 301 and its later variants came about because the revisionists believed that the only way to deal with the Japanese was to get them to commit to specific results.[10]

Despite the Reagan administration's shift to a more activist trade policy in 1985, many members of Congress did not believe that the administration was moving fast enough or far enough. Congressman Richard Gephardt thus proposed an amendment that would have required the USTR to (1) identify countries with "excessive and unwarranted" trade surpluses with the United States, and (2) then to identify those that also engage in unreasonable or discriminatory practices that have a negative impact on U.S. commerce. Once these countries were identified, the USTR would have six months to negotiate an agreement with the identified countries to eliminate the unfair practices and reduce the U.S. bilateral deficit. Finally, the USTR would be required to retaliate against countries that either failed to reach an agreement or did not reach their surplus reduction targets.

As expected, the Reagan administration strongly opposed the Gephardt amendment and threatened a veto. But the Congress wanted to send the president a strong message about trade priorities, settling on Super 301 as an alternative. Super 301 required the president (in 1989 and 1990) to enumerate trade priorities and identify countries with unfair trade practices. Unlike the Gephardt amendment, retaliation was discretionary if trade agreements were not violated.

In 1989, Carla Hills, George Bush's USTR, began implementing Super 301 and targeted six practices in three countries:

• Japanese exclusionary government procurement involving both *supercomputers* and *satellites*, and technical barriers to trade in *forest products*;
• Brazilian *quantitative import restrictions;*
• Indian *trade-related investment measures* that prohibit or burden foreign investment and barriers to trade in services, specifically the closure of India's *insurance* market to foreign firms.[11]

In 1990, Hills essentially ignored congressional intent by citing the Uruguay Round as the administration's top trade priority and failed to list any new Super 301 violations. Super 301 expired at the end of 1990 and was not renewed by Congress.

Shortly after his election, however, Bill Clinton promised that he would renew Super 301 by executive order and he did so in March 1994. Bayard and Elliott have called it a "kinder and gentler super 301." It was kinder because it did not require or encourage the labeling of entire countries as unfair traders. It was gentler because it gave the USTR more time to conduct negotiations before designations were due and because the USTR was not required to designate practices that had already been addressed or were under negotiation.[12]

Cases

The four cases that follow illustrate the application of trade remedies as examples of American industrial policy. Three of the cases are 301 actions and illustrate U.S. attempts to open up Japanese markets for American manufacturers and suppliers. The fourth case is an example of the application of an antidumping procedure in an attempt to protect an agricultural product, cut flowers, from foreign competition.

Motorola and the Sale of Cellular Telephones in Japan

Motorola first explored the idea of selling cellular phones in Japan in 1984. Nippon Telegraph and Telephone (NTT), the nation's publicly owned monopoly provider of telephone service, was in the process of privatizing. According to new laws issued by Japan's Ministry of Posts and Telecommunications (MPT), technical standards were to be established by the Telecommunications Deliberation Council, appointed by and attached to MPT. The Council recommended that any of three protocols, including those of NTT and Motorola, could be adopted for cellular service in Japan.

To implement cellular service, MPT decided that Japan should be divided into regions. NTT would be allowed to operate in all regions and one additional company would be allowed to compete with NTT in each region. However, only NTT's protocol could be used throughout the nation. Motorola was working with a Japanese partner—Daini Denden (DDI)—in an attempt to obtain a license to compete with NTT. In 1986 DDI began discussions with MPT relative to obtaining a license. But soon a rival appeared. A new consortium, Nippon Idou Tsushin Corporation (IDO), composed of Toyota, NEC, Japan Highway Authority, and Tokyo Electric Power, emerged with much stronger industrial and government connections than DDI. MPT attempted unsuccessfully to promote a merger. Once that failed, MPT announced in 1987 that licenses would be granted to IDO for the eastern half of Japan, including Tokyo—60 to 70 percent of the market—and to DDI for the remaining part. DDI accepted but Motorola was unhappy and complained to U.S. officials. After months of protracted negotiations between American and Japanese trade officials, DDI was given a license to operate throughout Japan, except in the populous Tokyo–Nagoya corridor. MPT claimed that there were insufficient frequencies to allow DDI to compete in Tokyo–Nagoya. This meant that NTT's protocol was the only one licensed for the Tokyo–Nagoya corridor and therefore the only company capable of delivering service throughout Japan. Motorola customers could still not use their phones in the Tokyo–Nagoya region. But Motorola reluctantly accepted the allocation.

However, shortly thereafter MPT allocated a 40-megahertz band width to a new and politically well-connected service, Convenience Radio Phone (CRP), for operation in the Tokyo area. Motorola once again complained to American trade officials.

This time Motorola's position was strengthened by the passage of the 1988 Omnibus Trade and Competitiveness Act and Super 301. Motorola filed a petition with the USTR, complaining that Japan was violating the MOSS (market-oriented, sector-specific) telecommunications agreement of the early 1980s in which Japan promised to open its markets and bring Japan's regulatory practices more in line with America's. MPT argued that it had not violated MOSS and also contended that the problem in the Tokyo–Nagoya area would disappear in a few years when digital cellular phones replaced the analogues currently in use. Motorola, however, saw this as another delaying tactic.

On April 28, 1989, the USTR announced that Japan had violated the MOSS agreement and that MPT had unfairly limited the access of American companies for third-party radio and cellular telephone systems. Telecommunications was the first sector slated for Super 301 retaliation. One hundred percent duties were to be levied on a variety of Japanese imports in thirty days if negotiations failed to resolve the dispute. Motorola's right to compete in the Tokyo–Nagoya market was a major bone of contention. After two months of bitter negotiations MPT finally agreed to reallocate frequencies in the region to allow Motorola to compete in the Tokyo–Nagoya market.

However, MPT designated IDO to serve as Motorola's operating company in the corridor. MPT made 20 percent of IDO's spectrum allocation available to Motorola. IDO was also ordered to erect the infrastructure necessary to service the Motorola equipment. In other words, IDO was ordered to operate a system that would directly compete with its already operating NTT system and its Japanese suppliers. IDO had every reason to delay, and it did—taking almost a year to order the necessary equipment from Motorola. And it was another year before it was installed. So not until the end of 1991 was Motorola up and running—more than two years after the 301 agreement. Overall, Motorola was finally able to establish a viable, although not fully equitable, place in Japan's cellular telephone market.[13]

The Sale of Wood Products in Japan

The wood products case is one of the best illustrations of how the Congress wanted Super 301 to be used to peel away the onion-like layers of Japanese protection. It is also meaningful because annual export gains from opening up the Japanese wood products market were estimated to be as high as $2 billion.

This Super 301 case was the culmination of a series of efforts beginning back in the late 1970s to open up the Japanese wood products market. U.S. suppliers had long complained about both tariff and regulatory obstacles to Japan's market. In particular, U.S. producers complained about:

- product standards that discriminate against imports;
- standards based on aesthetic qualities (e.g., appearance) rather than performance characteristics;
- unnecessarily restrictive building and fire codes;
- subsidies, including low-cost loans and tax incentives, for inefficient producers;
- government tolerance of cartels and restrictive business practices.[14]

In 1985, after several years of unsuccessful bilateral discussions, President Reagan and Prime Minister Nakasone initiated market-access negotiations under what became known as the MOSS talks. MOSS was relatively successful in liberalizing wood products trade with Japan. Japan reduced tariffs on some fabricated wood products, modified its building code to allow greater use of 4x8 panels in construction, and allowed the establishment of foreign testing offices in the United States to certify that U.S. products met Japanese standards. Overall, the United States viewed these agreements as very productive. U.S. exports of wood products to Japan grew by 133 percent between 1986 and 1989.

Despite this growth in exports, industry officials and their supporters in Congress pressed for further market openings and urged USTR Hills to make Japanese wood products a Super 301 priority. On May 26, 1989, Hills designated Japanese technical barriers on wood products as a priority under Super 301. Her complaint focused exclusively on regulations and standards that had discriminatory and trade-restricting effects on U.S. producers. One particularly egregious example involved fireproofing certification:

> [A] wood product was developed with a clear coating which, when heated to a particular temperature, would turn to foam and douse a flame. Japan required, however, that the product be subjected to a flame for a certain period before it could be certified as fire-proof. Since the wood product doused the flame before the time expired, it was not certified. As foreign [test] data are not accepted, although based on performance and quality of materials, this product was not certified.[15]

Japan made a number of concessions in response to the Super 301 designation. It accepted, in principle, that building standards should be performance based. It agreed to revise its building and fire codes to permit the greater use of wood products. In addition, Japan agreed to reclassify some laminated products into a 3.9 percent tariff category—down from the previous 15 to 20 percent duties. It also established several committees composed of both U.S. and Japanese officials to monitor implementation of the agreement.

U.S. industry and the Congress were both reportedly pleased with the agreements although immediate quantitative results were not forthcoming. Increased U.S. sales were not evident until 1993—possibly due to weakness in the Japanese economy. In 1993, however, there was a substantial growth in U.S. wood product exports to Japan.[16]

Probably the most important influence on the outcome was Japan's desire to avoid being designated a Super 301 priority again in 1990. The deadline for the United States to announce its new Super 301 priorities was April 30, 1990. In late March and early April, Japan and the United States reached agreement on satellites and super-computers, and in late April the wood products agreement was reached. This agreement was reported to be an important factor in Hills's decision not to redesignate Japan in 1990.

Colombian Cut Flowers

As discussed earlier, Section 301 and its variants are not the only industrial policy tools in the U.S. trade arsenal. Section 301 is not the most frequently used tool, antidumping is. The Colombian cut flower industry case is an example of the politics of antidumping. The Colombian cut flower industry emerged from nowhere in the late 1960s. The United States cut flower industry had historically been based in the East near the market for cut flowers. The eastern location was necessary due to the short life of the cut flowers and, therefore, the necessity for the industry to be located near the market. Once the airline industry had matured, however, the industry was able to move to less hostile climates in the South and in the West. Colombia, with its attractive environment and labor conditions, was a logical extension of this movement. American entrepreneurs were the first to identify Colombia's potential for cut flower production, focusing on the plateau region surrounding Bogota, with its moderate year-round temperatures, twelve-hour days, high light intensity, fertile land, and low-cost, low-skilled labor. From the late 1960s, when production was virtually zero, the industry emerged to become one of the most important in Colombia. Furthermore, the industry is now largely Colombian owned. Over 400 firms have almost 4,000 hectares under cultivation, directly employing 70,000 workers and indirectly supporting another 50,000 in ancillary activities. The industry exports 90 to 95 percent of its production, with more than 80 percent of these exports going to the United States.

Faced with intense competition from Colombia, U.S. growers in the 1970s first sought to limit imports, regardless of whether the flowers were fairly or unfairly traded. The domestic industry filed two escape clause petitions, one in 1977 directed at all cut flower imports and one in 1979 against the import of roses. Both escape clause petitions failed.

During the 1980s the industry turned to unfair trade practices legislation. In the early 1980s the focus was on roses. In one countervailing duty case, the Commerce Department determined that Colombian roses were receiving a 4 to 5 percent subsidy under a national tax certificate program. The case was settled when Colombian growers agreed not to use the subsidy.

In response, in 1986 U.S. growers changed their strategy. They made a mass filing of antidumping and countervailing duty petitions against seven types of flowers. The petitions covered 98 percent of the imports of these flowers. The mass filing was a success. The Commerce Department determined that exports of all seven types of flowers had been subsidized or dumped. But the U.S. industry was hardly satisfied—they received only modest levels of protection, much less than they had requested.[17] The case is of particular interest, however, because it illustrates the apparent ease with which dumping charges are upheld.

The U.S.–Japanese Auto Accord of 1995

Finally, one of the most highly publicized trade actions was the 301 action in 1995 attempting to open up the Japanese market to U.S. autos and auto parts and to convince the Japanese to purchase more U.S. parts for their transplant assembly operations in the United States. The June 1995 agreement was the culmination of almost two years of on again–off again negotiations in which, ultimately, the threat of retaliation by the United States seems to have played a role in the final reaching of an agreement.

The conflagration began on May 6, 1995, when President Clinton's economic advisors recommended that he impose significant sanctions against Japanese imports in retaliation for Tokyo's refusal to open its auto markets to the United States. The recommendation came the day after negotiations had broken down between USTR Mickey Kantor and MITI Minister Ryutaro Hashimoto (now prime minister).[18] Several days later President Clinton ordered an unfair trade complaint to be filed with the World Trade Organization (WTO). The United States then formally notified the WTO that it would file its case within the next forty-five days.[19]

In late May the United States announced that its sanctions for failing to reach an agreement by the end of June would be a 100 percent punitive tariff on thirteen Japanese luxury car models. The tariffs, worth about $5.9 billion, would be retroactive to May 20.[20] The U.S.-imposed deadline was June 28, 1995. The Japanese, in turn, filed their own complaint with the WTO.

As has been typical with so many of the U.S.-Japanese negotiations, agreement was not reached until the very last minute—the day before sanctions were to go into effect. The agreement came after three days of intensive talks between Kantor and Hashimoto. With the new agreement in hand, the United States did not impose the threatened sanctions based on 301 and Tokyo withdrew its complaint filed with the WTO.

The sticking point in the agreement was over the issue of "managed trade." The United States wanted measurable, quantitative targets on the opening of the Japanese auto market while Tokyo insisted that it would not agree to quantitative targets because they constituted "managed trade." In the end, Japan claimed it would not set numerical targets for implementation but that the United States would do so for its own assessment of the opening of the Japanese market. In fact, in the joint announcement the statements regarding targets were issued with blanks instead of the actual figures. The figures were added later.[21]

Both sides, of course, claimed victory. Trade chief Hashimoto said that the figures included in the agreement were merely Washington's projections and would not become targets.[22] Kantor, on the other hand, announced at a news conference, "We have a voluntary plan, we have objective criteria and we have the ability to verify progress. . . ." And President Clinton is reported to have said: "It is specific. It is measurable. It will achieve real concrete results."[23]

But how could these officials put such different spins on what should seem so clear? The answer is in the text of the agreement and in the two side statements, one from Kantor and one from Hashimoto. It appears that the different interpretations are of the following excerpt from the agreement:

> [T]he two ministers reaffirm that the framework addresses various governmental actions called "measures" to be taken by the two governments, including deregulation of repair garages that affect the repair parts market in Japan. . . . The assessment of the implementation of the measures, as well as the evaluation of progress achieved, will be based on the overall consideration of qualitative and quantitative criteria. Among other things, such criteria addresses trade in motor vehicles and parts, parts procurement by Japanese vehicle manufacturers in the United States, market conditions including exchange rates, and the efforts of U.S. motor vehicle and parts manufacturers to offer competitive products under competitive terms and conditions.[24]

Japan's insistence that it could not accept quantitative targets in opening up its auto and auto parts markets because that would be "managed trade" flies in the face of reality when it comes to Japanese auto trade with Europe. The Europeans have limited Japanese imports by allocating market share and growth rates. In Italy, the Japanese share of the market has been limited to about 5 percent thanks to lobbying by Fiat, while in France Renault and PSA Peugeot Citroen SA have been effective in getting the French government to limit Japanese imports to 4 percent. In contrast, in nonrestrictive European nations Japanese imports have a significant market share (e.g., Switzerland—24 percent; Ireland—37 percent; Finland—29 percent). And, unlike the United States, Europe got Japan to agree to 60 percent domestic content in any Japanese cars made in Europe.[25]

But that issue is an aside. What were the details of the agreement and the expected outcomes? First, the major Japanese car makers, with MITI guidance, announced plans to open up their dealerships to American cars. Toyota and Nissan agreed to establish a new section to respond to foreign manufacturers' complaints about gaining access to their affiliated dealers to sell American cars. All five major automakers said that they would reassure their dealers that they are totally free to deal in products of other companies both at home and abroad.[26] This is a far cry from past practices. (Eighty percent of American dealers handle both U.S. and Japanese cars; only 7 percent of Japanese dealers handle foreign cars.)

With regard to autos and parts, Toyota agreed to increase North American production by 200,000 units between 1996 and 1998, start up a fourth plant in North America with initial production of 100,000 units, and increase the export of vehicles assembled in North America by 27,000 units from 1994 to 1998. Nissan will consider producing transmissions in Tennessee at a future date and will establish a forklift engine plant in the United States with an annual production of 20,000 units. Honda will start up a parts development division for the purchase of after-market parts. Mazda will expand the number of vehicles produced by Ford plants in the United States, and Mitsubishi will invest an additional $300 million in U.S. production facilities.[27] (The Japanese companies, in announcing these plans, were quick to claim that these moves were already in the works and were not in response to U.S. pressures.)

The Japanese Transport Ministry will partially deregulate the car inspection and repair system. It will ease requirements for specially designated garages, which are currently required to have their own inspection facilities. (The Japanese take auto inspections very, very seriously.) Under the new rules, these garages will be able to share their inspection facilities with other garages. (But, will they do so?) The Ministry will also reduce the required number of licensed mechanics from three to two at the government-designated garages. Within the next year, the Ministry will review the category of "key safety parts," such as brakes. It has already announced that it will remove shock absorbers from the category.

But what are the outcomes that the Clinton administration expects? Washington estimated that by 1998 Japanese transplants will increase their auto production in the United States by 550,000 units, increase purchase of U.S. parts by $6.75 billion, and raise the local content of transplant-assembled vehicles to 56 percent. Washington also expects Tokyo to import $6 billion worth of parts for assembly operations in Japan.

USTR Kantor was also optimistic about Japan opening its market to Big Three autos. He said that the number of Japanese dealerships handling foreign cars should increase by 200 during the first year of the agreement and should reach 1,000 by the year 2000.

Finally, deregulation of the complex auto inspection system will drive a wedge in the Japanese companies' monopoly. Kantor believes that will result in the opening of 7,000 to 8,000 new garages, many of which will use U.S.-produced parts.[28]

Results of Aggressive Unilateralism

Table 4.1 shows that the number of administrative remedy cases investigated between 1979 and 1994 was more than 1,200. Countervailing duty (CVD) cases ballooned in the first half of the 1980s, peaking in 1982 and 1984. After 1986 the number of investigations dropped to a very low level and has stayed at that low level with the exception of 1992, when there were 43 cases investigated. This apparent upsurge in cases is the result of steel industry activity. In the 1990–92 period, the steel industry filed 43 CVD cases—three-fourths of the total for the period. A foreign subsidy was found in all 43 cases, although 27 were ultimately rejected because the United States International Trade Commission (USITC) did not find material injury.

The escape clause has historically been a sparingly used remedy. There were only twenty-five escape clause cases filed during the entire period. Most of these were prior to 1986.

Antidumping cases peaked in 1984 and 1986 and again in 1992. The

Table 4.1

Antidumping, Countervailing Duty, and Escape Clause Investigations Initiated, 1979–1994

Year	Antidumping cases	Countervailing duty cases	Escape clause
1979	26	40	4
1980	21	14	2
1981	15	22	1
1982	65	140	3
1983	46	22	0
1984	74	51	7
1985	66	43	4
1986	71	27	1
1987	15	8	0
1988	42	11	1
1989	23	7	0
1990	43	7	1
1991	51	8	0
1992	99	43	1
1993	42	5	0
1994	43	7	0
Total	742	455	25

Source: I.M. Destler, *American Trade Politics,* 3rd ed. (Washington, DC: Institute for International Economics, 1995), p. 166.

1992 peak is explained by the fact that the steel industry, in response to President Bush's ending of steel quotas in the spring of 1992, filed forty-eight separate petitions on June 30, 1992. But overall, antidumping has been very popular. A significant number of new cases were filed every year throughout the period.

Most recently, industries have been more successful in winning relief under the antidumping statute. In the first half of the 1980s, only 41 percent of the petitioners were successful. During the later half of the decade, 63 percent were successful. And when petitioners have been unsuccessful, it was rarely because they did not show dumping, it was because they did not prove "material injury." (Material injury is defined as harm that is not "inconsequential, immaterial or unimportant.")

It is therefore understandable that escape clause petitions have almost disappeared. If the finding of dumping is virtually automatic, the antidumping procedure has the advantage of a lower injury threshold, no presidential power to overturn the decision of the trade commission, and relief of indefinite duration.[29] Finally, Bayard and Elliott evaluated the "success" of seventy-two regular, special, and Super 301 cases completed between 1975 and 1992. They found that U.S. objectives were achieved 49 percent of the time. But the success rate has been going up in recent times. Just under one-third of the cases were successful from 1975 through the first half of 1985. More recently, from September 1985 through 1992, 60 percent of the cases resulted in reaching some or all of the negotiating objectives.[30]

The Free Trade Context

The brief descriptions of trade remedies and the cases cited above present a one-sided view of American trade policy. The discussion makes it seem as though protectionism for individual industries (industrial policy) is the norm and not the exception. But trade remedies clearly are the exception. Free(er) trade has been the dominant U.S. paradigm for more than fifty years. This is obviously underscored by the most significant trade actions of the decade—NAFTA and the Uruguay Round.

NAFTA

On December 17, 1992, the United States, Canada, and Mexico signed the historic trade accord—the North American Free Trade Agreement (NAFTA). NAFTA went into effect on January 1, 1994. It has been called "the most comprehensive free trade pact (short of a common market) ever negotiated between regional trading partners, and the first reciprocal free trade pact between a developing country and industrial countries."[31] It provides for the phased-in elimination of tariffs and most nontariff barriers over a ten-year period (in some cases fifteen years).

NAFTA was not an easy victory largely because of fears that it would lead to job losses in the United States and downward pressures on U.S. wages. Presidential candidate Ross Perot predicted that equilibrium would not be reached until average Mexican wages had risen to $7.50 an hour (up from $2.17) and average U.S. wages had fallen to $7.50 (down from $15.45).

This is essentially the "pauper labor argument," which claims that imports by a wealthy country from a poor country will reduce the standard of living in the wealthy country. But in spite of Perot's opposition, NAFTA was ratified by Congress and became law.

The trade in automobiles and automobile component parts is one of the more significant parts of the agreement. Autos and auto parts are the largest component of merchandise trade between both Canada and the United States, on the one hand, and Mexico. NAFTA has already cut automotive tariffs and will eliminate the remaining tariffs and nontariff barriers over ten years. Mexico's tariffs on autos and light trucks were cut from 20 percent to 10 percent immediately and are now being phased out over ten– (autos) and five– (light trucks) year periods. Mexico also reduced its trade balancing requirements from $2 of car exports for every $1 of car imports to 80 cents. This will go down to 55 cents in the year 2003 and then will be completely eliminated in 2004. In addition, Mexico's domestic content requirements as applied to autos will be phased out slowly over ten years.

NAFTA also resulted in significant trade liberalization in agriculture. Most tariffs on U.S.-Mexico farm trade will be phased out over 10 years. Tariffs were immediately eliminated on 57 percent of the value of bilateral trade. After 5 years the figure will rise to 63 percent, then to 94 percent after 10 years, and 100 percent at 15 years.

In the long run, NAFTA will also dramatically improve access to Mexican markets for U.S. and Canadian financial firms. The right to establish a business presence in Mexico will be phased in through 2007. A significant number of firms were allowed to enter the Mexican market when the agreement went into effect. And by the year 2000, all Mexican restrictions on entry into the financial service market will be eliminated. Finally, all temporary safeguards on banking and securities will be removed by 2007.

NAFTA, of course, is much more than the three examples just presented. The agreement is, after all, almost 2,000 pages long. Nevertheless, the examples presented here are representative of the changes made in the trade relationships between the three countries.[32]

The opposition to NAFTA eventually quieted and the proponents and opponents generally adopted a "wait and see" attitude toward the treaty. But after the first six months of NAFTA, early evaluations were generally positive. After its first six months, NAFTA was credited with boosting U.S.-Mexico trade in both directions. U.S. exports to Mexico went up almost 17 percent and imports rose by nearly 21 percent.

Autos were a major beneficiary. The U.S. Big Three automakers shipped 23,275 cars and trucks to Mexico in the first half of 1994, as compared to only 3,791 for the same period in 1993. (But the auto trade balance was still in Mexico's favor. U.S. automakers exported 143,756 cars and trucks from Mexico during the first half of 1994, as compared to 127,566 during the first half of the previous year.)[33]

NAFTA then pretty much died as a public issue until Pat Buchanan raised it as a campaign issue in his quest for the Republican presidential nomination in 1996. But again, establishment evaluations of the treaty are overwhelmingly positive.

The Uruguay Round

The completion of the Uruguay Round of the GATT was the second of the two significant trade opening agreements completed by the United States during the 1990s. The negotiations began in Punta del Este, Uruguay, in September 1986 (hence the name Uruguay Round) and were finally concluded on April 1994, taking effect in January 1995. The round produced a plethora of agreements that open new trading opportunities and create new trading rules and institutions.

In the area of trade liberalization, the Uruguay Round opened up trade in areas like agriculture and textiles, which had long been resistant to multilateral agreement. The agreement capped farm export subsidies and required a reduction of such subsidies by 36 percent and the volume of subsidized exports at 21 percent over six years. It required 20 percent reductions in support provided to farmers, and it converted nontariff barriers into tariff equivalents.

World trade in textiles had been covered by various iterations of the Multi-Fiber Arrangements (MFA). The Uruguay Round phases out the MFA. In the United States, textiles receive higher levels of protection than any other manufacturing industry. Textile tariffs in the United States will be cut an average of 24 percent; however, more than fifty items will still have tariffs above 15 percent. Apparel tariffs will be cut by only 9.2 percent and will still average about 18 percent.

Until the Uruguay Round, trade in services had never been subject to multilateral rules. The new General Agreement on Trade in Services (GATS) for the first time established multilateral rules for trade in services and liberalized barriers to investment and services trade.

The Uruguay Round also transformed GATT from a trade accord

serviced by a professional staff into a membership organization—the World Trade Organization (WTO). The WTO is to consolidate the results of previous negotiations under a common framework and provide a new mechanism for settling disputes. The new Dispute Settlement Understanding, or DSU, establishes a unified system to settle disputes arising under multilateral or plurilateral trade agreements. It is the WTO and the DSU that caused Pat Buchanan to complain that the United States has given away its sovereignty. In the past, if a dispute panel under GATT had found the United States guilty of some trade violation, the United States could simply block the panel report and avoid formal censure. Not so under WTO. But this really poses little threat to the United States as the costs of noncompliance are minimal.

First, if a panel finds the United States in violation and it takes no action, the aggrieved country would have the right to retaliate. But most countries do not present the United States with a credible threat of retaliation (with the notable exceptions of the European Community, Canada, and possibly Japan). The U.S. market is simply too important to them to risk a trade war. Essentially, the WTO can reprimand but not severely punish major trading powers.[34]

It is impossible at this early date to quantitatively assess the outcome of the Uruguay Round. It is, however, expected to open important new trading opportunities for the United States. Yet, at the same time, gains to the economy will probably be modest.[35]

Conclusion

Freer trade has long been the goal of American economists and it is still the dominant trade paradigm. But the day of the unconditional acceptance of free trade is a thing of the past. That became clear in the debate surrounding the 1996 presidential campaign.

Aggressive unilateralism, a form of national industrial policy, has become increasingly common. President Clinton, in his 1996 State of the Union Address, spoke to this issue: "Through tougher trade deals for America, over 80 of them, we have opened markets abroad, and now exports are at an all-time high, growing faster than imports and creating good American jobs."[36]

Aggressive unilateralism relies on the rules of trade remedies. And these rules provide the basis for numerous industrial policy decisions. If one looks only at the rhetoric, it appears that the United States has moved from an era of free trade to a period of trade deals in a free trade envelope. This surely would seem to be the case given some of President Clinton's first-term political appointments (e.g., Laura Tyson as chair of the Council of Economic Advisers and Robert Reich as secretary of Labor), and initial assessments of the outcomes of his policies.

The Clinton administration has negotiated a whole series of market-opening deals with Japan—twenty-one in his first three years in office.[37] Among the most import are those that have expanded air cargo service between the two nations (to the immediate benefit of Federal Express and United Parcel Service [UPS]), and a new computer chip agreement.[38]

But it is the auto agreement that the whole world is watching. And the Clinton administration has been quick to claim success, pointing to a 33 percent increase in the sales of U.S.-made cars in Japan between August 1995 and February 1996. The administration is also expecting to see an increase of 14 percent in the North American content of 1996 models produced by Japanese transplants.[39] Many analysts acknowledge Clinton's role in these increases, while others believe that much of the improved climate for U.S. cars in Japan is due to natural market forces, like the stronger yen, making American goods cheaper.[40]

But, as this chapter has shown, once outcomes and not rhetoric are examined, industrial policies have been a major component of the actual trade policies of Ronald Reagan and George Bush as well as Bill Clinton. The protection and promotion of individual industries in the realm of international trade has been a U.S. policy for quite some time.

And while agriculture and manufacturing industries have been the major beneficiaries of trade rules, U.S. industrial policy is hardly that limited. As the following chapter will illustrate, construction, real estate, and business services have been major recipients of government largess.

5

Rebuilding Urban America

There is one incredible statistic in Joel Garreau's recent book, *Edge City*. Garreau notes that there are more than 200 new (less than thirty years old) edge cities in the United States and that each one of these edge cities is larger than the downtowns of cities like Portland, or Tampa, or Tucson. But the incredible statistic is: "two thirds of all American office facilities are in Edge Cities, and 80 percent of them have materialized in only the last two decades."[1] And much of this development has been supported by the federal government both through direct subsidies for real estate construction and through tax benefits stimulating this development.

This chapter focuses on two policies that were designed to stimulate employment and general business activity (and they may have). But the main consequence of both programs was the subsidization of the construction of commercial and multi-unit residential complexes in urban places. One of these policies was a traditional subsidy activity—the federal Urban Development Action Grant (UDAG) program. The other was a tax action—the Economic Recovery Tax Act (ERTA) of 1981.

Urban Development Action Grants

The UDAG program never exactly targeted real estate development. It was actually the keystone to President Jimmy Carter's urban policy—an early initiative of his administration. UDAG became law under

90

Section 119 of the Housing and Community Development Act of 1977, signed by the president on October 23, 1977. The purpose of this discretionary grant program was to alleviate central city decay in the nation's most economically depressed urban areas through strategic use of direct capital subsidies.[2] Federal grants were to be targeted to communities with the greatest need for economic and physical revitalization by stimulating private investment in specific development projects. Six criteria were originally applied to determine a community's eligibility for the UDAG program: percentage of housing constructed before 1940, per capita income change, percentage of poverty, population growth lag/decline, job lag/decline, and unemployment rate. A seventh criterion, location in a labor surplus area, was added in 1984. The minimum threshold for each criterion was the median value for all large cities. Thus, half of the large cities would receive an eligibility point for meeting or exceeding each criterion. With some exceptions, cities needed three points (later four) to be considered "distressed."[3]

A central city could apply for a grant if it met either the program standards for distress or had a "pocket of poverty." Applications submitted by eligible communities were reviewed by HUD's staff, not only for the eligibility criteria but against other program goals as well. An applicant had to meet the minimum requirement for firm public and private commitments; a ratio of private investment to UDAG funds of at least 2.5 to 1; and the requirement that "but for" the program funds, the project could not be undertaken (i.e., that the UDAG funds were necessary to make the project feasible).[4]

The San Antonio Hyatt Regency Project

A San Antonio development gives a flavor of typical UDAG projects. The goal of the Hyatt project was to initiate a comprehensive revitalization of about six city blocks in the heart of San Antonio's historic downtown commercial area. The major components of the project included a *Riverwalk linkage.* This was a multi-level pedestrian walkway at both the San Antonio River and street levels to connect the Alamo Plaza with the river. Amenities also included were fountains and cascading waterfalls from the street to the river level.

The heart of the project was a *convention hotel*—the Hyatt Regency—a 600–room luxury convention hotel located on the banks of the San Antonio River. The lowest level of the hotel is a part of the

Riverwalk linkage to Alamo Plaza, serving as a mall providing sidewalk dining, entertainment, and shopping to the general public.

Designed concurrently with the Riverwalk linkage and the convention hotel is a *small commercial development*. It consists of 11,600 square feet of leasable commercial space in a partially enclosed shopping and entertainment mall.

Other components of the project include a five-level, 500-car *parking garage*. The garage also provides about 7,500 square feet of retail space and a cafe on the Riverwalk side. A major *historic facade restoration* was accomplished on historic buildings facing the Alamo, as was *other commercial revitalization*.

As was stated earlier, the subsidization of the development of downtown hotels and office structures was never an explicit goal of UDAG, it was simply the unintended outcome—the result of thousands of independent decisions by local and HUD officials. In this particular case, the UDAG project resulted in a new 600-room convention hotel and a total of 19,100 feet of leasable commercial space (actually not very much commercial space).

But the project also met its stated goals. It generated about 690 new jobs and about $2.1 million in new property taxes (in 1984). About $37 million in private funds was invested in the Hyatt Regency hotel with another $14 million used to.restore ten historic properties.[5]

UDAG's Demise

In its early years, when Jimmy Carter was president, UDAG proved enormously popular. When the program was enacted in 1977, Congress initially authorized $400 million per year for the first three years. When UDAG was reauthorized for another three years in 1980, Congress increased appropriations to $675 million annually.

President Reagan, however, had different ideas. The gist of his urban policy was to strengthen the overall economy through macroeconomic policies like tax cuts, deregulation, reducing inflation, and generally providing a healthy climate for business investment. He was opposed to direct subsidy programs like UDAG. As a consequence, he proposed termination of the program in each of his budget submissions. And, while he was not successful, he did manage to reduce UDAG appropriations from $675 million in 1981 to $216 million by 1988.

In the end, it was Congress, not the Reagan administration, that ended UDAG. In the budget deliberations in 1989, Congress was faced with the choice between funding a space station for NASA or funding UDAG. Congress elected to zero out UDAG. The UDAG funds that were awarded in 1989 were recaptured funds from projects that had been approved in the past but were never implemented. In 1990 President Bush sealed the coffin when he earmarked recaptured UDAG funds for the Community Development Block Grant program.[6]

UDAG Outcomes

The Urban Development Action Grant program awarded $4.6 billion to communities over the twelve-year life of the program (1978–89). It was responsible for about 3,000 projects in more than 1,200 cities during its lifetime. UDAG generated more than $30 billion in private investment in American cities (of all sizes).

But in spite of this massive effort, UDAG was barely evaluated. HUD conducted one evaluation of the program in the early years of the Reagan administration, hoping to convince HUD Secretary Samuel Pierce and President Reagan that the program had value.[7]

In 1992, however, political scientist Michael Rich wrote what seems to be the only published summary of the program's outcomes.[8] HUD classified projects into one of three types: neighborhood, industrial, or commercial. For our purposes, the typology is useful, but confusing. What makes it confusing is the fact that about one-half of all of the projects in major cities were mixed-use.

Nevertheless, about half of the major city projects were commercial projects and they received almost two-thirds of the dollars awarded. Furthermore, in the last three years of the program, commercial projects received about three-fourths of all metro cities UDAG funds.

In order to more closely examine the UDAG projects, Rich conducted a content analysis of the nearly 1,600 metro cities UDAG projects that were active through 1987. He found that among all projects, retail stores and office buildings were the two most frequently funded activities. Of the 1,578 projects examined, 487 (or 30.9 percent) included the development of some form of retail activity and 502 (or 31.8 percent) included office building construction or renovation. These two activities accounted for more than 40 percent of all program dollars spent. Multipurpose UDAGs accounted for about 30 percent of all projects although they received half of the funds awarded. Again, retail trade and office buildings dominated the activities.

Hotels, particularly downtown hotels, were also dominant UDAG activities. Almost half of the cities receiving UDAG awards received at least one grant for a project that included a hotel. One out of every four UDAG dollars spent went to a project that included the construction or rehabilitation of a hotel. Also, 40 percent of the dollars awarded to multipurpose projects went to projects that included a hotel. In major cities, the UDAG program aided in the construction or renovation of 236 hotels between 1978 and 1989, adding about 60,000 hotel rooms.

Overall, UDAG in its application was a commercial program. About one-third of UDAG grants involving slightly more than half of the funds went to downtown projects, and these projects were typically heavily weighted toward office buildings, retail stores, and hotels.

More office space was constructed in the downtowns of the thirty-three-largest metropolitan areas during the first four years of the 1980s than was built in the previous three decades. But to credit UDAG alone with this building boom would be a mistake. For one thing, much of this construction took place in cities not eligible for UDAG. On the other hand, UDAG certainly contributed to the boom in a lot of places. Baltimore alone, for example, received a total of 78 UDAG grants. New York had 63, Chicago 59, Cleveland 44, and even Rochester had 33. In these and many other cities, UDAG clearly had an impact.

The Economic Recovery and Tax Act of 1981

The Economic Recovery and Tax Act of 1981 (ERTA) was a product of the Reagan administration and its supply-side policies. It was designed to reduce tax rates and thus stimulate the economy to recover from a serious recession. Both inflation and interest rates were very high and the unemployment rate had been rising. Productivity and savings were stagnant.

The objective of ERTA was to upgrade the nation's industrial base, stimulate productivity and new business, lower personal taxes, and restrain the growth of the federal government.[9] As a result of ERTA's focus on investment, the real estate sector of the economy was a major beneficiary of the law. ERTA included provisions that provided incentives for real estate investors by reducing their tax liabilities. The act also reduced the marginal tax rate on long-term capital gains.

Chicago CPA Irving Blackman wrote of the impact of ERTA on real estate investments: "Real estate investors should rejoice. The new fast write-offs move real estate to or near (depending on your viewpoint) the top of the good-guy tax shelter list."[10]

ERTA introduced a new section into the Internal Revenue Code (Section 168) and a new depreciation system for various classes of property—the Accelerated Cost Recovery System (ACRS). The most revolutionary part of the system was that it discarded the accounting concept of spreading the cost of an asset over its useful life. The new class of property determined the period of time over which it could be recovered. Actual useful life became irrelevant.[11]

The ACRS turned real estate into a true "tax shelter." A tax shelter in real estate is property with the following characteristics: (1) it can be depreciated over a shorter period of time than its useful life, (2) when sold, the profit will be taxed as a capital gain, and (3) the tax loss deducted (probably over several years) is greater than the amount of cash that the investor has in the deal.

Generally, real estate had a fifteen-year recovery period[12] (although some realty was included in the ten-year property class, and low-income housing had special rules). The ACRS schedule of depreciation was based on the 175 percent declining-balance method of accounting with a switch to the straight-line method at a point that would maximize the deduction.[13] There were separate rate schedules depending on the month that the building was placed in service. An example of a depreciation schedule is shown in Table 5.1.

Note that, depending on the month the building was placed in service, the asset is about 50 percent depreciated by the end of the sixth year. Component depreciation (e.g., separate depreciation of the electrical wiring, plumbing, etc.) was no longer allowed with one exception—substantial improvement to the building. If the costs added to the building over two years were at least 25 percent of the adjusted basis of the building, then the improvements could be treated as a separate building.

In addition, within certain limits, new real property was eligible for a 10 percent investment credit. The investment credit on rehabilitated buildings was even higher, as is shown below:

	Credit
1) Nonresidential building, 30–39 years old	15%
2) Nonresidential building, 40+ years old	20
3) Certified historic structures	25

Table 5.1

15-Year Depreciation Schedule Under ERTA

Depreciation year	Percentage of depreciation by month asset placed in service		
	January	September	December
1	12	4	1
2	10	11	12
3	9	10	10
4	8	9	9
5	7	8	8
6	6	7	7
7	6	6	6
8	6	6	6
9	6	5	6
10	5	5	5
11	5	5	5
12	5	5	5
13	5	5	5
14	5	5	5
15	5	5	5
16	–	4	5

When there was an early disposition of the property, a 2 percent credit was not recaptured for each full year the property was held.[14]

But from an investor's standpoint, the 1981 Tax Act did not have all of the positive consequences speculators (as opposed to long-term investors) might have desired. As has been shown, the rapid depreciation rule allowed investors to make lots and lots of money through tax savings. But it did not always allow speculators to make bundles of money on the sale of property. Accelerated depreciation proved beneficial for nearly all regular residential property, but disadvantageous for all commercial property, unless it was held for a long time.

Prior to the Tax Act, for residential property, accelerated depreciation was generally inferior to straight-line under most circumstances. With the Tax Act, however, accelerated depreciation provided "unambiguous financial advantage for residential property."[15]

For commercial property however, the advantage of accelerated depreciation had to be weighed against the recapture penalties. Accelerated depreciation allowed the investor to defer the realization of income from early to later years. But with the optional straight-line method, ordinary income could be converted to capital gains.

Table 5.2 illustrates examples of recapture rules. Assume that the properties shown in the table were purchased in 1981 for $100,000 and

Table 5.2

Examples of Recapture Rules Under ERTA of 1981

	Type of Realty and Cost Recovery Method			
	Residential		Commercial	
	Regular ACRS	Optional 15–year Straight-line	Regular ACRS	Optional 15–year Straight-line
1/1/81 to 12/31/92	$ 85,000	$ 80,000	$ 85,000	$ 80,000
Tax basis, 12/31/91	$ 15,000	$ 20,000	$ 15,000	$ 20,000
Recognized gain when sold on 12/31/92	$105,000	$100,000	$105,000	$100,000
Nature of recognized gain:				
Ordinary income	$ 5,000	0	$ 85,000	0
Capital gain	$100,000	$100,000	$ 20,000	$100,000

Source: Gailen L. Hite and Raymond J. Krasniewski, "The 1981 Tax Act: Cost Recovery Choices for Real Property," *Journal of the American Real Estate and Urban Economics Association* 10 (Summer 1992), 203.

Note: Purchase price as of 1/1/81 was $100,000; selling price as of 12/31/91 was $120,000. These numbers reflect the allocated value of the building and structures only.The value of the land component is treated separately since it is nondepreciable and not subject to recapture.

sold twelve years later for $120,000. Depreciation using the ACRS method would be $85,000 as compared to $80,000 using the straight-line method. With the residential property under ACRS, only $5,000 of the excess depreciation is recaptured as ordinary income with the remaining $100,000 being capital gain. With a tax rate of 50 percent on ordinary income and 20 percent on capital gain, the tax upon the sale would be $22,500.

With the commercial property under ACRS, however, the difference between the selling price ($120,000) and the depreciated value of the property ($15,000) is taxed as $85,000 of ordinary income and $20,000 capital gain. This produces a tax upon sale of $46,500.

While these tax differences favored residential property over commercial, one thing should not be forgotten. The ability to write off the cost of real estate in depreciation favored all real estate investors—speculators included—regardless of type of property.[16]

These changes significantly enhanced the tax incentives for investing in real estate and, consequently, the real estate sector of the economy boomed. The result was significant overbuilding in the real estate sector, resulting in high vacancy rates, foreclosures, and the savings and loan crisis. For example, in terms of commercial space from 1983 to 1986, there were 937 million square feet in new construction starts but the market could absorb only 575 million square feet. In the residential market, the apartment vacancy rate went from 5.5 percent in the second quarter of 1984 to 6.9 percent in the first quarter of 1986. Five years after ERTA, Congress would conclude that the ERTA tax incentives had contributed to the overbuilding of office space, high vacancy rates, and distorted business decisions at all levels.[17]

What ERTA did was give several million wealthy people the opportunity to invest in real estate that actually produced a large cash return but, once depreciation was taken, produced a paper loss that individuals then used to reduce their reported ordinary income and thus their taxes. Nice work if you can get it. These "tax shelters," the common term used for such activities, led to unfairness and inefficiencies in the tax structure. But the shelters were perfectly legal. In fact, the law encouraged real estate investors not only to reduce income from that particular investment but also to shelter income from unrelated sources.

Although tax shelters could be employed through a number of different legal entities, limited partnerships became the main vehicle. They were attractive mainly because of the limited liability of the partners (excluding the general partner). General partners who put together such schemes were called syndicators due to the many limited partners who were solicited for each partnership. Table 5.3 illustrates the magnitude of the net losses reported to the Treasury by limited partners from 1982 to 1986. Net losses reported by limited partnerships increased from $17.5 billion to $35.5 billion. The Treasury indicated that this magnitude of losses could only be attributed to the excessive use of tax shelters by limited partnerships.

Limited partnerships also showed a large increase in the number of partners as compared to the growth in the number of general partners during the 1981 to 1986 period. And, the number of limited partners reporting losses on their tax returns also increased dramatically—from 2.55 million in 1981 to 5.11 million in 1986. One thing about wealthy Americans—they are quick learners.

But limited partnerships and high-income individuals were not alone in skimming the Treasury; corporations were also able to take advantage of these tax preferences to reduce their tax liabilities. Major

Table 5.3

Net Income (Loss) By Type of Partnership, 1982–1986 (in billions of $)

Year	Limited partnerships	General partnerships
1982	−17.5	10.2
1983	−18.7	16.1
1984	−22.6	19.1
1985	−26.9	18.0
1986	−35.5	18.1

Source: California Department of Real Estate, *The Impacts of Tax Reform on Real Estate Investment in California* (Sacramento, CA: California Department of Real Estate, December 1991), 14.

U.S. corporations were significantly reducing their tax liabilities, paying little or no federal income taxes, while their financial reports to stockholders showed strong earnings.

As time progressed, Congress, and even the Reagan administration, began to find politically unacceptable inequities in ERTA. The generally accepted view was that ERTA had created a situation whereby middle-income Americans were carrying an unfair share of the tax burden. They either could not take advantage of the tax incentives because they did not have the income or investment funds to participate, or they did not know anything about the tax shelters that were available. Congress also came to believe that the tax law promoted inefficient investment decisions because resources were diverted from higher-value uses to lower-value uses that were only more profitable to the investors due to the tax benefits.

Preferential capital gains taxation was another tax incentive believed to be causing inefficiencies. Critics argued that investment was also being steered to projects where the returns were eligible for capital gains treatment, and thus lower taxes.

By the mid-1980s, the Reagan administration and congressional leaders believed that broad-based tax reform was necessary. The president also insisted on revenue neutrality. Revenue neutrality meant increasing the tax base and decreasing tax rates at the same time so that there would be no change in tax revenues.

In late 1984, President Reagan sent a new tax plan to the Hill. After receiving congressional and public comment, a revised plan, "The President's Tax Reform Proposals to the Congress for Fairness, Growth and Simplicity," was sent to Congress in May 1985. On October 22, 1986, the Tax Reform Act of 1986 (TRA) was signed into law.

It has been called "the most significant change in the Federal income tax system since broad-based taxation was introduced during World War II."[18]

Describing the many changes to the tax law brought about by the TRA is well beyond the scope of this chapter. However, it is important to show how the changes in tax law affected real estate and related interests. As part of its equity objective, Congress imposed new restrictions on the use of losses to offset unrelated income and reduce depreciation and interest deductions.

One of the major provisions of the TRA was the prohibition imposed on individuals, estates, trusts, closely held C corporations (5 or fewer individuals holding 50 percent or more of the stock), and personal service corporations from deducting losses from passive activities (with limited exceptions) to offset income and tax liability from nonpassive sources (like wages and portfolio income). Passive activity is any business in which the taxpayer does not materially participate, and any rental activity, whether or not the taxpayer materially participates.

Next, depreciation provisions were changed significantly. The tax lifetime of residential properties was extended to 27.5 years and that of commercial properties was extended to 31.5 years; in addition, the straight-line method of depreciation was required. This reduced the potential maximum depreciation deductions for residential and nonresidential properties over a ten-year period by 41 and 49 percent respectively.

In order to illustrate what a plum ERTA had been for passive real estate investors, let us take the cases of two passive investors—one purchased a new multifamily apartment building on January 1, 1983, and the other purchased a new building on January 1, 1990. Both paid $150,000 for the property, which included $130,000 for the structure and $20,000 for the land. Both put up $50,000 of their own money and borrowed the remaining $100,000 at 12 percent over a twenty-five-year term. Both have the same revenues and expenditures. Both depreciate their buildings at the maximum allowable rates. Table 5.4 shows the impacts of these investments on the owners' personal taxes.

Assuming a principal payment of about $670 or so for the first year, both received a nice cash profit on their investments. Their cash income was net operating income (NOI) ($21,520), less interest ($11,984), less principal ($670), or $8,866. Not a bad cash return on a $50,000 investment—17.7 percent.

Table 5.4

Comparison of Tax Treatments Under ERTA (1981) and TRA (1986)

	A's investment 1983	B's investment 1991
Gross revenue	$32,000	$32,000
Vacancy allowance	1,680	1,680
Operating expense	8,800	8,800
Net operating income (NOI)	21,520	21,520
Less interest	11,984	11,984
Less depreciation	15,600	4,727
Allowed as deduction against nonpassive income	100%	0%
Allowable deduction against nonpassive income	−6,064	0
Taxable income/Marginal tax rate	40%	28%
Federal income tax	$−2,426	$1,347

Source: Derived from Donald R. Epley, *Highlights of the 1986 Tax Reform Act and Its Impact on Real Estate* (Chicago, IL: Society of Real Estate Appraisers, 1987), pp. 52–60.

But then we come to their tax returns. Individual A gets to deduct interest plus $15,600 depreciation (12 percent) from NOI for a paper loss of $6,064. Individual B's depreciation, however, is only $4,727 (3.6 percent), giving B a paper profit of $4,809. But, it is just as well for individual B—she might as well show a profit. Being a passive investor she could not deduct a loss from her ordinary income anyway. So, in 1991, with B in the 28 percent bracket, she would have to pay $1,347 in additional income taxes on her $4,809 profit from her real estate venture.

But A was operating under the old rules. With his 12 percent depreciation under ACRS (see Table 5.2), and with the lenient tax laws regarding passive investment, A was able to deduct the full $6,046 paper loss from ordinary income on his tax return. Being in the 40 percent tax bracket, A saved himself a cool $2,426 in taxes, which he would have had to pay on his ordinary income without the real estate investment. Not at all bad when you add it to his $8,866 cash return.

The act also modified investment tax credits for real estate development. The new credits were for rehabilitated property only. A 10 percent credit was authorized for buildings placed in service prior to 1936 and a 20 percent credit for certified historic properties.[19]

The tax law with regard to capital gains was also changed by the Tax Reform Act. Prior to TRA the highest capital gains tax rate applicable to noncorporate taxpayers was 20 percent. For corporations it was 28 percent. Both rates were lower than regular income tax rates, causing taxpayers to try to have income streams treated as capital gains rather than ordinary income. However, under TRA there is no differentiation between capital gains rates and ordinary rates—effectively raising capita gains rates. For individuals the maximum rate became 28 percent and for corporations 34 percent. Thus the happy ride in real estate was slowed with the passage of the Tax Reform Act of 1986.

Conclusion

The question left unanswered at this point is: Did the industrial policies of the early 1980s, which promoted the construction of commercial buildings and multifamily dwelling units, have the distorting effect on the American economy that economists would suggest? Another way to ask the question might be: Did the industrial policies of the early 1980s that were geared to aid the construction and real estate industries work? Those analyzing the savings and loan debacle certainly thought so. They attributed the speculative overbuilding generated by ERTA as one of the contributing causes of the debacle.[20]

For example, the National Commission on Financial Institution Reform, Recovery and Enforcement concluded:

> The 1981 Tax Act, the Reagan Administration's major tax-reduction initiative, reduced the depreciation life of real property to 15 years, replacing the previous complex schedules that had depreciation lives of up to 60 years for structures, and it made depreciation available to passive investors. The shortening of depreciation lives greatly increased the profitability of real estate investments. By leveraging a real estate investment, it was possible to get more tax deductions than the entire amount invested. This made the after-tax return on real estate investment so attractive that initial investments would be earned back in only a few years. The 1981 Tax Act relating to real estate investment produced a boom in real estate development, in which many S&Ls, along with banks and insurance companies, experienced enormous losses when the inevitable bust occurred.[21]

Recent construction statistics seem to bear this out. Figure 5.1 shows the value of construction of commercial buildings (e.g., offices, retail complexes) for the fifteen-year period of 1980 through 1994. Between 1980 and 1985 the value of construction of these structures virtually doubled from $27.7 billion to $54.6 billion. Then, begin-

Figure 5.1. **Value of Construction of Commercial Buildings, 1980–1994**
(in billions of $)

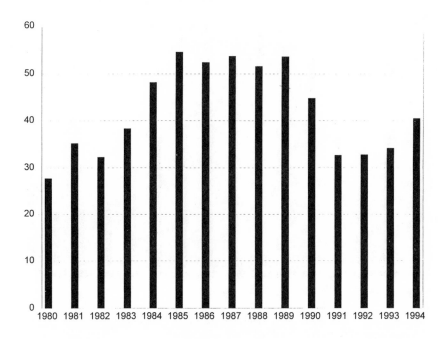

Source: U.S. Bureau of the Census. *Statistical Abstract of the United States: 1995*
(Washington: Government Printing Office, 1995), p 276.

ning in 1986 when the Tax Reform Act was passed, commercial construction declined slightly and remained fairly constant through the
1980s. It then declined to $32.7 billion in 1991, undoubtedly in re-
sponse to the 1990 economic recession. Figure 5.1 thus strongly suggests some precipitating events in the early 1980s stimulating
commercial construction.

  A similar trend holds true for the construction of multifamily housing units. Figure 5.2 shows the trend for multi-unit (five or more units)
housing starts for the same fifteen-year period. Construction again increased dramatically from 1981 to 1985. The number of starts doubled
during that time period from 288,000 to 576,000 units. Starts then
began a precipitous decline, reaching a low of only 133,000 in 1993.

  Of course these figures do not "prove" that UDAG and ERTA
"caused" the construction boom of the early 1980s, and economists
would argue that other factors were involved. There was, after all, a

Figure 5.2. **Housing Units Started: 5 or More Units, 1980–1994**
(in thousands of $)

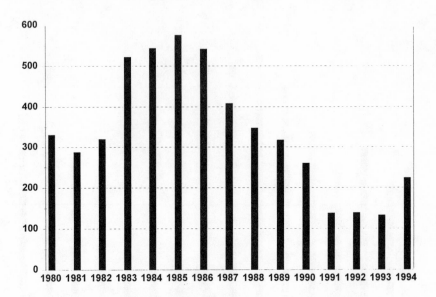

Source: U.S. Bureau of the Census. *Statistical Abstract of the United States: 1995* (Washington: Government Printing Office, 1995), p 276.

serious recession going on from 1980 to 1982 and unemployment was substantial. Interest rates were also out of sight, further depressing construction. Thus it was only natural that construction and real estate activity would pick up as the economy improved and interest rates plummeted.

But why did all of this activity peak in 1985 and level or decline through the remainder of the 1980s and early 1990s? After all, times were very good. Unemployment was low, interest rates were low, and inflation virtually nonexistent. Was it because of changes in the tax laws brought about by the Tax Reform Act of 1986? It would certainly appear so. And, in fact, economists have come to this conclusion—claiming that ERTA had certainly distorted investor behavior and stimulated the construction boom (and TRA had ended it). James Poterba of MIT, for example, looked at the relationship between tax policy and housing construction. Poterba found that the 1986 Tax Reform Act did indeed "correct" the amount of rental construction going on in the United States. He based this conclusion on several pieces of evidence.

First he examined data on sales of publicly traded real estate partnerships. (Recall that prior to 1986 investors in rental properties that generated tax losses could use these losses to shelter taxes from other sources of income.) He found a 37 percent decline in real estate partnership sales between 1985 and 1988. Real estate partnerships accounted for over 55 percent of new sales before the 1986 act but only 44 percent by 1988.

Second, Poterba used multifamily housing starts in Canada as a control for nontax events. He recognized that simply comparing the number of housing starts before and after the Tax Act was a very weak test because it failed to control for other changes that may have altered the incentives for housing construction. Canadian housing starts, however, provided a natural "control" because Canada has a similar demographic mix and is subject to economic shocks similar to those experienced in the United States, but it had a different and stable tax policy with respect to housing.

A comparison showed that Canada had an upturn in the construction of multifamily housing while similar starts in the United States declined. Furthermore, the pattern of single-family housing starts remained quite similar, all suggesting that tax policy accounted for the decline in construction of multifamily housing units in the United States.[22]

This leaves us with one unmistakable conclusion. UDAG and ERTA were industry policies initiated by the Carter and Reagan administrations, respectively. Both were successful in moving investment into activities that, without them, would not have occurred—a clear example of industrial policy, perhaps unintended, but industrial policy nevertheless.

Chapter 6, which follows, provides a very different example of American industrial policy. The chapter deals with industrial policy promoted and carried out in the name of national defense. The Defense Department over the years has supported the development of many industries with civilian as well as national defense applications. Chapter 6 will examine some of these industries and their industry policies.

6

Industrial Policy Through National Defense

Writing in 1980, military analyst Jacques Gansler documented the structure of the defense industry, the impact of that structure on research and development (R&D), and the peculiar problems of the industry faced by subcontractors and parts suppliers. The defense industry is a peculiar beast indeed. It is both oligopolistic and monopolistic and yet it differs significantly from the traditional oligopoly and monopoly market, in which the buyer and seller are essentially in adversarial bargaining positions. In defense, the buyer and seller have a far greater mutuality of interest—one in which price plays a relatively reduced role.[1] The Harvard Business School's George Lodge once said, "It is a dangerous delusion to keep mumbling the old myths of free enterprise when they are irrelevant."[2] In defense, they are irrelevant.

Defense procurement (or demand) is basically created in two ways: from a military requirement for a more advanced weapons system, or from a new technological opportunity, usually developed by a contractor. Yet neither the supply nor demand determines how much of the product is purchased; it is Congress. And Congress is often affected by other factors like the mood of the country, elections, or domestic or international events.

The defense market is also extraordinarily concentrated. A very few programs take a huge share of the money. By the end of the 1970s, for example, some twenty programs were consuming over 40 percent of the Department of Defense (DoD) procurement dollar. Since there was no "share of the market" in a procurement sense, the magnitude of these programs produced a unique oligopoly among defense suppliers.

The fact that military programs are concentrated means that the typical military product will have a single prime contractor, producing fierce oligopolistic competition for these contracts. As of this writing, for example, the major aircraft companies were bidding on a new jet aircraft contract for the Joint Advanced Strike Aircraft (JAST)—a contract that could eventually be worth $750 *billion*. The Air Force, Navy, Marines, and Britain's Royal Navy are expected to buy about 3,000 of these fighters once they go operational in 2008. This will be the military's biggest contract ever, the reason being that the aircraft will have to perform missions for all of the services. It must be able to take off conventionally from land or a carrier deck as well as vertically.

Given the fact that there will not be another fighter built for decades, the competition is fierce. The winner will be guaranteed military aircraft work for years to come while the losers may have trouble staying in business. Three teams were competing for the business— Lockheed Martin, Boeing, and a consortium made up of McDonnell Douglas, Northrop Grumman, and British Aerospace.

The military cut the competition down to two in November 1996 with the McDonnell Douglas consortium being the surprise loser (surprise because Boeing has never built a fighter aircraft). The two survivors will now spend tens of millions of dollars building prototypes to compete in a fly-off before the final selection is made in the year 2000. Lockheed Martin CEO Norman Augustine said "You're bidding your company's life."[3] That was no exaggeration.

Why Defense Work?

But why do these oligopolistic firms stay in the defense business given the high risk? Why don't they diversify? The answer is, most do. Most hold controlling interests in firms that are not so heavily defense dependent, and Boeing's main business is civilian aircraft anyway. But defense work has its drawing cards. These include: (1) government funding of research and development, (2) a huge volume of business, (3) long-term multiyear contracts, and (4) countercyclical funding against business downturns.

The R&D Factor

The impact of government funding of military R&D has long been of concern to policymakers. Military R&D is thought to distort national research capacity in ways that damage national economic competitiveness. In terms of spending alone, for example, the military controls about 12 percent of basic research, 15 percent of applied research, and 45 percent of development. And 97 percent of federal R&D funds that go to corporations are for military-related purposes.

Historically, the most active aspect of this debate is the rate of spin-offs into the civilian market from military products. A post–World War II history of spin-offs would suggest that military R&D spending has important ramifications for the civilian economy. Examples include commercial jet aircraft, computers, semiconductors, communications satellites, nuclear power, and, of course, Teflon.

The aircraft industry is the most obvious example. The civilian benefits of defense research and spending were once very large and had much to do with America's current dominance of the commercial aircraft industry. Jet engines were developed by the military during World War II and were significantly improved by the military over the next twenty years. The C-5A transport project provided the technological breakthrough for the high-bypass-ratio engine used in commercial wide-bodied jets.

Military research also aided in the development of commercial airframes. With the KC-135 tanker aircraft, military requirements substantially reduced the cost of commercial development and tooling for the Boeing 707.[4]

In fact, it is just such spillovers that caused the Europeans to argue that European governmental support for the Aerobus was no different from what the United States had done for the commercial aircraft industry in the United States under the guise of defense spending. In March 1988 Aerobus released a document in which they claimed that the U.S. civilian aircraft industry had been subsidized by defense spending. Aerobus essentially argued that the civil part of the industry had benefited from the manufacture and sale of military aircraft and that the stability and long-term nature of the military revenues cushioned the manufacturers against the cyclical nature of the civilian side of the industry.[5]

Yet evidence today suggests that there is a much lower rate of civilian spillover from military spending than in the past. The divergence between military design requirements and civilian product characteristics is widening as technologies become more sophisticated. Also, military technology itself is pushing into more exotic and arcane areas.[6]

Even more important is the fact that today, in some areas, the spin-offs have reversed. That is, the civilian sector is ahead of the military in technology. This is particularly true in semiconductors and computers.[7]

The Department of Defense and Industrial Policy

Up until the late 1980s, Department of Defense support for specific industries was seldom a topic of discussion. But in 1988 the Defense Science Board brought the relationship between the Pentagon and industrial policy out into the open. The board held that "There is no military, economic or industrial base that is predominately separate from the civilian economy."[8] It recommended that "The Secretary of Defense should take an active role in the formation of national economic policies, including tax and trade. . . . The Secretary of Defense should request formal membership on the Economic Policy Council. . . . The President should create an Industrial Policy Committee chaired by the National Security Advisor."[9] This all confirms Lester Thurow's long-held argument that the Defense Department has often acted as America's MITI.[10]

But the larger Defense Department can never be a lead player in industrial policy because they are not only defense oriented but are defensive in character. They focus on threats, not opportunities. With DoD, risk reduction is an underlying premise. For MITI, economic development is the dominant goal.[11]

But there has always been a DoD role of some kind in industrial policy. And the Pentagon office (although it is not located in the Pentagon) that has historically bridged the gap between the military and industrial sectors is the Defense Advanced Research Projects Agency (DARPA). (Note: From 1992 to 1996 the agency was called the Advanced Research Projects Agency; Defense was dropped from the title. In the interest of keeping things simple, the agency will be referred to as DARPA, whether or not it was in its ARPA days.) Until very recently, Glean Pascall and Robert Lamson's assessment of DARPA held true: "More than any other, this agency can be seen as America's MITI."[12]

The Defense Advanced Research Projects Agency

In a shabby building in Rosalyn, Virginia, a couple of miles from the Pentagon, a few hundred people are in the industrial policy business, and they have been in that business for about thirty years. Defense Advanced Projects Research Agency project managers essentially hire private companies and academics to do research. Spending about $100 million a year on basic research makes DARPA America's premier venture capital company.

Beyond the military, DARPA attempts to influence U.S. industrial development as it shapes military innovation. This has particularly been true with the electronics industry. DARPA has invested time, energy, and money into the promotion of the U.S. semiconductor and high-definition display industries. One of the biggest examples has been DARPA's $100 million a year support of Sematech.[13]

It was noted earlier that most government support for R&D comes through the Department of Defense, which supports technologies with military potential. Within DoD, much of the funding for cutting-edge technologies is sourced from DARPA. DARPA was founded in 1958 and has an annual budget just short of $1.5 *billion*. It searches the nation for new technologies with military potential. When it identifies a promising new concept or product, DARPA contracts out research in the area to universities, government labs, and private corporations. The private firms provide the research to fulfill DARPA's military needs, but are free to fully exploit commercial applications of any unclassified research results.

The results of the majority of the agency's projects fall into this "dual use" category—whereby innovations have both important defense and civilian applications. The computer mouse is a good example. This technology came out of DARPA's research in the 1960s designed to help the Army speed up its paperwork flow.[14]

Because it funds individual companies, DARPA has been criticized for "picking winners and losers" in the commercial sector; it has. In fact, former DARPA Director Craig Fields lost his job during the Bush administration over his industrial policy activism. Fields invested $4 million of DARPA's money in Gazelle Microcircuits, Inc., a super-high-speed microchip developer. Gazelle manufactured gallium arsenide computer chips used to transmit and receive data at speeds up to one gigabit/second in fiber-optic communications systems. DARPA support allowed the company to extend the speed of its chips up to 1.5 gigabit/second. DARPA's return on this venture was 1–3 percent of net sales of the product over fifteen years, or cash payments based on an increase in Gazelle's stock price.[15] This partnership was the first under legislation that Fields had championed that allowed DARPA to participate in ventures like a true venture capitalist.

For Fields, however, the deal was the straw that broke the camel's back. To the Bush administration this was industrial policy and not to be tolerated. The White House fired Fields and moved some of DARPA's money into "mainstream" DoD. It also forced DARPA to slow its participation in Sematech (more about that shortly) and reduced its commitment to research on high-definition television (HDTV).[16]

Background

In 1986, Casper Weinberger, then secretary of Defense, was appalled to learn that half the chips in the F-16's fire-control system came from Japan. American companies simply could not make chips to the specifications required. So defense led the way in designing the recovery of the semiconductor industry.[17]

The United States absolutely dominated the semiconductor market up through the 1970s. During the early 1980s, however, the U.S. share of worldwide semiconductor sales fell from 58 to 37 percent. At the same time, Japanese sales rose from 26 to 49 percent of the world market. Even worse, the Japanese gains were in leading-edge markets.

Many reasons have been given for this success, including a government-led research consortium, a government-protected domestic market, and the dumping of semiconductors on the U.S. market. However, geographer David Angel holds that the Japanese success has less to do with these factors and more to do with the superior manufacturing performance of the Japanese semiconductor producers and some luck.

The luck was a market opening created by the U.S. semiconductor firms in the 1970s. Following a 1974–75 slump in semiconductor sales, U.S. firms dramatically reduced their capital investment in new production facilities. When demand for semiconductors began to increase in the late 1970s, shortages developed. Then, many high-volume U.S. producers turned to Japanese suppliers. These sales to U.S. firms allowed the Japanese firms to engage in high-volume production and created opportunities for the Japanese to realize economies of scale in production and move rapidly up the learning curve. By the end of the 1970s, Japanese firms had captured 40 percent of the U.S. market for 16K DRAMs.

This entry into the U.S. market was critical to the ultimate success of the Japanese. They were able to demonstrate to the American computer manufacturers that they could produce high-quality products and deliver them on time. By 1990 Japanese firms held over 70 percent of the world market for DRAMs.

One of the reasons for Japanese success was the close relationship between semiconductor producers and their equipment suppliers. In the United States, the relations between the giant semiconductor manufacturers and their equipment suppliers were often strained. Rather than developing strong linkages with equipment suppliers, U.S. manufacturers constantly switched among the many competing suppliers for the most technologically advanced equipment. They also had the nasty habit of transferring much of the cost of fluctuating demand to their equipment suppliers in the form of reduced or canceled orders for equipment. Thus, U.S. equipment manufacturers remained weak, small, and undercapitalized. In contrast, Japanese producers formed strong partnerships with their suppliers, fostering a strong equipment industry. Semiconductor manufacturers often took the lead in promoting and introducing new equipment into the manufacturing process. The semiconductor engineers worked closely with equipment manufacturers adapting new equipment into the actual production environment. And the semiconductor manufacturers' strong financial and ownership ties with their suppliers provided a pool of investment capital available for research and development. (Most manufacturers and suppliers are part of the *keiretsu*. See the appendix.)

Under these conditions it became increasingly difficult for U.S. equipment manufacturers to compete, resulting in Japanese dominance of the semiconductor equipment industry. Between 1983 and 1989, the U.S. share of the market in wafer fabricating equipment tumbled from 62 to 41 percent. The share going to Japanese firms increased from 28 to 48 percent of the world market.[18]

The appendix documents the effort the Japanese government put into developing their semiconductor industry. Angel asserts that "where industrial production is characterized by dynamic economies of scale, imperfect competition, and a cumulative and territorially embedded knowledge base, government intervention can decisively shift competitive advantage from one national economy to another."[19] This was exactly the case of the Japanese semiconductor industry. "Through a combination of investment incentives, coordination of R&D, and market closure, the Japanese government helped to secure the rise of the Japanese semiconductor industry to a position of market leadership, thereby undermining the profitability of, and employment in, the U.S. semiconductor industry."[20]

Sematech

The U.S. took a slightly different tack toward remedying the situation vis-à-vis the Japanese. It formed a research consortium—Sematech. It appears that the U.S. government's willingness to initiate an industrial policy for the semiconductor industry stemmed from two sources. First, there was the widespread belief that the problems of the U.S. semiconductor industry were the direct result of unfair trade practices of the Japanese. And second was the dynamic lobbying and public relations campaign of the semiconductor firms conducted by the Semiconductor Industry Association to convince federal officials that the prosperity of the semiconductor industry was a national security issue. This was not a difficult task.

So Sematech was born. Sematech (an acronym for semiconductor manufacturing technology) is a nonprofit research consortium of U.S. semiconductor firms established in 1987. It is a research partnership between the U.S. government and the largest semiconductor manufacturers.

Sematech was made possible by the 1984 National Cooperative Research Act (NCRA). NCRA facilitated research cooperation among firms by excluding "pre-competitive" research from the triple damage provisions of antitrust laws.

Two reports influenced Sematech's creation. In 1987, the Defense Science Board (DSB), a committee of scientists and engineers that advises the undersecretary of Defense for Research and Engineering, issued a report documenting the fact that U.S. semiconductor manufacturers were falling behind the Japanese in manufacturing process technologies for chips. The DSB argued that this had important implications for national security. It argued for the creation of a manufacturing facility for producing semiconductor components to be jointly owned by the government and industry.

This report came out shortly before a second report issued by the Semiconductor Industry Association (SIA), which recommended the formation of an industrywide consortium to conduct research, rather than manufacture chips. Shortly thereafter, in May 1987, a fourteen-member committee of the SIA proposed a research consortium with matching federal contributions. These fourteen companies became the founding members of Sematech. Among them, they controlled 80 percent of the semiconductor component manufacturing capacity in the country.[21]

Sematech was originally funded with a $100 million annual appropriation from Congress for its first five years and fees ranging from $1 million to $15 million from its members. The funding was provided through DARPA, although the agency had little direct involvement in either Sematech's creation or the initial $100 million annual appropriation. It was the semiconductor industry itself that lobbied successfully for federal support. Essentially in response to the push from the industry, Congress gave $100 million to the secretary of Defense to support the semiconductor industry. Defense concluded that support of Sematech was the most effective way to use these funds. DARPA's involvement was a marriage of convenience. DARPA was the most convenient way to pass through these funds and, at the same time, provide oversight.[22]

The government has been a limited partner in the management of Sematech. While DARPA and the General Accounting Office (GAO) provide oversight, and several representatives of federal agencies sit on Sematech's governing board, the organization has clearly been member driven. The engineering staff of Sematech is made up of both Sematech employees and engineers on loan from partner firms. About two-thirds of the 300-member professional research staff are engineers on loan from the partners. Sematech conducts research at its own facilities in Austin, Texas, as well at the facilities of member firms and equipment suppliers.[23]

At the same time that Sematech was founded, the semiconductor materials and equipment suppliers (SME) formed Semi/Sematech to facilitate linkages between the suppliers and Sematech. Semi/Sematech has about 135 member firms, accounting for more than 80 percent of the SME business. The organization is funded by dues and fees generated from sponsored conferences. The president of Semi/Sematech sits on the board of Sematech, and the boards of Semi/Sematech and Sematech meet jointly once each quarter.[24]

The original mission of Sematech was to "demonstrate the feasibility of manufacturing leading-edge semiconductors using only U.S.-made equipment."[25] Sematech was to establish a state-of-the-art wafer manufacturing plant (which it did). Lessons learned from the effort were to be initially shared with the member firms, and subsequently with other U.S. manufacturers.

However, within two years, Sematech's mission had dramatically changed to one of providing developmental assistance to U.S. semiconductor equipment manufacturers. This shift in focus was due to the poor competitive position of the equipment manufacturers, which made it virtually impossible to establish a leading-edge semiconductor manufacturing facility using American-made equipment. During the 1980s virtually the entire supplier industry declined, with the United States losing its leading-edge position in lithography, etching, materials purification, as well as in other key areas. The worldwide share held by U.S. equipment manufacturers declined from 72 percent to 42 percent during the period, while the Japanese share went from 20 percent to 48 percent.

The causes of the declining fortunes of the equipment manufacturers were twofold: the small size of the firms and low levels of R&D spending. Most were unable to allocate sufficient capital for development—in part because of their small size. In 1990 only 6 percent of the equipment suppliers had sales of over $100 million, with most having sales of less than $25 million. All of these firms combined were only spending $50 million on R&D. (This compares to $3 billion spent on R&D by the semiconductor firms.)

In an attempt to solve the manufacturing equipment problems, Sematech spent $371 million over the period 1987–89 on equipment improvement projects. By far the largest amount ($145 million) was spent on the development of lithography equipment with contracts to two manufacturers—Silicon Valley Group and GCA.[26]

The consortium's focus shifted from the development of a state-of-the-art production process to knowledge diffusion and technology transfer. The revised research strategy is illustrated by Sematech's announcement in January 1993 that it had achieved its goal of manufacturing 0.35 micron line-width integrated circuits. Rather than developing a process that could be adopted by member firms, it developed a generic technology that was not product-specific or firm-specific, yet could be adapted to a multitude of uses.[27]

Sematech's emphasis is clearly now on suppliers. It has increased its spending on supplier contracts to over 50 percent of its funds. Sematech's interaction with SME suppliers falls into four categories: joint development projects, equipment improvement projects, provision of technology "road maps," and efforts to broaden communications between members firms and suppliers. Joint development projects fund the development of new equipment by suppliers (Sematech typically funds about 25 percent of the project's costs).

Equipment improvement projects were started in response to complaints about poor reliability of U.S. semiconductor manufacturing equipment. A Sematech engineering team manages each equipment improvement project from start to finish. The results are passed on to member firms who can improve their utilization or maintenance techniques for such equipment. Both joint development and equipment improvement projects include efforts to "qualify" new or improved equipment. Qualification is generally conducted at Sematech's Austin facility with the participation of Sematech engineers and supplier personnel.

"Roadmaps" for suppliers are set through formal meetings between Sematech managers, member firm representatives, and project managers in each research area (such as lithography). They meet several times a year to discuss project performance and future requirements. The roadmaps set the Sematech research agenda and coordinate its selection of research projects.

Sematech and Semi/Sematech have also attempted to improve communications between SME suppliers and the semiconductor manufacturers. This is done through formal conferences and programs. An example is the "Partnership for Total Quality," which focused on improving supplier management and financial practices and the development of world-class capabilities.[28]

To What Effect?

Although a comprehensive evaluation of Sematech has not yet been done, Angel believes Sematech can be credited with aiding the recovery of the semiconductor industry by contributing to the increased competitive position of the equipment suppliers. U.S. equipment firms increased their share of the worldwide market by 5 percent in 1991 (to 47 percent). And major U.S. semiconductor firms such as Motorola and Intel reported significant purchases from U.S. equipment producers. Angel reports that according to a U.S. government report, "Sematech is widely credited by member firms with improving communication within the semiconductor industry, shifting the culture of firms toward long-term partnerships with equipment suppliers, and helping to establish common standards for software and manufacturing equipment."[29]

Angel is not alone in declaring Sematech a success. An article in *IEEE Transactions on Engineering Management* declared Sematech a total success. The author, Sandia Lab's James Gover, concluded that "Sematech has demonstrated that government-sponsored R&D programs can have economic impact on the competitiveness of a critical industrial sector," and "Sematech has evolved as the optimum model for government to use in helping U.S. industry regain their competitiveness."[30] And, while not quite as effusive in their praise, three Berkeley researchers reached essentially the same conclusion in a comprehensive article in the *Journal of Policy Analysis and Management*.[31]

Even one of Sematech's most serious critics, T.J. Rodgers, CEO of Cypress Semiconductor, now offers constrained praise: "There are a lot of good things you can say about Sematech. A lot of its programs and developments are valuable. . . . My objection isn't to what Sematech does; my objection is that I don't think taxpayers ought to be footing the bill."[32]

And they won't be footing the bill much longer. After the initial five years of support of $100 million per year, government funding has all but been eliminated. It was $90 million in 1994 and 1995 and was reduced to $39 million in 1996. As of 1997 federal funding is expected to end and Sematech will be on its own.

High-Definition Television (HDTV)

DARPA's interest in HDTV was, in part, an outgrowth of its interest in developing and protecting the semiconductor industry. According to Craig Fields, then DARPA's deputy director for research, in a statement before the House Committee on Science, Space, and Technology, federal support for HDTV will also support the semiconductor and computer industries—industries critical to national defense.

> HDTVs will consume large quantities of semiconductors. . . . The country whose companies supply those semiconductors for HDTV will

enjoy a significant economy of scale of production, and will have the massive revenues needed for refining manufacturing and the ever increasing expense of R&D required for developing next generation semiconductor products. In turn, that will give those companies competitive advantage in supplying semiconductors for products other than HDTV, e.g. automobiles and telecommunications, and in fact will give them leverage in gaining market share in those other "down stream" industries. . . .

Further, to the extent that HDTVs evolve to be computers, as digital technology inexorably replaces analog technology, an evolution that is inevitable even if its speed is debated, the companies that produce HDTV will have a competitive edge in capturing market share in the computer industry.[33]

But supporting the semiconductor and computer industries was hardly the only reason for DARPA's interest in HDTV. The Defense Department has for many years acquired high-definition displays for such applications as training simulators, command and control systems, weapons displays, and intelligence work stations. Support for HDTV is merely a logical outgrowth of R&D and procurement in those areas.

With this in mind, DARPA took the position that national security requires an assured domestic supply of the highest performance and highest quality technology in our industrial base. HDTV fits this bill. Defense does not believe that the military industrial base can be separated from the larger volume commercial and consumer base. In other words, it is hard to separate our national security and economic strengths.[34]

But from the consumer point of view, exactly what is high-definition television anyway? Some of the features of HDTV are: higher picture sharpness, larger picture, more colors, wider picture, and multichannel digital CD-quality sound. Pictures will have six times the resolution of current TV. Motion will be seen as smooth and the picture will be clear enough for the viewer to be able to sit very close to a very large screen.

Specifically, the current generation of televisions has an optimum viewing distance of eight to ten times the height of the picture. This means that if the screen is one foot tall, the ideal viewing distance is eight to ten feet. The present sets provide about a ten-degree field of vision for the viewer. With HDTV the optimum viewing distance is only three times the height of the screen. (One can sit very close to

HDTV and still get a "great picture.") In addition, the field of vision will be 30 degrees at that distance. In other words, for a given room we can now add a much larger screen (and wider picture) and not suffer the distortion we see now on big screen sets when we are too close. HDTV is about big screens and field of vision.

At present, HDTV is available commercially only in Japan. Technologically, it is not easy to integrate transmission signals into the current system because of bandwidth problems. But these problems will soon be solved. HDTV will soon be coming to the United States. But it will not be cheap. The first generation of sets will be the toys of the rich (and the sports bars). Sets will be priced between $5,000 and $10,000.[35]

But what were the specifics of DARPA's involvement in HDTV? In November 1988, DARPA announced a new $30 million grant competition for the development of high-definition displays and display processors. The $30 million was split equally between display and processor research. DARPA received eighty-seven proposals and in June 1989 announced that thirteen grants had been awarded for research on high-definition displays. However, HDTV ran into trouble in the Bush White House. In November 1989, the Bush administration announced plans to sharply curtail DoD programs to support R&D. Included in this announcement was DARPA's high-definition technology project. In addition, the Office of Management and Budget (OMB) asked DoD to put a hold on several of the research contracts already awarded under the project.

In the meantime, Congress had authorized an additional $20 million for HDTV research at DARPA contingent on receiving a report explaining the need for the funds. DARPA had not been able to supply this report to Congress because the administration blocked its release. Things came to a head when Fields (now DARPA's acting director) decided to fund the high-definition research out of DARPA's discretionary funds in April 1990 and continued to speak out in favor of civilian technology programs. Then, on April 20, when DARPA announced its decision to invest the $4 million in Gazelle Microcircuits, Fields was fired and the initiative to purse HDTV policy moved to the Federal Communications Commission (FCC).

The FCC made a number of policy decisions regarding HDTV, one of which was crucial to the support of American firms. The United States was late getting into high-definition television. Japan and Europe were ahead in defining their systems. Both had opted for the delivery of analog signals via satellites. The FCC, however, decided that the United States should adopt a digital delivery system. FCC chairman Alfred Sikes hoped that an all-digital HDTV would be something the United States electronics firms could do better than the Japanese or European firms.

So DARPA got the HDTV ball rolling and the FCC kept it in play. Only time will tell how the American firms will do.[36]

Flat Panel Displays

One of the current contributions of the military to national industrial policy is a process called civil-military integration (CMI). With CMI, common technologies, processes, labor, equipment, materials, and/or facilities are used to meet both defense and commercial needs.[37] The theory behind CMI is that a strategy aimed at making greater use of commercial technology and industrial base to help meet national security needs has the potential both to save money and to improve technology. Flat panel displays is one of the technologies being supported by the Defense Department under CMI.

Flat panel displays (FPDs) are thin electronic devices that present images without the bulk of a picture tube. Flat panel displays have allowed the development of devices such as digital wristwatches, video cameras, and, of course, the laptop and notebook computers. They will soon be part of wide-screen televisions that are so light and so thin that they can be hung on a wall. FPDs are also critical to the military. They are used in displays in aircraft, ships, and vehicles.

There are many different, competing panel technologies. They fall into four broad categories: liquid-crystal displays (LCDs), electroluminescent displays (ELDs), plasma-display panels (PDPs), and field-emission displays (FEDs).

Liquid-crystal displays are by far the most common type of flat panels. Liquid crystals are organic molecules that have crystal-like properties but are liquid at normal temperatures. The molecules can be realigned by weak electromagnetic fields. An LCD consists of a layer of liquid-crystal material 1.5 to 6 microns thick sandwiched between two layers of glass or polymer. When an electronic field is applied in quick succession to different areas, the display produces illuminated dots known as pixels. There are passive- and active-matrix LCDs. Passive-matrix displays (PMLCDs) are currently the most common. In a passive matrix, multiple pixels are turned on, and, like a cathode ray tube (CRT), it paints the display in rapid horizontal strokes. Active-matrix displays (AMLCDs) do not have to be multiplexed and the pixels are individually activated. They are shallower, weigh less, consume less power, are more reliable, and easier to maintain than PMLCDs. They are also the wave of the future. Passive displays, on the other hand, are less costly and therefore continue to dominate the field in low-information-content (simple) displays.

The advantage of electroluminescent displays is resolution. Visually, they are bright and highly readable, with fast response. They are reliable, long-lived, and extremely thin. In ELDs, layers of thin phosphor films are deposited onto a sheet of glass, then covered with another sheet. One of the films is luminescent, emitting light when struck by electrons. ELDs are currently used in tanks and command centers by the military and commercially in ATM machines. They are not now used in computers or consumer electronics.

Plasma displays are composed of front and back substrates with phosphors deposited on the inside of the front plates. An inert gas placed between the glass plates of each cell generates light, with the color depending on the phosphor used. Plasma displays are currently used in submarine and command centers, and in portable medical equipment.[38]

The demand for flat panel displays is large and increasing. The market exceeded $10 billion in 1995 and is growing at a rate of more than 10 percent per year. It is estimated that the market will be between $20 and $40 billion by the turn of the century. While critical to the U.S. military, flat panels for military systems represent less than 1 percent of the worldwide market. This figure is not likely to increase.

At the moment, the Japanese dominate the market. While there are over fifty firms worldwide producing flat panel displays, the U.S. industry remains quite small. No U.S. firms currently produce LCDs for the commercial market.

U.S. Concerns

There are two major concerns for the nation:

- Economic Benefit. Some observers say that the lack of a high-volume domestic FPD industry could harm the nation because domestic firms will be unable to: (1) sell to a large and growing FPD market; (2) compete in product markets that rely on FPDs as a critical component; and (3) benefit from the spillovers of FPD technology to other semiconductor-based products.

- National Security. According to DoD, the domestic FPD industry is not able, and leading foreign suppliers are not willing, to provide the military with *early, assured, and affordable access* to leading-edge FPD technology, which DoD asserts is critical to national security.[39]

The DoD states specifically that it "cannot currently rely on the overseas supply base to furnish customized or specialized products or capabilities that will be required to support future DOD needs, or to provide leading edge technology to DOD before it is in widespread commercial use."[40]

The fundamental technologies used in military FPDs are the same as in the commercial market. However, military displays differ in their size, shape, and the extreme operating environments they will be exposed to. One area of military display applications is portable battlefield information and communications systems. Another is large area workstation displays in aircraft, surface ships, submarines, and stationary positions. Very large area displays are used for presentations, briefings, and for strategic map displays. Military avionics displays present critical flight, targeting, and communications information to the pilot in a harsh environment. There are literally hundreds of thousands of display uses in the military.

The U.S. flat panel display industry is currently comprised of a number of relatively small and innovative firms that carry out leading-edge research, some prototype development, and manufacturing for niche and custom markets. There is essentially no domestic mass manufacturing for commercial markets.

Given this background, flat panel displays were deemed a critical CMI technology. The industry stands to grow by leaps and bounds over the next few years and yet the military makes up a very small part of the industry. The fundamental technology is the same for both the commercial and military sectors, yet the military has special needs. So it is logical that U.S. government funding for FPDs is dominated by DoD.[41]

Flat panel displays first became a concern of the U.S. government in 1989, when the government was concerned with high-definition television. Flat panel displays were an integral part of this concern.[42] In 1989 DARPA initiated the High-Definition Systems (HDS) program, originally called High-Definition Display Technology. Program funding started with $5 million and rose to $30 million the following year. Funding was then increased to $75 million in 1991 and 1992 and then to $161 million in 1993 including $25 million specifically for AMLCD technology. In 1994 and 1995 Congress funded (through DARPA) FPDs to the tune of $85 million and $82 million, respectively.

DARPA's HDS program was designed to develop the domestic capability to manufacture FPDs by bringing together firms from three levels of the industry: materials and equipment, display manufacturers, and end-users. The first phase (from 1990 to 1992) focused on developing the materials and equipment sector of the industry and also supported research into advanced displays technologies. A number of technological breakthroughs resulted. Examples include a thirteen-inch diagonal AMLCD with 6.3 million pixels (the most to date) developed by Xerox, a full-color HDTV format digital micromirror display (first of its kind) by Texas Instruments, and a full-color, thirty-inch diagonal high-resolution plasma monitor developed by Photonics Imaging.

Phase two of the program began in 1993 with the objective of adding manufacturing testbeds to the ongoing R&D programs. The first manufacturing testbed award ($48 million) went to OIS. The manufacturing plant was built in Northville Township, Michigan. Its production is about 160,000 AMLCD displays annually, with about one-fourth going to the military.

The second award ($50 million) went to a partnership of AT&T, Xerox, and Standish Industries in 1994. This testbed will be distributed at four sites among the firms and will develop high-resolution displays and advanced packaging for intelligence applications.

DARPA has also funded the National Center for Advanced Information Components Manufacturing (NCAICM), a cooperative research program in flat panel displays and microelectronics technologies operated by Sandia National Laboratories in conjunction with Los Alamos and Lawrence Livermore National Laboratories. The goal of the display portion of the program is to develop flexible manufacturing technologies that can be applied to low-cost, high-volume production of large area emissive flat panel displays, mainly plasma, FED, and ELD.

But, in general, DARPA has tried to stay out of the manufacturing end of projects, largely because of the expense involved. An investment in prototype development might require ten times the funds available for research, and a manufacturing facility one hundred times. For this reason, DARPA has tried to avoid projects that move very far beyond prototype development.[43]

The National Flat Panel Display Initiative

The latest move in the flat panel arena is the Clinton administration's National Flat Panel Display Initiative (NFPDI), announced on April 28, 1994. The announcement was made by former DARPA official and long-time proponent of government support for the flat panel industry, Kenneth Flamm. Flamm was assistant secretary of Defense for Dual-Use Technology and International Programs and is credited with being largely responsible for the flat panel initiative.[44] Flamm announced that the government would be spending $587 million over the next five years to promote U.S. *manufacturing* of flat panel displays.[45] NFPDI was ostensibly initiated to meet defense needs by developing a high-volume commercial flat panel display industry. While the justification related to national security, the initiative came under the administration's dual use policy. Recall that this calls for DoD to use commercial capabilities wherever possible and to focus on capabilities that will support both defense and the commercial technology bases. The thrust of NFPDI is threefold: continuation of the DARPA R&D and testbed programs, awarding grants to firms planning to manufacture flat panel displays, and applying DoD funds to procurement programs if they use domestic flat panel displays. Spending under the initiative is expected to be in the neighborhood of $610 million over the five-year period 1994–98.[46] The goal of the initiative is to develop a flat panel display industry equaling 15 percent of world production by the end of the decade (from about 5 percent).[47] The key, of course, is manufacturing. The innovation in the initiative was an explicit plan to encourage new commercial production facilities rather than just new R&D efforts.

The flat panel display initiative relied on a task force (chaired by Flamm) report. Not surprisingly, the report came to be known as the Flamm Report. In terms of government reports, it broke new ground by suggesting general principles under which government might be justified in creating new, viable domestic industries. These "overriding principles" are:

1) The initiative must be of sufficient scope and duration to attract significant industry participation.

2) Industry must be willing to share in the costs of the initiative. The extent of industry willingness to undertake such costs is one of the most important measures of the initiative's value.

3) The initiative should be based on principles of competition among firms and technologies. Central to this principle is the notion that the initiative will go forward only if industry responds with acceptable proposals and plays a lead role in determining the technologies to pursue.

4) Given the international nature of modern, high-technology industries and the emphasis on achieving leading-edge capabilities, DoD programs should have the flexibility to consider participation by foreign-owned entities that satisfies program objectives.

5) The initiative should be consistent with other government policy objectives. In particular, given the leading role of the United States in supporting an open international trading system and the benefits that such a system has for our economic security, the initiative should be consistent with U.S. obligations under the General Agreement on Tariffs and Trade and the World Trade Organization.

6) The initiative must be subject to sunset provisions and include clear measures of success to force and guide decisions about the continuing necessity of the initiative over the medium to long term.[48]

The Flamm Report then went on to state that the goal for the initiative was to establish at least four new production facilities for high-volume production of flat panel displays in the United States. It expressed hope that the U.S. share of world production would rise from its current level of 5 percent to 15 percent.[49]

Comments

The reaction to the initiative has been mixed, as one would suspect. A number of editorials and op-ed pieces have been negative. In *Newsweek*, economist Robert Samuelson opposed the plan. An op-ed piece in the *New York Times* also opposed the idea, as did ABC's Brit Hume, writing in the *Washington Post*. On the other hand, *Business Week* provided a glowing endorsement.[50]

The reactions of American companies were also mixed. Many of the commercial users of the displays have developed stable relationships with Japanese suppliers of displays. They did not want to do or say anything that would upset the apple cart. But the Advanced Display Manufacturers Association, the trade association of the display industry, was, of course, thrilled.[51]

Conclusion

The DoD has been in the industrial policy business for some time now, with DARPA its lead agency. Presidents have come and gone, but DARPA and its mission have survived. At one time, for example, George Bush tried to do in Sematech. Bush took a minimalist approach in terms of economic policy. He has been quoted as being "darkly pessimistic" about government's ability to change anything for the better.[52] His troika of economic advisors (called "the Iron Triangle") had a rigid allegiance to the free market ideology and opposition to governmental intervention. The three were John Sununu, White House chief of staff; Richard Darman, director of the Office of Management and Budget; and Michael Boskin, chairman of the Council of Economic Advisers. The three tried to shoot down even modest proposals for technological development. In 1989, for example, the three recommended an abrupt end to government support for Sematech. But when confronted with a bipartisan howl of protest from Congress, Bush backed off.[53]

And while most reasonable analysts now give Sematech at least some credit for helping to rescue an industry in trouble, not all such initiatives will pay off. The flat panel initiative is probably a long shot. DARPA's flat panel efforts under the initiative are being administered by its Electronic Systems Technology Office, headed by Dr. Lance Glasser. Glasser calls the initiative "a long shot. It's a hedge. We should have started in 1983 but we missed it. Now we are trying to repatriate a technology. We have to learn how to do that, because each year there are more candidates for repatriation. The problem now is to get the big users on board."[54]

DoD has clearly moved industrial policy initiatives into the high-technology arena. But DoD is no longer the only player in town. Other executive agencies have recently been flexing their industrial policy muscles, as the cases in the next chapter illustrate.

7

Industrial Policy for New Technologies: Pitfalls and Foibles

Richard D. Bingham and Maria Papadakis

The previous chapter may convey the wrong impression—that industrial policy, at least as it pertains to technological advances, is the exclusive purview of the Department of Defense, and in particular to the Defense Advanced Research Projects Agency (DARPA). DARPA is clearly an important player in industrial policy for certain technologies, but it is hardly the only player. There are other agencies, like the Department of Commerce and Department of Energy, which also play important roles, as do White House offices like the Office of Science and Technology Policy.

This chapter is about some of those other players and government efforts to promote two new technologies—an entirely new, highly fuel-efficient automobile, and high-temperature superconductivity (HTS). It is also about government by committee.

Maria Papadakis is associate professor of Integrated Science and Technology at James Madison University and co-editor of the *Journal of Technology Transfer.*

In some ways DARPA is atypical. It controls such a (relatively) vast amount of money that it can virtually develop an industry all by itself. This is the case with flat panel displays, as was shown in Chapter 6. But the reality of government is not usually that uncomplicated. It is typically the case that by the time officials high enough up in government to make things happen decide that government should become involved in the commercialization of some technology, numerous federal agencies are already involved. What then? Is that technology then centralized in one agency? Rarely. Agencies are hardly prone to give up something they already have that is receiving a lot of (favorable) high-level attention. So what typically emerges is some form of government by committee, as the two cases presented here clearly illustrate.

The Clinton/Gore Auto Initiative

In late September 1993, the Clinton administration and the Big Three automakers announced a new joint research project designed to triple the fuel efficiency of U.S. autos to about 80 miles per gallon (mpg) over the next decade. Vice President Gore likened the project to NASA's Apollo lunar program in its scope and daring.[1]

The seeds of the project grew from the thoughts and ideas presented by President Clinton and Vice President Gore at a technology conference held on February 22, 1993, very shortly after the new administration had taken office. They identified six "new initiatives" for rebuilding America's economic strength. One of these new initiatives was to develop a new generation of automobiles: "a new generation of vehicles could be on the market—preserving jobs, expanding growth—that would be safe and perform as well, if not better than existing automobiles, cost no more to drive than today's automobiles, consume only domestic fuels such as natural gas and renewables, and produce little or no pollution."[2]

Why Autos?

The auto industry was certainly a good place to start a new industrial initiative. For one thing, more than 13 million Americans are employed in motor vehicle–related industries with over 2 million employed directly by the U.S. automakers and their suppliers and dealers. The industry accounts for almost 5 percent of the gross domestic product. It was felt that the development of the breakthrough technologies required to achieve the Clinton/Gore objectives could not be realized through the marketplace alone; that a partnership between government and industry was needed to address this challenge.[3]

The partnership required an all-out effort. A multitude of research projects would have to be coordinated and everything must eventually come together in prototype vehicles. The scope of the problem is shown in Figure 7.1. The figure shows the distribution of energy in a current mid-size vehicle. It is clear that major advances must be made in a number of technologies simultaneously in order to achieve an 80 mpg vehicle. Given that in a current automobile only 12.6 percent of the energy turns the wheels after engine, standby, driveline, and other losses, improvements will require a three-pronged approach: energy must be converted more efficiently, regenerative braking must be implemented to recapture energy, and overall energy demands must be reduced.[4]

Figure 7.2 shows a parametric model illustrating the various ways in which these approaches could be combined to achieve the 80 mpg goal. It is unlikely that the targeted fuel economy will be attainable through engine improvements alone. The needed thermal efficiency is twice that of today's engines. Even with advanced fuel cells, which have higher efficiencies than heat engines, other improvements will be needed.

Regenerative braking must be developed to recover, store, and reuse energy currently lost by braking. This will reduce the amount of energy that must be converted from fuel, which is normally the most inefficient step of the energy cycle.

In addition, the goal will only be met by reduction of 20 to 40 percent in the mass of today's vehicles. This will require more than refinements of today's frame and body construction, it will call for entirely new classes of structural materials.[5]

Vice President Gore was quick to follow up on the speech, meeting with John Gibbons, the president's new science advisor and head of the Office of Science and Technology Policy (OSTP). Gibbons set up several interconnected working groups to decide what auto improvements were technically possible over the next decade.

USCAR

It was obvious from the beginning that if any auto effort were to succeed it would need the full cooperation, if not enthusiastic partici-

130

Figure 7.1. Energy Distribution of Typical Mid-Size Vehicle

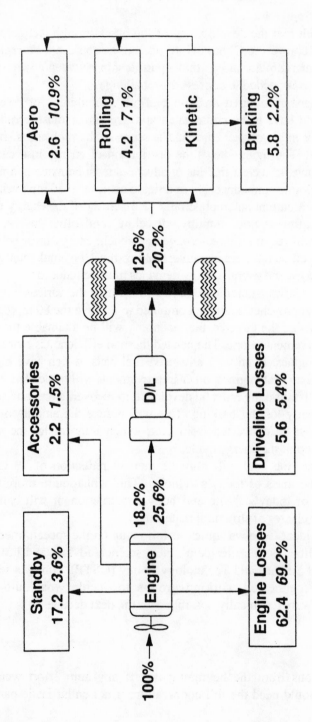

Source: Partnership for a New Generation of Vehicles.

Figure 7.2. **Design Space for "3X" Fuel Efficiency**

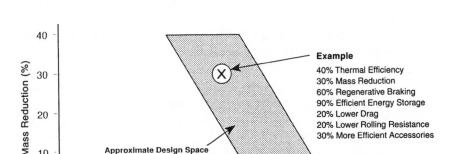

Source: Partnership for a New Generation of Vehicles.

pation, of the Big Three automakers. Fortunately, USCAR, an organization that might foster government/industry cooperation, was already in place. USCAR is an acronym for United States Council for Automotive Research, a partnership between the Big Three auto firms, designed to carry out cutting-edge automotive research. The passage of the Cooperative Research Act of 1984 (see Chapter 6) allowed the major automakers to work together on research problems without violating antitrust laws. This legislation enabled Chrysler, Ford, and General Motors to first come together (in August 1988) to form a consortium to conduct joint research on structural polymer composites. The development of such materials for structures and body panels was a major undertaking—more than any one of the companies was willing to spend on its own.

As the manufacturers found that the consortia were useful tools in addressing a wide variety of long-range technical problems, more consortia were spawned. As the number of consortia grew, it became evident that an organizational entity was needed to direct and coordinate their work. Thus the birth of USCAR in 1992. USCAR's cooperative research and development programs permit the leveraging of resources to address common technical issues, thereby sharing competitive research without compromising the ability of members to compete in the marketplace. By 1994 some fourteen consortia had been formed.[6]

And the federal government has been heavily involved in the funding. Take the United States Advanced Battery Consortium (USABC) as an example. The USABC was formed in 1991 to develop advanced battery systems for commercialization that will provide increased range and improved performance for electric vehicles in the later part of the 1990s.[7] Costs of the program are split evenly between the federal government and private sector participants. Through FY 1994 the federal government had obligated $77 million toward the government's share of the $260 million joint program.[8] The chair of the Consortium calls progress to date "very encouraging." All USABC developers are producing actual batteries that are undergoing testing in the national labs.[9]

The Partnership for a New Generation of Vehicles

During the summer of 1993, Gibbons's representative began negotiating in earnest with the representatives of the auto industry (the three directors of USCAR), Gibbons, the vice president, and working group members from the various federal agencies with interests in the project. The task was to identify the components of an auto project that were "doable" within a decade. For example, auto efficiency became an immediate point of contention. The industry believed that a doubling of auto efficiency was easily possible during the decade. Government representatives wanted to hold out for a quadrupling in efficiency.

About a month before the September announcement of the Partnership for a New Generation of Vehicles (PNGV) initiative, Vice President Gore and Science Advisor Gibbons met with the three CEOs of the American auto companies and reached agreement on the goals of the initiative. Newly appointed Commerce Undersecretary for Technology Mary Good was put in charge. Good was an excellent choice. She had recently retired from Allied Signal and had a sound reputation with industry.[10]

On September 29 the president, vice president, and the chief executive officers of the Big Three automakers announced a partnership to develop technologies for a new generation of vehicles. The federal government and USCAR agreed on the following three specific but interrelated goals:

Goal 1. Significantly improve national competitiveness in manufacturing.
Improve productivity of the U.S. manufacturing base by significantly upgrading U.S. manufacturing technology, including adoption of agile and flexible manufacturing and reduction of costs and lead times, while reducing the environmental impact and/or improving quality.

Goal 2. Implement commercially viable innovation from ongoing research on conventional vehicles.
Pursue advances in vehicles that can lead to improvements in the fuel efficiency and emissions of standard vehicle designs, while pursuing safety advances to maintain safety performance. Research will focus on technologies that reduce the demand for energy from the engine and drivetrain. Throughout the research program, the industry commits to apply those commercially viable technologies resulting from this research that would be expected to increase fuel efficiency and improve emissions.

Goal 3. Develop a vehicle to achieve up to three times fuel efficiency of today's comparable vehicle (i.e., the 1994 Chrysler Concorde, Ford Taurus and Chevrolet Lumina).
Achieve fuel efficiency improvement of up to three times the average of Concorde/Taurus/Lumina, with equivalent customer purchase price of today's comparable sedans adjusted for economics. Note: While costing no more to own and drive than today's automobile, adjusted for economics, while meeting customers' needs for quality, performance, and utility.[11]

Organization

Mary Good had a new program but no organization. How was this public–private partnership going to be run? What was its administrative structure to look like? Ms. Good met with the three auto vice presidents (the directors of USCAR) at the Greenbriar Resort in White Sulphur Springs, West Virginia, and developed the organizational structure for PNGV. Organizational decisions were to be made by an Operational Steering Group composed of officials from both government and industry. The chair of the group was to be rotated between government and industry. The Operational Steering Group was composed of two subgroups—the government steering group and the industry steering group.[12]

The industry steering group was fairly straightforward and essentially represented USCAR. The Government Steering Group was larger and a little more complicated. Its explanation requires a short digression. The PNGV program was a coordinating program with no real staff or money of its own. Federal agencies participating in PNGV were essentially expected to reallocate some of their research funds to the program's priorities—but they would not lose control or ownership of their funds. And, in fact, some of these federal agencies were already funding automotive research that dovetailed nicely into PNGV. All this led to the fact that it was necessary to have a representative of each of the funding agencies (and a few others like OSTP and OMB) on the steering group.

On November 11, 1993, the Operational Steering Group held its first meeting at the headquarters of USCAR in Dearborn, Michigan. The steering group's first task was to develop its declaration of intent, which identified in detail the organization's goals and objectives. It also decided that it needed a technical team to identify the various technical tasks that had to be accomplished. The group decided on a Technical Team structure that very much mirrored the Operational Steering Group.[13]

The PNGV organizational chart is shown in Figure 7.3. There is no doubt that it is cumbersome, but it seemed to work—at least during the early years of the program.

The Operational Steering Group had the following responsibilities: strategic planning, program review, assuring the availability of program resources and funding, coordinating of legal and public affairs functions, and providing direction to the Technical Team. The Technical Team was responsible for plan development and implementation, project management, coordination of technical expertise among government and industry, and communicating progress to the Operational Steering Group.[14]

In mid-January, 1994 PNGV had its next meeting in Washington—a meeting hosted by Vice President Gore. The purpose of the meeting was to bring all participants up to speed on the state of the art in vehicle research. The vice president played an active role as host—leaving no doubt in anyone's mind that the administration was totally behind the initiative.[15]

The next item on the agenda was to identify the technical tasks necessary to meet PNGV's goals. This was done by the industry side of the organization. Industry identified the research priorities. The priorities were worked into PNGV's first program plan, which was delivered to the

Figure 7.3. **Organization of Partnership for a New Generation of Vehicles**

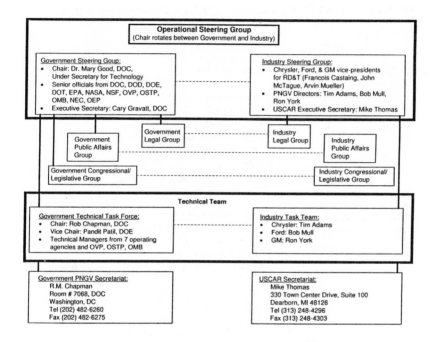

Source: Partnership for a New Generation of Vehicles.

public and industry in July 1944. Technological innovations were needed in advanced lightweight materials and structures, energy-efficient conversion systems (e.g., advanced internal combustion engines and fuel cells), energy storage devices (e.g., advanced batteries, flywheels, and ultracapacitors), more efficient electrical systems, and waste heat recovery.

Over the next six months the Technical Team and Operational Steering Group met regularly, refining the research priorities and identifying the innovations needed to make the new generation of vehicles a reality. This resulted in the publication of *Inventions Needed for PNGV*,[16] a guideline for firms interested in participating in the program. *Inventions Needed* laid out in detail the research areas of interest to PNGV and the agencies and contacts for each of these areas. Table 7.1 gives a brief listing of some of the technological areas and candidate technologies involved in the program.

Table 7.1

Innovations Needed for Partnership for a New Generation of Vehicles

Technology areas	Candidate technologies
Advanced lightweight materials and structures	• Design optimization • High strength steel • Polymer matrix composites • Metal matrix composites • Ceramics • Engineering plastics • Aluminum, titanium, magnesium • Joining technologies and adhesives • Recycling • Process/cycle time advancements in manufacturing
Advanced manufacturing	• Agile manufacturing (programmable machines and tools; near net-shape casting) • High-speed data communication and data management • Rapid prototyping and virtual manufacturing; high-performance computing; complex visualization techniques • Supercomputing • Advanced forming technologies • Advanced joining technologies
Energy conversion	• Four-stroke, direct-injection engines • Turbines • Fuel cells
Energy storage devices	• Advanced high-power batteries • Flywheels • Ultracapacitors
Efficient electrical systems	• Advanced electric motors • Power electronics • Efficient electric controllers (for regenerative braking, power management, signal distribution)
Waste heat recovery	• Thermo-electric systems
Advanced analysis and design methods	• Simulations • Fluid dynamics • Structural mechanics • Virtual prototyping • Trade-off studies

Table 7.1 *(continued)*

Reduction of mechanical losses	• Advanced lubricants • Low-friction materials
Aerodynamics/rolling resistance improvements	• Simulation tools • New materials
Improved efficiency of internal combustion engines (combustion management)	• Stratified charge/lean burn engines • Direct injection • Transient fuel control/fuel injection
Emissions control	• Advanced NO_x exhaust catalysts • On-board diagnostics (evaporative systems, catalyst diagnostics, engine misfire) • Advanced particulate traps)
Fuel preparation, delivery, and storage	• Pressure vessels • Hydrogen storage alternatives • Reformers/fuel processors
Interior thermal management	• Low-emissivity windows • Efficient heating, ventilation, and air conditioning (HVAC)

Source: Partnership for a New Generation of Vehicles, Innovations Needed for PNGV (Washington: Government Printing Office, March 1995), pp. 5–6.

Figure 7.4 gives the time line for the PNGV program. In order to meet the goal of producing prototype vehicles by 2004, a number of high-risk research and development programs are ongoing simultaneously. It is hoped that this will enhance the probability of achieving the needed technological breakthroughs. Technology developments will narrow at the end of 1997, when technologies will be selected for refinement and incorporation into concept vehicles. A further narrowing will occur around the year 2000, as manufacturing developments are assessed and selected for use in the design and manufacture of production prototype vehicles. The complexity of the program is obvious.

Government funds are available through existing programs within the eight participating federal agencies. Each program is empowered to award research funds to different types of organizations and for different types of research projects and research topics. In addition, the programs employ different types of funding mechanisms (e.g., grants, contracts).

138

Figure 7.4. **PNGV Master Program Schedule**

ID	Name	1992	1993	1994	1995	1996	1997	1998	1999	2000	2001	2002	2003	2004	2005
1	1 Component Technology Development														
2	1.1 Exploratory Research														
3	1.2 Vehicular Feasibility Assessment														
4	1.3 Maturation														
5	1.4 Refinement														
6	2 Systems Analysis														
7	2.1 Phase I														
8	2.2 Phase II														
9	2.3 Phase III														
10	3 Subsystem Technology Development														
11	3.1 Hybrid Propulsion Systems														
12	3.2 Ll Weight Vehicle Structure														
13	4 Concept Demonstration Vehicle														
14	4.1 Concept Definition														
15	4.2 System Design														
16	4.3 Fabrication														
17	4.4 Assembly														
18	4.5 Vehicle Test & Development														
19	5 Production Prototype														
20	5.1 Requirements Definition														
21	5.2 Preliminary Design														
22	5.3 Detailed Design														
23	5.4 Fabrication														
24	5.5 Assembly														
25	5.6 Validation Testing														

Source: Partnership for a New Generation of Vehicles.

Assessment

How is PNGV doing? It is really too early to tell. There is a peer review committee that will assess progress annually. But the real question is: Can a program that is really only a coordinating mechanism maintain its initial momentum? There is some indication that it cannot. For one thing, the Operational Steering Group no longer meets as frequently as it once did. It initially was meeting monthly. Then it started meeting every other month; then quarterly; now, reportedly, something less than that. Also, the level of participation is no longer what it once was. Originally, the senior officials appointed to the Steering Group attended meetings themselves. Now they often send lower-level participants as stand-ins.

On the one hand, this could mean that PNGV is beginning to lose its effectiveness. But on the other hand it could mean that the program is actually running very smoothly and no longer requires frequent meetings or the participation of the highest level personnel. Only time will tell.

There is one other comment worth making. It appears that the program really got off the ground because the vice president took an active interest in it. His personal attention seems to have given the program the visibility and push it needed to get the bureaucracy moving. It will probably take a continuing high level of interest on the part of the vice president or president to keep the program on track.

High-Temperature Superconductivity

Federal government interest in high-temperature superconductivity stemmed from two acclaimed scientific discoveries in the mid-1980s. In 1986, George Bednorz and K. Alex Mueller, research scientists at IBM Zurich, discovered that a Lanthanum-based material superconducted electricity at 30 Kelvin (K); in February 1987, Paul Chu (at the University of Houston) announced that he had induced superconductivity in an Yttrium-based compound at 93 K.

Superconductivity is the state in which an electric current passes through a material with no resistance, meaning no loss of energy. A simple illustration is to note that when electricity passes through copper wire, the wire gets extremely hot; heat is the physical manifestation of electrical resistance and its associated loss of energy. The "practical" significance of superconductivity principally involves three technological fields—electric power generation, electromagnetics, and microelectronics. The no-resistance property of superconductors means conceivably (a) that electric power can be transmitted with near-perfect efficiency, (b) very high magnetic fields may be generated by much smaller electromagnets, and (c) electronic signaling and filtering is controllable to virtually the atomic level.

The catch, however, is that the phenomenon of superconductivity normally occurs only at extremely cold temperatures. "Low-temperature" superconductors have been around since the early twentieth century, and are typically metallic wires made of Niobium and related alloys that operate between 4 and 10 K, or about –447 Fahrenheit. Keeping low-temperature superconductors cool to such a degree requires the use of liquid helium, which is costly and awkward to work with. Consequently, commercial low-temperature superconductors emerged in a very limited way: first as electromagnets for nuclear accelerators, and later as the highly sensitive electromagnetic sensors that are used in biomedical MRI machines. Low-temperature superconducting devices are also used in several transportation system prototypes, including electromagnetic ship propulsion and maglev trains.

This is essentially why the high-temperature discoveries were so significant. Not only did they bust a temperature barrier that scientists considered physically impossible, but in the case of Chu's discovery, demonstrated that superconductivity was viable in the "high-temperature" range. What makes high-temperature superconductors substantially different from low-temperature ones is that they operate above the critical cooling threshold of 77 K (or –320 F), the boiling point of liquefied nitrogen. High-temperature superconductors can be cooled with liquid nitrogen, eliminating the fundamental economic constraint that cooling with liquid helium imposes.[17]

The HTS discoveries thus moved superconductivity out of the realm of science fiction into the real world of possibility. All of the imagined applications of superconductivity that seemed somewhat fantastic—infinite energy storage; frictionless bearings; magnetically levitated objects and people; and ultra-refined sensors, signalers, filters, and processing devices—suddenly appeared within human grasp. Significant improvements in energy conservation and efficiency, noninvasive medical diagnostics, and precision cellular telecommunications are but a few of the considerable social and economic contributions that high-temperature superconductors can make. Unlike some new technoscience discoveries, the utility of high-temperature superconductors was immediately apparent.

The United States Reacts

The worldwide reaction was swift and decisive. In the United States R&D spending by government and industry on HTS increased dramatically and within just a few months of Chu's February 1987 announcement.[18] The U.S. government in particular behaved in an entirely uncharacteristic way, which was to identify HTS as a critical technology field deserving of intense strategic attention. The rhetoric was not only followed by money but also by the development of (a) quasi-strategic planning committees, and (b) a number of new R&D programs in the national labs.

In relatively short order—and by reprogramming funds in the middle of the 1987 fiscal year—the government went from negligible R&D spending on HTS to $45 million in FY 1987. This budget doubled to roughly $93 million in FY 1988, and increased by nearly another 40 percent to $128.8 million in FY 1989. By 1994 funding was up to almost $150 million. Although heavily concentrated in the Department of Defense and the Department of Energy (DoE), which together account for about three-quarters of all HTS R&D funds, HTS research is also supported by NASA, the National Science Foundation, the Department of Commerce (through the National Institute for Standards and Technology), and the Department of Transportation.

These monies were not spent willy-nilly. Coordinating and strategic mechanisms were put in place to facilitate superconductivity R&D planning. A presidential commission was appointed in February 1988 (the Committee to Advise the President on Superconductivity); it recommended at the end of that year that funding for superconductivity be increased and that R&D consortia (composed of industry, government, and academia) be formed. The National Superconductivity and Competitiveness Act of 1988 (PL 100-697) was passed late in the 100th Congress and mandated the White House Office of Science and Technology Policy (OSTP) and the National Critical Materials Council to develop a five-year national action plan for superconductivity. The Omnibus Trade and Competitiveness Act of the same year temporarily formed the National Commission on Superconductivity for the purpose of providing an assessment of U.S. capabilities in superconductivity. By 1988, and on paper at least, the following institutional mechanisms were assigned responsibility for superconductivity planning and coordination:

- Committee to Advise the President on Superconductivity (now disbanded);
- National Commission on Superconductivity (now disbanded);
- National Action Plan for Superconductivity (delivered in December 1989);
- National Critical Materials Council;
- Committee on Materials (COMAT, under the aegis of OSTP);
- Defense Superconductivity R&D Working Group (the internal DoD coordinator);
- Energy and Materials Coordinating Committee (the internal DoE coordinator);
- Superconductivity Working Group (NASA's in-house coordination committee)

At the agency programmatic level, response was equally quick. DoD created major HTS programs in DARPA and the Strategic Defense Initiative Organization, while DoE formed three Superconductivity Research Centers in 1987 (at Argonne, Lawrence Berkeley, and Ames national laboratories) and three Superconductivity Pilot Centers in 1988 (at Argonne, Los Alamos, and Oak Ridge national labs). The National Institute of Science and Technology (NIST) also instituted a superconductivity research center, and NASA subsequently organized a consortium based out of the Jet Propulsion Laboratory.

Within two to three years of the HTS discoveries, there was an almost astonishing government momentum with respect to funding, organizing, and coordinating federal R&D for superconductivity. To a very large extent, the response was genuine. R&D expenditures increased significantly, many recommendations were adopted (such as the creation of consortia and dedicated research facilities), and a modest strategic capability was put in place, particularly within the agency and departmental R&D establishment.

Assessment

The key question is whether these efforts have moved the United States toward the competitiveness and commercialization goals underlying the government's actions. In this respect, performance is somewhat troubling, in spite of otherwise good appearances. First, the five-year National Action Plan delivered to Congress was not really an action plan. It contained no budget analysis, no long-term targets (technological or commercial), and merely tipped its hat to the need to coordinate the federal R&D programs. There is thus still no central national coordinating mechanism for this technology, although COMAT has provided a valuable role as facilitator of HTS status meeting. Second, HTS R&D is heavily concentrated in the national laboratories, and successful commercialization will rely on their ability to implement effective technology transfer mechanisms, something that the labs continue to struggle with.

Third, it appears that the research agenda for HTS may still be heavily preoccupied with classification and pushing the temperature envelope of the materials, neglecting the need to generate commercially viable HTS prototypes. Fourth, key partnerships with industry and potential HTS "consumers" are limited. Fifth, there are ongoing concerns about the Japanese and their outspending of the United States in superconductivity R&D.[19] Finally, government HTS R&D funds have not only been relatively stable since FY 1990, but they dropped by about one-third in FY 1995 when DARPA, one of the few government agencies that directly funds industry, ceased its HTS program.

These weaknesses and their impact on competitiveness and commercialization become more apparent when we focus on one area of HTS applications—electric power generation and transmission. What the story of this application reveals is that the United States has reached the limits of what technology policy can accomplish. Missing is a complementary set of industrial policies that can effectively pull HTS out of the R&D system and into the commercial marketplace.

Electric Power Commercialization Efforts

HTS promises to overcome many well-known and long-identified problems in energy transmission and storage. There are three particular problems with electric power generation and use. First, the generation and distribution of electricity are inefficient: energy is lost through transmission lines due to resistance, and there is an imbalance in the amount of electricity generated by a utility relative to what is consumed. This latter problem is commonly known by the peak/off-peak load cycle, in which electricity demand is high during the day but low at night. Utilities must be able to provide boosts of energy during peak work hours, and store the excess electricity that is generated after dark.

Second, motors (especially the large industrial variety) consume most of the electricity in advanced industrialized countries—about 65 percent in the United States.[20] They too are inefficient due to resistance, and their life cycle is not extensive. Third and finally, many industries experience significant, costly disruptions in their manufacturing processes due to current surges and losses in the electric power supply.

HTS can potentially create extraordinary cumulative energy savings within the electric power and use infrastructure by conserving, storing, leveling, and regulating power. HTS transmission lines may operate at about 90 percent or higher efficiency, superconducting magnetic energy storage systems (SMES) can store excess electricity and boost it (again with roughly 90 percent efficiency), HTS motors can produce more horsepower with less energy and longer life cycles, and fault current limiters can better regulate the flow of electric current. The net result is lower fuel consumption, reduced emissions, energy savings, and less vulnerable manufacturing processes. In a fully deployed HTS power system, not only could cost savings amount to billions of dollars per year nationwide, but HTS power equipment could be a significant new growth industry. One estimate places the global market for such equipment at $31 billion by the year 2020.[21]

HTS is an undeveloped technology that could be intensively and systematically pursued to meet the future energy needs of the country. Indeed, this potential is regularly highlighted in government and industry policy and planning documents. But because HTS is not by any means a proven technology, significant R&D efforts and technical advances are required to get HTS to the prototype stage. Moreover, the critical enabling cooling technology—cryogenics—also needs to be substantially advanced.

To some extent, the U.S. government is acting on these R&D and technical needs with at least three programs. The largest effort is based out of the DoE's Office of Utility Technologies, and is reflected in its planning document, *Superconductivity Program for Electric Power Systems*, FY 1994–1998 *Multiyear Plan*. The Office of Utilities has consistently been funding HTS electric power R&D at about $20 million per year.[22] However, virtually all of these funds go to the associated DoE national laboratories. The banner program of the Office of Utilities is the Superconductivity Partnership Initiative, which funds four separate research consortia (industry–government partnerships) to move HTS toward electric power commercialization. The average cost over the life of each of the consortia's projects is about $4.5 million. The partnerships are focused on the development of discrete power system components, namely an HTS (1) fault current limiter, (2) generator, (3) motor, and (4) direct current transmission wire.

A second effort is the building of a prototype low-temperature superconducting SMES, an energy storage system that allows electricity load leveling during the peak/off-peak cycle. The system was slated for demonstration in 1995, at a total cost of about $30 million. Support comes from several DoE sources, including the Bonneville Power Administration and the DoD's Ballistic Missile Defense Organization. Finally, although the amount of support is relatively small, NIST has been funding some HTS companies through its Advanced Technology Program (ATP), and several HTS companies also participate in cooperative R&D projects (CRADAs) with the national lab superconductivity centers. What makes CRADAs and the ATP efforts unique is that companies themselves define the needs and nature of research to be performed.

But what the United States is missing is the policy component and perspective that focus explicitly on commercializing the technology once it is developed. There is very nominal government support for the development of prototype power generation systems. In FY 1995 the United States was spending about $5 million per year on four small industrial consortia composed of a few firms and utility companies. Two core companies—American Superconductor Corp. and Intermagnetics General—are both highly innovative HTS wire and related systems firms, yet they are disadvantaged in market power relative to Japanese *keiretsu*[23] and by their isolation from a broader network of HTS product adopters and users.

Relatedly, the end products of these consortia are pre-prototype devices, not the development of a power system. In the absence of a full-scale government commitment to a demonstration project, the United States can be expected to only incrementally produce superconducting HTS devices that will not accumulate into a power system. There will additionally be no collective experience and know-how among the potential user community, and the barriers to market adoption and diffusion will still not have been eliminated.

Conclusion

In terms of government policy, there is a technical difference between America's attempt to produce a new fuel-efficient automobile and high-temperature superconductivity. The auto effort is clearly an industrial policy, but superconductivity is still a technology policy. Technology policies are not industrial policies. The differences are both nuanced and explicit. Specifically, technology policies are designed to develop technologies, or at least remove the obstacles and uncertainty related to creating technologies. Technology policy is predicated on the assumption that markets will fail to adequately invest in new technologies that are characterized by high technical risk, cost, and uncertainty, or when the technology has a strong public goods (defense, space, energy) component to it.[24] Government support of technology is therefore strongly warranted when the potential social good content of a new technology is transparent, but the market cannot properly respond given its inherent conservatism and/or inability to sustain long-term financial investments without reward.

Industrial policies are designed to increase the competitiveness and efficiency of specific industries and sectors.[25] Industrial policy is predicated in part on the assumption that markets will fail to adequately adopt new technologies once they are developed because of uncertainty about how to use the technology and the amount of profit that it will generate relative to other technological alternatives. The latter problem of uncertainty about rewards (or "rents") is exacerbated by public goods technologies, which have a high degree of inappropriability. Moreover, industrial sectors that are highly oligopolistic (e.g., the U.S. auto industry) or monopolistic (e.g., electric power) are especially innovation adverse, because they can readily pass costs on to consumers. Government industrial policies are therefore strongly warranted when it is the only institution capable of inducing the commercial adoption of new technologies under imperfect market conditions.

Both industrial and technology policies are clearly based on market failure principles. The nuance that distinguishes them is that industrial policy recognizes that market failure can occur in both the production of the technology and in its commercial adoption. U.S. economic philosophy has generally regarded failures to commercialize otherwise attractive technologies as rational market outcomes: economic actors decided that relative to other considerations, the new technology was not a sufficiently profitable or certain innovation. This is why technology-push strategies are considered to be sufficient efforts for competitiveness: a compelling new technology will inevitably be commercialized, and if it is not, it is because the market was acting for good reasons.

The Japanese—and other governments—have alternatively viewed such market decisions as market failures. They constitute sticky points that may be rational in a static sense, but are nonetheless obstacles to long-term dynamic efficiency.[26] Industrial policy may then step in to pull the technology out of the R&D system and into the marketplace; this is a particularly common Japanese practice with respect to high and emerging technologies. Industrial policy is designed to alter the uncertainty that potential adopters confront about a new technology relative to best practice and other alternatives; it is also designed to reconfigure issues of cost and/or appropriability to make adopting the technology less of a financial hardship.

Nonetheless, the subtle distinction between technology policy and industrial policy is not the main concern here. It is the organization and administration of industrial policies for new technologies.

When a new and potentially important industrial discovery emerges, the various federal agencies having overlapping interest in the discovery immediately rush in to establish their presence and stake out territorial claims. The result is a host of overlapping projects and a dramatic increase in funding. This is exactly what happened in the case of high-temperature superconductivity.

In this respect, the weakness with U.S. superconductivity policies—their lack of a central coordinating mechanism—shows its impact. With no one overseeing the full scope of applications for HTS, research activities will reflect the mission interests of each cabinet agency. This, in turn, spills over to the second and third weaknesses: HTS R&D spending will thus represent the differential bureaucratic power of the agencies to get funds, and not necessarily a more "objective" set of national priorities for HTS research. Because HTS R&D is also conducted primarily in the national labs, commercialization becomes vulnerable to lab skills in technology transfer and cooperative R&D.

Government–industry partnerships try to overcome these institutional weaknesses, and the Superconductivity Partnership Initiative (SPI) within the DoE mimics the PNGV initiative for autos in two crucial ways. First, it is a vertically integrated consortium of industry and government labs, with clear technological goals and milestones related to commercializing HTS in the electric power sector. Second, the industrial partners are also corporations with market clout—General Electric, General Dynamics, and Southern California Edison, to name a few.

The superconductivity partnership is, however, distinctively *different* than the PNGV in three crucial ways. First, there are no economic constraints on the development of the HTS technology. In the case of autos, the new car must sell within the same price range as current vehicles, allowing for inflation and changing cost structure in the industry. In electric power HTS, this is not the case. Second, the SPI is a DoE-initiated program, whereas the PNGV is managed with the explicit support of the Vice President and President. Third, commercialization of new HTS electric power technologies will have to occur in a monopolistic industry on the verge of major and rapid deregulation. For autos, the new vehicle will diffuse in a mature industry with a clear understanding of market psychology.

What are the implications of these differences? Taken altogether, they suggest that one partnership is primed for commercial success. The other, however, may be doomed to failure because of inadequate funding, lack of executive support, an inability to be price competitive against next-best technological alternatives, and grossly uncertain market conditions.

Does the government intend such an outcome? Undoubtedly not. In both the auto and HTS partnerships, the government has clearly attempted to set up an effective coordinating structure and to try to institutionalize momentum by integrating industry into the planning and implementation process for the technology strategy. However, the challenge is in maintaining momentum for both programs and in developing adequate industrial diffusion and commercialization policies for the new HTS technologies (it is quite unlikely the market will uptake them on its own within the next decade). The need to maintain momentum highlights the fundamental structural tension in U.S. industry policies: bureaucratic diffusion, the need for executive branch support, and the long-term payoffs of policies may all be working against one another.

An industrial program is fairly easy to manage (and maintain interest in) if it is totally under the control of one agency. But in this day and age such a luxury is not possible, and widespread support may even be vital to the success of major industrial programs. Everyone wants a piece of the action, and it is much easier to provide diffused resources, such as with the PNGV, than to try to centralize the activity in one agency. And, while centralization in one agency may be administratively attractive (such as with the Superconductivity Partnership Initiative), R&D funds are intensely vulnerable to intra-agency program competition. As the HTS partnership also illustrates, technology push industrial policies do not always address the market weaknesses that may prevent the technology from being readily commercialized.

These weaknesses pave the road for executive leadership. Yet executive attention is notoriously strained by the long-term payoffs of industrial policies themselves. Policies for new-generation autos will not come during the Clinton/Gore administration, even in the second term. For Clinton and Gore there is no political payoff (although in the long run there may be for Gore). And when a program has no political payoff, it is difficult to keep it on the front burner—no matter how important it may be for the nation's long-term interests.

Bureaucratic rescue is likewise constrained. Long-term payoffs are well beyond the horizon of political appointees in the upper echelons of bureaucracy. Turnover here is horrendous, with typical longevity being about three years. It is thus career bureaucrats who must rise to the occasion; with their institutional memories, they must constantly prod their political leaders to maintain a continuing long-term interest in high-technology industries.

Given these structural constraints of government, industrial policies for new technologies are stuck between a rock and a hard place. Their success depends upon either ongoing high-level attention to policy-making, the institutionalization of a new form of intra-organizational policy network (the public-private strategic technology partnerships), or the ability of career bureaucrats to stimulate and maintain focus on industrial issues. In all instances, momentum will be hard to maintain.

8

Why All the Fuss?

George Bush announced to the world that he did not have an industrial policy. Presumably Jimmy Carter and Ronald Reagan would have said the same thing of themselves. Even Bill Clinton, who is consistently more active in promoting specific industries than any of his three predecessors, would presumably also deny that he has an industrial policy. And all four would be correct to some degree. As presidents, they never articulated a coherent and comprehensive industrial policy.

And yet, while these presidents may not have had an industrial policy, the country they have governed certainly does. And it is actually fairly coherent and reasonable.

But the presidents would not be alone in thinking that the United States lacked an industrial policy. Much of the policy community has been vocal in its criticism of any government efforts at industrial development.[1] Mainstream economists are critical because these proposals usually violate some of their theories. Conservatives are critical because they see industrial policy as nothing more than meddling with the free enterprise system—the only "perfect" system known to humankind. Liberals are not much happier. They see industrial policy efforts as disconnected and uncoordinated, sometimes working at cross purposes.

But industrial policy in the United States is actually fairly consistent—it is a fairly coherent policy with a number of identifiable dimensions. And the United States has had plenty of experience honing this policy. Chapter 2 documented America's long history of industrial policy by looking at how the nation supported the growth, development, and sustenance of the aircraft, airline, railroad, motor carrier, shipping, agriculture, oil, and banking industries. Other examples certainly abound, but one fact is excruciatingly clear. America's industrial policy efforts go back a very long time. However, while history is both important and interesting, contemporary industrial policy is the focus here.

The previous chapters have shown that there are regularities in the ways in which the United States government supports specific industries. These regularities are a useful way to view America's industrial policy. Empirical investigation of the nation's industry policies suggests that they fall into five categories, or variations, which, taken as a whole, constituted America's national industrial policy from 1976 through 1996. They are: (1) Too Big to Fail, (2) Hardball in the Trade Arena, (3) Supporting Urban Real Estate, (4) The DARPA Component, and (5) Technology Commercialization.

Too Big to Fail

In the early 1970s, Kenan Jarboe took an initial stab at describing the literature surrounding the industrial policy debate and coined the term *functional problem solving*. With functional problem solving, a problem facing a specific firm or industry is identified and government actions are taken to alleviate it.[2] Many of the policy initiatives Jarboe describes are in response to the economic and political pressures caused by those that are Too Big to Fail. Too Big to Fail is a policy in response to firms or industries whose dominant position is so large that their failure would create havoc in the industry or in the country, as the case may be. This was the case with the failure of the Continental Illinois bank. It was such an important part of the banking industry, particularly in the Midwest, that failure was never a possibility. The Federal Reserve and the FDIC were never going to let Continental go out of business. So, with Too Big to Fail, any major player in an important industry will not be allowed to fail.

Too Big to Fail also concerns matters of public convenience. Penn Central was Too Big to Fail and Amtrak was created because of the millions of railroad passengers on the East Coast. Events like the failure of Penn Central would have created not only economic havoc but political havoc as well. Congress would have none of that.

Similarly, Chrysler was Too Big to Fail for political reasons. Economically, there probably would have been little fallout if Chrysler had failed in the early 1980s. Another car company might have bought Chrysler out, or its assets might have been sold to a number of auto manufacturers. In any event, Ford, GM, and the Japanese would have quickly stepped in to fill the void.

But politically Chrysler could not have been allowed to fail. Chrysler parts suppliers, banks, and dealerships were spread throughout the country—virtually in every House and Senate district in America. If Chrysler failed, businesses in all of these districts would be hurt and some of them might also fail. The pressure on Congress was thus simply too great to allow failure to occur.

Finally, Too Big to Fail is also a policy response to failing industries whose position in American life is so important that failure is unthinkable. This is exactly what happened with the savings and loans. Their failure would have put much of the nation's economic system at risk. The government had no choice but to effect a bailout.

Hardball in the Trade Arena

The second major dimension of American industrial policy occurs in the area of international trade. Playing Hardball in the Trade Arena refers to the U.S. policy developed over the past three administrations of negotiating market-opening agreements with foreign nations designed to open foreign markets to specific industrial goods or services. This, of course, antagonizes economists to no end but pleases the CEOs of the companies in the affected industries. Economists see this as a violation of trade theory and the doctrine of comparative advantage. (More will be said about this later.) The CEOs view such market openings as an attempt to "level the playing field" and as part of the new competitiveness movement sweeping the business schools of the nation. (Again, more of this will come.)

There have been some giant market-opening efforts over the past two decades, all made in the name of fairness and competitiveness. Prince among these were the three semiconductor negotiations of the early 1980s. A side letter to the September 1986 agreement (third agreement) promised the U.S. companies a 20 percent share of the Japanese market by 1991—clearly managed trade.[3]

But if the semiconductor industry is the prince, the automobile industry is the king. The U.S.–Japan Auto Accord of 1995 is one of the biggest market-opening moves ever negotiated. If all of the cards fall into place by 1998, the U.S. should be exporting an additional $200 million plus in autos and auto parts to Japan. Increased Japanese transplant production of motor vehicles and parts can also be expected to reduce imports by over $200 million (that is, if it all works).

Hardball makes an important and controversial assumption—that foreign trade is a zero-sum game. It assumes that nations are like corporations competing for the same dollars. Every additional car that the American auto industry sells in Japan means one less car that the Japanese buy from their own companies. But is this hardball assumption valid? The issue will be examined shortly.

Supporting Urban Real Estate

The board game "Monopoly" has been endearing to Americans young and old for generations. Monopoly gave Americans the chance to pretend to be big-time real estate speculators, even if for only a few hours. Supporting Urban Real Estate, however, gave some Americans the actual opportunity to be big-time real estate speculators—and to make a lot of money while they were at it.

It was easy enough for the political system to single out real estate and its related industries for favored treatment. Real estate employs about 7.6 million people if one includes all of the related activities like finance, construction, building supplies, brick, lumber, and the like. This is about 8 percent of the American work force. And as with the Chrysler network, these workers are well represented in all congressional districts. So the politics was right.

The real estate industry is also an important economic indicator. Congress thus saw Supporting Urban Real Estate as a sure-fire way to get, or keep, the economy moving.

The real estate initiatives under Presidents Carter and Reagan all worked out just the way they were supposed to. The UDAG program and the Economic Recovery Tax Act of 1981 led to massive commercial and multifamily real estate development. The trouble is that it all worked too well. Construction and real estate boomed. Unfortunately the excesses were so gross that they created an embarrassment to both the Congress and the Reagan administration. So the Tax Reform Act of 1986 (TRA) was finally required to rein in the real estate speculative boom created by this leg in the industrial policy stool.

The DARPA Component

There has always been a defense role of some kind in industrial policy. Historically, the obvious example has been the contribution of military aircraft development to the civilian aircraft industry. But in recent years the relationship between the military and the development of selected civilian industries has been close and direct. This is because of the increasing influence and importance of the Defense Advanced Research Projects Agency (DARPA). It is also because the DoD has moved closer to the manufacturing end of the spectrum.

DARPA influences industrial development as it shapes military innovation—and this has been particularly true in the electronics area. DARPA has been called America's MITI.[4] And while this is something of an exaggeration, the point is well made. DARPA's recent emphasis on "dual use" innovations gives the agency its industrial policy focus. (Recall that dual use innovations are those having both defense and civilian applications.)

The DARPA Component was the mechanism by which the government supported Sematech. And while Sematech has its detractors, virtually all who have evaluated it give it high praise. What Sematech has done is to move government closer to the manufacturing process. Sematech's concentration on improving the products of the semiconductor equipment manufacturers has helped incorporate new and/or improved equipment into the manufacturing process. This has made both U.S.-produced semiconductors and SME internationally competitive.

DARPA's efforts to develop a flat panel display commercial production capability also illustrates the government's attempt to develop a manufacturing capability in an area where none had existed. DARPA's High-Definition Systems (HDS) program was designed specifically to develop the domestic capability to manufacture flat panel displays. DARPA has made several large awards with the objective of adding manufacturing testbeds to ongoing research programs.

Technology Commercialization

Sematech seems to be serving as a model for the commercialization of new technologies in that the new non-DoD efforts are all partnerships between government and industry, with industry setting the agenda. These efforts all strive for international leadership for U.S. industries and rapid commercialization of technologies. They are all driven by market failures of one kind or another.

Most Americans would agree that developing a reasonably priced, fuel-efficient automobile should be one of the country's top priorities. Yet before PNGV it simply was not being done, and with very good reason. Common sense may be calling for a fuel-efficient car but the market is not. Gasoline prices remain reasonable, and there is no gasoline shortage in sight. Consumers are not crying for highly fuel-efficient automobiles. In short, the market does not demand such a new vehicle. Furthermore, a tripling of fuel efficiency is no small undertaking. Radical changes in automotive design will be required. None of this will be cheap. All of it is well beyond the scope of reasonableness for auto industry decision makers.

Yet from an environmental standpoint such a vehicle is more than reasonable. And from a competitiveness standpoint it might be nice to see thousands of Fords, Chevrolets, and Chryslers being driven around downtown Tokyo. But the fact is that no reasonably priced 3X (3 times the current gas mileage) car was on the horizon without government intervention.

The situation with high-temperature superconductivity (HTS) is similar. There are potentially huge savings possible through HTS in power generation and transmission. But power companies are typically local monopolies under state control. They generally operate on a cost plus system with rates approved by the states. The market does not demand that they be innovative. And it is a rare instance that power companies want to save electricity (although it occasionally does happen). They want to sell it.

Thus, there is no market demand for HTS in power generation and transmission. It may be good government policy to reduce utility consumption but it is not particularly good business policy from the power companies' perspective. If the industry is ever going to have HTS power systems, it is going to require government action.

Whither Industrial Policy?

So national industrial policy is a reality. It is the sum of our industry policies, and these industry policies from 1976 through 1996 had a regularity to them. But what does the future hold? Is industrial policy on its way out, or is it evolving, or is it a little bit of both? Chapter 2 traced the history of some industries in the United States that have had long-standing industry policies. The specific industries discussed were the railroads, trucking, the maritime industry, air carriers, agriculture, oil, and banking.

There is one thing common to most of these industries other than their long history of industrial policy and that is their recent histories of deregulation and withdrawal of government support. Today there is far less government intervention in these industries than there was one or two decades ago. But does this signal the demise of industrial policy in general, or merely a shift in it? After all, these are all mature industries. Perhaps when industries mature they no longer need an industrial policy. Perhaps industrial policies best serve emerging industries. And what about the dimensions of industrial policy that this book has identified? Are they all active today?

Too Big to Fail

At the moment, Too Big to Fail is inactive. The federal government is not now bailing out any industry or large company. Yet it is impossible to say that Too Big to Fail is gone for good. It is impossible to believe that the U.S. government would let General Motors, or Boeing, or Lockheed Martin go under just as it is impossible to believe that the government would let the semiconductor or commercial banking industries go under. No, the sleeping bear, Too Big to Fail, is simply hibernating.

Hardball in the Trade Arena

It is clear that our use of trade remedies is down. It is also obvious with the recent conclusion of the Uruguay Round of the GATT and the implementation of NAFTA (and the discussion concerning expanding NAFTA to South America) that trade is becoming much freer. On the other hand, aggressive unilateralism seems to be getting more aggressive. Nontariff trade barriers are as strong as ever with respect to Japan, and are very common in the economies of the newly emerging economic powers like China, Korea, and Thailand. These are among the nations we are counting on to help us increase exports. And it is going to take enormous pressure to open up these markets. The U.S.-Japan auto accord was just the tip of the iceberg. Hardball in the trade arena is a dimension of industrial policy that is going to be around for a long time.

Supporting Urban Real Estate

The passage of the Tax Reform Act of 1986 unquestionably reduced the favored position of real estate in the investment world and corrected a gross industrial policy mistake. It reduced the industry's favored position but it did not eliminate it. After all, home mortgages, mortgages on second homes (or boats), and home equity loans are still deductible on federal income taxes. But it is absolutely clear that the industry policy for the promotion of real estate investment is not what it was fifteen years ago.

The DARPA Component

In these post–cold war days, with the size of the military being reduced, is DARPA's industrial policy role likely to be changed or reduced? It could well change if two of the authors cited in Chapter 6 are correct. Glen Pascall and Robert Lamson held that there is a much lower rate of civilian spillover than in the past, that the divergence between military design requirements and civilian product characteristics is widening, and that military technology is moving into more exotic and arcane areas.[5] If this is true, it might suggest a lessening of DARPA's role as America's answer to MITI.

Also recall that in 1996 DARPA changed its name back from ARPA—adding back an emphasis on defense. Is this because it now sees its mission as being more "defense only" and less "dual use?" Or did it change its name at the whim of a new director, or to please a conservative Republican Congress?

On the other hand, "dual use" is a clever concept. It suggests all kinds of efficiencies and is a very popular idea. Even if the differences between civilian and military technologies are widening, there are certainly enough dual-use applications around to keep DARPA busy for many years to come.

Technology Commercialization

Of the dimensions of industrial policy, this is the one that seems likely to be most emphasized in the future. At all levels of government, public-private partnerships are "in." The apparent success of Sematech provided the model for PNGV. The National Flat Panel Display Initiative will also be a public-private partnership. Recall that the first three "overriding principles" in the Flamm report are:

1. The initiative must be of sufficient scope and duration to attract significant industry participation.
2. Industry must be willing to share in the costs of the initiative. The extent of industry willingness to undertake such costs is one of the most important measures of the initiative's value.
3. The initiative should be based on principles of competition among firms and technologies. Central to this principle is the notion that the initiative will go forward only if industry responds with acceptable proposals and plays a lead role in determining the technologies to pursue.[6]

So, Whither Industrial Policy?

There is no question but that the use and intrusiveness of specific industry policies is down from what it was twenty years ago. This is due to the maturation of the industries involved, changes in multilateral trade rules, deregulation, and the end to many subsidies, like agriculture. Though industrial policy is hardly dead, it is more focused. Modern-day industrial policy concentrates on specific problems—Too Big to Fail and Hardball in the Trade Arena—and on high technology—The DARPA Connection and Technology Commercialization.

The need to concentrate on specific problems is obvious. If something is seriously wrong with a specific industry or very large firm, or another nation is not treating a specific industry or firm fairly (in our judgment), something must be done to correct the problem.

High technology is something else altogether. Industry policies supporting high technology are derived from the benefits these industries provide to American society. Laura Tyson, President Clinton's former chair of the Council of Economic Advisers, believes that success in high-technology industries bestows national benefits in productivity, technology development, and job creation, and that the United States must devise industry policies that promote our high-technology industries.[7] The DARPA Connection and Technology Commercialization are designed to do this.

So industrial policy has changed in focus over the past several decades. There is an increased emphasis on functional problem solving and aggressive unilateralism. There has also been a significant shift in industrial policy away from supporting basic industries and into the support of high technology. Also, today's generation of industrial policies are of shorter duration. In the past, industry policies were forever, until changed by Congress. Today, on the other hand, federal support for Sematech has already ended and PNGV is destined to terminate in 2004.

Can anyone argue that today's policy is better? It may be. It is certainly more limited and more focused.

The Steady Hand of Industrial Policy

Another of the more interesting parts of this investigation was the finding that industrial policy sailed along on the sea of politics no matter who was captain of the ship. Over the past two decades it made no difference who was in the White House, Republican or Democrat— industrial policy changed little. Republicans have been as likely as Democrats to develop industry policies. Jimmy Carter, Ronald Reagan, and George Bush all played Too Big to Fail. Hardball was a favorite tool of the Bush administration and has been adhered to faithfully by President Clinton. Supporting Urban Real Estate was popular with Jimmy Carter but experienced its heyday under Ronald Reagan. The DARPA Component was important to both Reagan and George Bush. Only Technology Commercialization is the primary tool of one party and one president, Bill Clinton—and that is only because it is the newest of the industrial policy dimensions.

But at the same time that the presidents were being industrial policy activists, they were talking a different game—with George Bush being industrial policy's most vocal critic. However, it is their behavior that counts. And all four presidents—Carter, Reagan, Bush, and Clinton— have shown themselves to be industrial policy moderates, no matter what their pronouncements.

But if industrial policy is in such a steady state politically, why is it that it engenders such debate? Why is it that the words "industrial policy" had to be abandoned in the 1980s in favor of "competitiveness" or "strategic trade?" Economists may be the problem.

Enter the Economists

It is the economists who really created problems for the industrial policy advocates. In the United States, the consumer is king, and that elevates the importance of economists in our society. Economists take the position that the overriding purpose of economic activity is to improve the welfare of consumers—a refrain the public likes to hear. Thus economists see foreign government subsidy to industries as benefiting American society to the extent that these goods are imported into the United States and provide consumers with lower prices.

The same argument can be made with regard to dumping. Dumping means that the American consumers are getting a bargain. Their consumption is being subsidized by Japanese businesses (for example) and the Japanese consumer (through higher prices at home). Dumping makes economists happy and, although they might feel some sympathy toward the industries in the United States that are the "dumpees," their underlying commitment to free trade overrides their concerns for the economic futures of a few companies.

The free trade rubric calls for multilateral agreements to break down all economic barriers between states and to promote free and open trade throughout the world. A laudable goal, but an unrealistic one. Nations are simply not willing to stand idly by while their industries are destroyed by a global marketplace in which firms (particularly multinationals) are on a constant march to find that one spot in the world where production costs are lowest.

There will always be protection and there will always be subsidies—even in the United States. For example, for more than fifty years this country has been protecting its sugar industry. The 1981 Farm Act required the United States to prop up the price of sugar through quotas. Because the country produces less sugar than it consumes, the price can be set almost at will by restricting imports. For example, in the late 1980s, the U.S. government maintained quotas on sugar imports to support the domestic sugar price that sugar farmers receive, which was about 22 cents per pound, in contrast with the sugar trade price of 11 cents per pound prevailing in the world market. The big beneficiaries of such government protection are obviously the sugar cane and sugar beet farmers.[8]

But if, like us, foreign nations erect barriers to protect their favored industries, or if they allow their industries to dump products on foreign soil while keeping prices high at home, or if these governments provide direct subsidies to these industries so that the prices of their products on foreign markets will be lower, what should we do?

Our free traders would say, "Nothing." Let the free market prevail.

Let the American consumer benefit. If foreign governments and companies want to improve the lives of American consumers, so be it. It matters little that some American companies are forced out of business and workers lose their jobs. The businesses can move into another industry and workers can be retrained for the jobs of the future.

This writer happened to be in Tokyo on the day after the United States reached the accord with Japan on opening up Japan to U.S. cars and auto parts. CNN International aired an interview with economist Richard Beason of the University of Alberta, then a visiting scholar at the Bank of Japan's Institute for Monetary and Economic Studies. The outcome was so predictable. Beason said that the agreement was a waste of effort—that market forces, with the strong yen and weak dollar, were opening the Japanese economy to U.S. autos and auto parts anyway. But someone needs to remind Mr. Beason that this dispute has been around for twenty years. Jimmy Carter, Ronald Reagan, and George Bush were all just as concerned as Bill Clinton with the trade deficit and with opening up the Japanese auto market. One only has to remember President Bush's pathetic trip to Japan in 1992, attempting to pry the Japanese market open. Accompanied by executives from the Big Three automakers, Bush seemed more car salesman than statesman.[9]

Someone needs to ask the economists: Why is the free market always just about to correct itself? Why has it not done so in the past? Why was the United States not able to sell auto parts to Japan in 1990? Why does the country have to wait until the year 2000 for market forces to work?

Economists United

Some government policy types have a deep-seated aversion to economists. Perhaps it is because they see economists as too dogmatic, or just plain negative. There was a Peanuts cartoon in the newspaper a couple of years ago showing Charlie Brown reclining in his beanbag chair and watching the news on television: "Thousands of people paraded happily through the streets, but economists predict the cleanup will be costly." "Skies were sunny today, but economists warn that this could cause an increase in the price of sunglasses. . . ." "Although audiences across the country love the film, economists are saying it will probably lose money." Charles Schulz has a knack for capturing public perceptions.

Former Reagan trade official Clyde Prestowitz, Jr., vents his frustration with economists in his book *Trading Places* in a section entitled

"Conversations with Economists." Prestowitz starts off his "Conversations" with the following, which clearly tells us what he thinks:

> U.S. economists of all stripes are bound together in opposition to any firm government response to questionable foreign trade practices regardless of the consequences to U.S. industry. Divided on almost everything else, the supply-siders, the Keynesians, the monetarists, and other breeds can all unite on this, opposing any trade actions except negotiations to open foreign markets. That such negotiations are doomed precisely because of the reluctance to consider alternative actions has not been a consideration. This attitude is not only the legacy of the Depression and the peculiar circumstances of the postwar era but also reflects a focus on consumers that ignores strategic economic objectives as well as other participants in the economy.[10]

Recounting his trade experiences, Prestowitz constantly complains that economists were always united against protecting U.S. industries, no matter what industries from other countries were doing in (and to) American markets. He complains that they were ardent champions of consumers but had little sympathy for workers or producers. He claims that economists were unconcerned if companies were forced out of business by dumping or other such practices, reasoning that Americans should be happy their consumer goods were being subsidized by others and that it did not matter if American firms were being driven out of business. If the Japanese quit their dumping and raised their prices, U.S. companies could go back into the business again. These sentiments, he tells us, were common to the members of president's Council of Economic Advisers and the Trade Policy Review Group, an interagency body at the undersecretary level.[11] Reflecting on his five years' experience with the Trade Policy Group, Prestowitz reports: "Never once did I hear an economist or a representative of any economic agency speak in favor of granting relief or of taking action to aid a U.S. industry. They sometimes bowed to political necessity, but never willingly."[12]

The Competitiveness Movement

Prestowitz did not know it at the time, but he was taking a position with regard to economists that would be characteristic of the competitiveness movement. Michael Porter of the Harvard Business School became the leading spokesperson for the movement with his book, *The Competitive Advantage of Nations*.[13] Over the years, Porter developed a strong conviction that the national environment plays a central role in the competitive success of industries. He thus saw a need for a new paradigm beyond that held by all economists—the theory of comparative advantage. For Porter:

> the assumptions underlying factor comparative advantage theories of trade are unrealistic in many industries. The standard theory assumes that there are no economies of scale, that technologies everywhere are identical, that products are undifferentiated, and that the pool of national factors is fixed. The theory also assumes that factors, such as skilled labor and capital, do not move among nations. . . . The assumptions underlying factor comparative advantage were more persuasive in the eighteenth and nineteenth centuries. . . . [14]

Porter then identifies a myriad of ways in which government can play a prominent role in developing a national competitive advantage for its industries.[15] Porter thus struck at the heart of the trade economists.

The Economists' Position

It was not long before replies were forthcoming—for example, from Paul Krugman, proclaimed by *The Economist* as "the most celebrated economist of his generation." Krugman is one of those rare economists who is capable of writing for the general public, which he does. He is also very blunt and straightforward in his criticism. He recently published two books that take on the competitiveness movement (including a derivative, the strategic traders). They are *Peddling Prosperity*,[16] published in 1994, and *Pop Internationalism*,[17] published in 1996. These books are essentially critiques of industrial policy. This discussion focuses on Paul Krugman only because he is a moderate economist who is well respected and widely read in his discipline and beyond. Economists come in all shapes and sizes. There are supply-siders and there are Marxist economists. It is impossible to focus on them all. So Krugman, because he is so mainstream, will have to do.

In *Peddling Prosperity*, Krugman takes on nonacademic economists, business types, and economic journalists for what he generally sees as promoting nonsense. He calls this group "policy entrepreneurs." These policy entrepreneurs include supply-siders like Arthur Laffer, Robert Bartley, Jude Wanniski, Robert Mundell, Paul Craig Roberts, George Gilder, and Irving Kristol. While Krugman spends some time on the supply-side movement and the supply-siders, he ultimately dismisses them. But Krugman's real wrath is reserved for liberal policy entrepreneurs like John Kenneth Galbraith, the Harvard Business School's Bruce Scott and George Lodge (but, curiously, not Michael Porter), Lester Thurow, and Robert Reich—particularly Thurow and Reich. Their sin was worse than the supply-siders' because, in Krugman's view, they knew better.

But what was their sin? Their sin was promoting certain sectors of the economy over others—"sunrise" industries or those termed "high value." Krugman calls these sinners "strategic traders." Strategic traders challenge the economic orthodoxy with the use of the analogy between the economy as a whole and an individual corporation competing in the marketplace. Thus, countries are seen as being in competition with each other in the same way that corporations are. Strategic traders are accused of overemphasizing the importance of trade in the economy and ignoring the theory of comparative advantage, under which nations benefit from trade.[18]

Pop Internationalism deals more directly with competitiveness. Krugman decries what he sees as a dangerous and misguided concern with international competitiveness. He claims that the idea that a nation's economic fortunes are determined by its success in world markets is "flatly wrong."[19] He holds that the world's leading nations are not in competition with each other to any important degree,[20] and points out that the United States is still almost 90 percent an economy that produces goods and services for its own use.[21]

Again, what particularly annoys Krugman are those who compare nations to big corporations competing in the global marketplace. He holds that the analogy between a country and a corporation is seductive but misguided, and that most people who use the term "competitiveness" do so without a second thought. To them the analogy between a country and a corporation is perfectly reasonable.

But why does Krugman find the competitiveness metaphor disturbing and the business analogy misleading? Because it suggests that nations are in an economic struggle against each other when mainstream economists hold that they are not, due to the theory of comparative advantage, which shows that, in theory, nations all benefit from trade due to specialization. Krugman is especially incensed by the subtitle to Lester Thurow's best-selling book *Head to Head: The Coming Economic Battle among Japan, Europe, and America.*

For Krugman, serious problems could develop from the growing emphasis on competitiveness. These problems include a potential misallocation of resources as the United States aids manufacturing industries while it is the service industries that have productivity problems. The most serious problem, however, may be trade conflict or even a trade war promoted by "old-fashioned protectionists" under the guise of competitiveness.[22]

In *Pop Internationalism,* Krugman has specific bones to pick with Thurow and Prestowitz. Both support interventionist trade policies, taking their cues from new (1980s) economic theories of international trade, suggesting "a possible role for strategic policies to promote exports in certain industries."[23]

Krugman, however, asserts that the empirical evidence weighs against interventionist policies. He claims that research overwhelmingly concludes that "to identify which industries should receive strategic promotion or the appropriate form and level of promotion is very difficult. Second, the payoffs of even a successful strategic trade policy are likely to be very modest."[24]

But what if some countries with high productivity across the board were to be compared to low-productivity nations. Why would a country with high productivity trade with one with low productivity? Krugman explains:

> A country that is less productive than its trading partners across the board will be forced to compete on the basis of low wages rather than superior productivity. But it will not suffer catastrophe, and indeed will normally still benefit from international trade. The point is that international trade, unlike competition among businesses for a limited market, is not a zero-sum game in which one nation's gain is another's loss. It is [a] [sic] positive-sum game, which is why the word "competitiveness" can be dangerously misleading when applied to international trade.[25]

So what happens if the United States, say, loses the "battle" with Japan for dominance in high-technology sectors? Will it still be able to compete? Krugman replies affirmatively—the principle of comparative advantage still applies. But the United States will "increasingly be forced to compete on the basis of low wages rather than high productivity."[26]

Krugman also acknowledges that new trade theory (first developed by Canadian economists James Brander and Barbara Spencer)[27] recognizes that government can, in effect, create comparative advantage. This is what happened with military procurement in the 1950s and 1960s, which created the U.S. comparative advantage in aircraft production. However, Krugman believes that most economists working on trade issues "have agreed that strategic trade policy can work in principle but have been highly skeptical about its importance and usefulness in practice."[28]

In spite of some warnings and objections, most mainstream economists do see a role for industrial policy. When you cut through all of the layers, even Paul Krugman (reluctantly) recognizes that in real life, markets are imperfect and industrial policies have their place—albeit limited.

> Now the fact that a policy issue is not of life-and-death importance does not mean it should be ignored. As Everett Dirksen said, a billion here, a billion there, and soon you're talking about real money. So by all means let us support the development of promising technologies and bargain toughly with foreign nations we believe are pursuing their own strategic policies. But let us maintain the right perspective and not imaging ourselves in the midst of some apocalyptic struggle over global supremacy.[29]

Conclusion

As the United States continues to pursue policies in support of specific industries, mistakes will be made. These, of course, will delight those who are quick to point out industrial policy initiatives that are less than successful. Conservative economist Murray Weidenbaum, for example, argues that direct government support for commercially relevant technology is wasteful or outright counterproductive. He believes that government has demonstrated little aptitude for choosing among promising new technologies. His examples include the now abandoned superconducting supercollider and the abortive attempt to develop a commercial synthetic fuels industry.[30]

But why should we not expect government to make mistakes? Should it be so much better than private industry? After all, for every group of companies that open their doors, only half will still be around in five years.[31] And just think about all of the trouble major corporations get into. One only has to think back a few months to remember Valuejet. Management errors of huge proportion were found during the investigations following Valuejet's Everglades crash.

The failure of a policy initiative need not necessarily be a failure of policy, as some may imply; it could be a failure of administration. The flat panel antidumping case is a splendid example. On July 18, 1990, the Advanced Display Manufacturers Association (ADMA) filed an antidumping suit against Japan. They charged twelve Japanese flat panel manufacturers with dumping in order to gain 90 percent of the U.S. market. They also charged that the dumping was responsible for driving many U.S. firms out of the market.

But representatives of American computer companies were opposed to the suit. Firms such as IBM and Apple argued that since any tariff duty resulting from the suit would apply only to the flat panel displays themselves, and not to an assembled product containing a flat panel display, duties could be avoided by assembling offshore.

In a three-to-one vote, the International Trade Commission found in favor of ADMA's claims. Antidumping duties were assessed. The outcome was exactly as the computer companies had predicted. Hosiden (a Japanese flat panel manufacturer) halted all flat panel exports to the United States. Apple announced plans to move all its computer assembly to Ireland. Toshiba moved its assembly operation from Irvine, California, to Japan. Dolch Computers of Milpitas, California, began assembly operations in Germany, and N.View Corporation moved its plant from Virginia to Toronto.

Thus, the Japanese companies named on the suit avoided the duty altogether by assembling offshore, as did U.S. computer companies. The net result was a significant loss in American jobs. Furthermore, the duty did nothing to improve the competitive position of U.S. flat panel producers, and the American computer industry still remained essentially totally dependent on the Japanese for flat panel displays.[32]

So the government sometimes makes mistakes. But sometimes they do things right too. In Chapter 2, political scientist Emmett Redford was cited as concluding that the results of America's industry policy for the airlines was threefold: A "more than normal" amount of resources were attracted to the airline industry, service was provided to more city-pair markets than could be sustained commercially, and there was a faster rate of development of commercial aircraft than market forces alone would have produced.[33]

Virtually everyone would agree that this is true. Of course the anti–industrial policy economists would argue that this diverted resources away from areas where they would otherwise have been used, and that consumers were forced to pay more for airline travel than they would have paid under a deregulated system. These arguments are both true. But, come on, who can seriously say that our airline industry policy was not a success?

Another example is the Harley case. The Harley-Davidson Corporation was once the premier motorcycle manufacturer in the world. But through a series of missteps, Harley quality deteriorated relative to other motorcycles, so that by the summer of 1983 Harley was down to a market share of only 3 to 5 percent of the U.S. market and was almost bankrupt. Harley asked for, and was granted, relief under Section 201 of the trade laws, which gives temporary protection to industries as they try to adjust to foreign competition. Harley was given help in the form of a five-year tariff increase on big bikes manufactured abroad. After three years of protection, Harley took the unusual step of asking the president to suspend the tariff, which still had two years to run. The president's economic advisors declared Harley's recovery a victory for Reaganomics (although they had vigorously opposed the tariff).[34]

Industrial policy is not about supporting American industry; it is about supporting a few American industries. For the sake of argument, let us say that all of America's industrial policy efforts are wildly successful. Trade-protected industries recover, the Japanese really do open up their markets to U.S. autos, a commercial flat panel manufacturing presence is established in America, the 3X car becomes a worldwide darling, and vast savings are achieved in the delivery of public power. How much might all of these industries mean to the United States economy? Probably not much. At the outside they might contribute perhaps 4 to 7 percent to the economy. And bear in mind that this is only a wild guess.

The point is that the use of industrial policy in the United States is limited. The tasks of industrial policy are in improving productivity, increasing the skills of the work force, upgrading jobs, avoiding chaos, and promoting technological development. The competitiveness/comparative advantage argument is not the issue. The issue is a steady improvement in the quality of American life.

Appendix

Japanese Industrial Policy: Does It Work?

In Chapter 1 of this book, a communitarian society was defined as one in which government's role is to determine the needs of society and to see that those needs are met. Thus, communitarianism produces a "developmental" state in which it is government's responsibility to define national priorities and see to their implementation. A communitarian society is a planned society, and Japan is the epitome of a communitarian society.

No aspect of Japan exemplifies its communitarianism more than the economy. Japan, in its propensity for long-range planning, has always rejected the West's theory of comparative advantage, which has been the foundation of America's trade policy. Western theory holds that countries should produce those products they make best and trade for other products. Thus, each nation ends up "specializing" in a series of industries. Japan's industrial policy has always rejected this viewpoint. It targets for development industries it believes are in the long-term interests of the nation to have.

Behind this thinking is Japan's strong desire to maintain its autonomy and hegemony. It believes that it cannot survive as a nation if foreign companies dominate its markets. For Japan, industrial policy is a matter of national security.[1]

For the past two decades scholars have debated the impact of

Japan's industrial policy on its economic success. "Explanations" for that success range across a broad political and philosophical spectrum. At the one end is the "Japan, Inc." explanation, which holds that Japan is run like a huge corporation with the national government minutely controlling all industries and all aspects of the economy.[2] At the other is the position put forth by the Japanese themselves—that Japan's economy is among the most open in the world and that Japan's success is the product of the free market economy, superior management, and hard work.[3]

The truth, of course, is that neither explanation is satisfactory. A more correct explanation is the following:

> In complete contrast to the United States, neomercantilist rather than neoclassical ideals and practices shape and fuel Japan's economy. Strategic industries are targeted for development and declining industries for protection, and those industries are nurtured through a dynamic mixture of corporate collusion and competition. Industrial policies are implemented with a range of subsidies, import barriers, technology infusions, and export promotions. These policies assumed a similar pattern: Japan imports a technology . . . from the West. It then protects the industry from foreign competition to whatever extent and by whatever means may be required while it gains scale, experience, cost parity, and momentum in Japan itself—the world's second largest and fastest growing market, exporting aggressively, further enhancing its cost position. Gradually it converts a part of its cost advantage into improved product quality. At some point the Japanese producer is able to offer a better product, profitability, and lower price.[4]

Japan's economic system is based not only on competition between Japan's largest firms but on extensive behind-the-scenes economic and political collusion among big business, politicians, and the economic ministries. Japan's corporate elite is dominated by a half-dozen huge industrial conglomerates (*keiretsu*) centered around a bank, trading company, and insurance firm. These are the predominant backers of the keiretsu's manufacturing arm, consisting of primary metals, automobiles, mining, electronics, and machinery components. Each of these firms sits on top of a network of hundreds of subcontractors and suppliers with which they have long-term commercial relationships.

Cooperation on industrial matters is assured through cross-ownership of stock. About 25 percent of a keiretsu firm's stock is owned by other companies in the keiretsu while another 5 percent is owned by firms in "competing" keiretsu. This natural cooperation fostered by extensive stock cross-ownership is reinforced by hundreds of cartels—over 500 legally sanctioned by the Japanese government and hundreds of others "overlooked" by the antitrust authorities. The more competitive the foreign products, the tighter the collusion among cartel members to restrict foreign competition to a tiny share of the market.

Up until very recently, continual reelection of the conservative Liberal Democratic Party (LDP) had allowed the LDP to concentrate on maintaining the neomercantilist economic policies that have been so successful in Japan. And today, even though the LDP has lost its absolute majority, conservative policies remain.

Japanese political scientists have attempted to develop a concept that adequately describes their political/economic system. The best labels they seem to be able to come up with are "bureaucracy-led mass inclusionary pluralism" (kanryoshudo taishu hokatsu-gata tagenshugi)[5] or "mixed, party-bureaucracy-led, compartmentalized pluralism" (jimin-kancho kongotai hoko-zukerareta, shikirareta tagenshugi).[6] In any event, the point is that the bureaucracy and the political system support and enhance each other's power.

Every sector of the Japanese economy is characterized by extensive cooperation between business and government and among businesses. Both are obsessed with an extraordinary nationalism, calling for Japan to be "number one." This cooperation is maintained through a web of formal and informal ties that

> include membership in LDP policy "tribes" (zoku) and party sections (bukai), "wise men" policy councils (shingikai) and research groups (chosakai), and Diet committees, the retirement of elite officials into the private and public corporations that they were formerly "regulating" as well as into the LDP (amakudari), the thousands of industrial associations, the hundreds of legal and extra-legal cartels, vast industrial groups (keiretsu), and business groups like the Federation of Economic Organizations (FEO Keidanren). Informal ties such as being alumni from the same elite universities (gakubatsu), particularly Tokyo University, inter-élite marriage (keibatsu), and other old boy networks (jinmyaku) can also be important.[7]

This is not to suggest that the relationship between business and government is all honey and roses—it is not. There is a dynamic tension between the two, with the economic ministries continually trying to increase their influence over business while business tries to keep government control at arm's length. But the tension seems to work, producing industrial policies that are among the most efficient in the world.

The Ministry of International Trade and Industry

It is the Ministry of International Trade and Industry (MITI) that continues to conceive and implement most of Japan's industrial policies. Although MITI's power has diminished over the years, even today it plays a visible and important role in selecting and nurturing strategic industries. And, even with its diminished influence, the ministry's power and authority are far beyond anything we are accustomed to in the United States. Its responsibilities include:

- consensus building and the articulation of long-term visions for those industries under its control;
- the setting of sectoral priorities;
- the allocation of subsidies and facilitation of financial flows to priority sectors;
- adjustments of industrial structure;
- infant industry protection;
- investment guidance in certain industries and under certain conditions;
- regulation of excessive competition;
- downside risk reduction and cost diffusion;
- export promotion and mediation of trade conflicts.[8]

Despite this formidable array of formal powers, much of MITI's work is accomplished behind the scenes through "administrative guidance" (*gyosei shido*). This provides a flexible way of securing voluntary compliance rather than having to go through legal channels or the Diet to implement policy. And both the government and industry prefer it—it can be adapted quickly to changing circumstances and makes the whole process seem "voluntary."

Over the years, Japan and MITI have used less overt power in industrial development largely in response to foreign charges of "unfair" industrial and trade practices. During the 1980s the régime shifted into a "neocorporatist" mold. Other ministries have successfully challenged MITI and the Ministry of Finance's (MOF) dominance of economic policy. Corporations have become increasingly powerful and wealthy and less inclined to blindly follow government directives. And the power of the dominant triad was eroded absolutely as a result of the political "reform" of 1993.

Nevertheless, Japan remains a neomercantilist state, and the success of its industrial policies depends on its careful management of trade relationships. Nothing makes this clearer than the auto negotiations between Japan and the United States in 1995 (see Chapter 4).

Japan spends millions of dollars annually on a global public relations campaign to convince its trading partners that its markets are open. Projecting this image is vital to Japan's neomercantilist policy as it must, at all costs, be able to export freely. Japanese goods must have relatively free access to world markets while competitive foreign goods remain locked out of Japanese markets. To date Tokyo has been very successful at restraining trade. David Bobrow and Stephen Chan suggest that restraint of trade is critical to Japanese success.

> Restraint entails knowing how much to push and where to stop. It calls for a willingness to compromise and to settle for half-a-pie. In contrast to a negotiation style that demands all or nothing, such a posture avoids antagonizing and rallying opposition groups in the target country. . . . Restraint also means avoiding "bad press" that focuses critical attention on one's policies and activities, and engenders domestic pressure in the target country to review and change its policy of cooperation.[9]

The ability of Japan to continue its mercantilist policies depends on a strong national government. A government can be considered strong if it can:

> (1) create a consensus in society sufficient to allow government to design and implement goals for the community as a whole; (2) change the behavior of important groups, such as businesses, to further its policies; and (3) change the structure of society—the nature of ownership, the degree of industrial concentration, and the importance of particular sectors—in pursuit of its goals.[10]

The Bureaucracy

The Japanese government does all of these things. And the way it exercises its power is through the bureaucracy. The Japanese bureaucracy is very different from America's federal bureaucracy in many important respects. One way in which it differs is in the number of political appointees in an agency. In the executive branch of the U.S. government there are literally thousands of political appointees at the highest levels of power. In each Japanese ministry there is only one genuine political appointee, the minister, who is selected by the prime minister and also becomes a member of the cabinet. All other positions in the ministry are filled by career civil servants—including vice minister. Thus the prime minister names only about 20 political appointees, compared to over 3,000 appointees the U.S. president names in his federal agencies. This is done in an attempt to isolate the ministry from "political interference." It is the norm in Japan "for the minister to fear his bureaucrats and to be dominated by them . . . what they [the bureaucrats] really want is a minister who will leave them alone while at the same time taking responsibility for the ministry and protecting it from intrusion by other politicians or outside interests, particularly business interest."[11]

The Japanese bureaucracy is a prestigious and elitist institution—a characteristic that permeates the system all the way down to its hiring practices. Prospective bureaucrats sit for either class A or class B examinations. Those who pass the class A exam are eligible to advance to the highest levels of the bureaucracy. Those who pass the B are generally restricted to the section chief level. University students who hope to enter the bureaucracy sit for the A examination during their last year at the university (very often their last year of graduate school). Those who pass and are selected by one of the ministries become a member of an entering class in that ministry—probably the most important event in an individual's life. Japan scholar Chalmers Johnson elaborates:

> The identification with an entering cohort becomes the bureaucrat's most important attribute during his entire bureaucratic life, and it follows him long after he leaves government service. Entering classes establish vertical relationships among all high-level, or "career" (*kyaria*), officials—or what are called *sempai* (seniors, those of earlier classes) and *kōhai* (juniors, those of later entering classes). Both promotion to the level of section chief and retirement are in accordance with strict seniority. This age grading (*nenkō joretsu*) and "respect for seniority" (*nenji sonchō*) among bureaucrats influences everything they do, not just their activities in a ministry.[12]

Not only are the young bureaucrats divided based on their exam scores but based on their college majors as well. There are again two career paths—one for administrative officials or generalists, and one for technical official or specialists. Only one ministry, the Ministry of Construction, promotes its technical officials to the top position.

Promotion to section chief (through seniority) is virtually guaranteed for every career officer who does not make a serious mistake. But beyond that, the competition between classes for positions is intense. Obviously, not everyone in each entering class can reach the top levels of the bureaucracy—there simply are not enough positions. Once a class reaches the section chief level, those not selected for the next rounds of promotion are required to resign—or to "descend from heaven" (*amakudari*) into a lucrative job in the private sector or politics. Ultimately, everyone must descend to ensure that new blood is constantly introduced into the systems. The process of separating out those who will resign early is known as *kata-tataki* (the tap on the shoulder).

The amakudari system has advantages both for the bureaucracy and for industry. The strong personal ties between class members provide preferential ties between government and the strategic industries that the "tapped" bureaucrats descend into. These are the bases from which sector strategies are developed and coordinated.[13]

Administrative Guidance

Implementing these strategies is known as *administrative guidance.* Administrative guidance differs from law in that it is not legally enforceable.

> Its power comes from government-business relationships established since the 1930's, respect for the bureaucracy, the ministries' claim that they speak for the national interest,[14] and various informal pressures that the ministries can bring to bear. The old Japanese proverb used to describe this threat of government retaliation is "To take revenge on Edo by striking at Nagasaki," meaning that the bureaucracy has the means to get even with a businessman who refuses to listen to its administrative guidance.[15]

Administrative guidance has historically taken many forms like coordinating capital investment priorities in an industry in "cooperative discussion groups" (cartels). Others include the promotion of mergers, the allocation of production targets, promoting the introduction of foreign technology into Japan, providing access to government financing, rationalizing industries,[16] and providing government assistance in the commercialization and sale of products.

In political science circles, this is known as the bureaucratic dominance theory. Most of the studies of Japan's industrial development subscribe to this theory, elegantly described by Chalmers Johnson. But not all. Most notably, books by Kent Calder,[17] David Friedman,[18] and Richard Samuels[19] strongly challenge the power of the bureaucracy (especially MITI) in Japan. The three books are a powerful critique of the bureaucratic dominance thesis. But theirs is a minority view, and a small minority at that.

The Semiconductor Industry

Thus far Japanese industrial policy has been described in general terms. Policy is much more vivid when it is illustrated by specific case studies, and two of the most frequently described examples are semiconductors and machine tools.

In 1957, Japan had a small but growing electronics industry. MITI then developed and had enacted a new law designed to nurture and develop that industry—the Extraordinary Measures Law for Promotion of the Electronics Industry. Under the law, MITI in cooperation with industry was directed to

> select products and projects in research and development for special promotion, to set production, quantity, and cost targets, and to ensure adequate funding of the programs both by providing subsidies and by directing bank lending activities. . . . The law also authorized the creation of cartels in cases deemed useful by MITI, and established under the control of MITI, an Electronics Industry Deliberation Council consisting of representatives of industry, academia, and the press, to develop plans and provide coordination.[20]

The Deliberation Council concluded that Japan's top priority must be to build a world-class computer industry. To do this it had to target IBM, which had about half of Japan's computer market.

MITI's first step against IBM was to raise the tariffs on computers.

When IBM tried to get around the tariffs by manufacturing in Japan, MITI refused to permit production in Japan until IBM licensed its basic patents to fifteen Japanese companies. IBM also had to agree to get MITI's permission on the number and types of computers it could produce. MITI was thus able to control IBM's market share to some degree.

The Japanese government controlled bank lending and saw to it that the companies it had targeted for support in the computer race were funded. It also provided tax incentives for them and established a government-backed leasing company to purchase Japanese computers as fast as they were produced. Finally, it used its powers of persuasion to force users to "buy Japanese."

By the mid-1970s, MITI had come to realize that the semiconductor industry was the key to computer superiority; it then began targeting the semiconductor industry.[21] Officials of the Japanese computer industry met with MITI to see what could be done about IBM's dominance of the market. At the time, the industry was divided into two groups. The seventy or eighty small companies in the industry had formed themselves into the Electronic Industry Promotion Association. The remainder of the industry was composed of the five mainframe producers—Hitachi, Fujitsu, Toshiba, NEC, and Mitsubishi.

In April 1976, Japan established the Very Large-Scale Integrated Circuit Technology Research Association (VLSI/TRA) on the initiative of MITI with the sole objective of developing VLSI for the computer. The core of the association was a joint effort encompassing six existing joint research laboratories with the research staff being drawn from the Electronics Technology Laboratory (attached to MITI) and from the five large companies. The life of the project was to be four years (1976–80); it was funded by 72 billion yen with 30 billion yen coming from the national government. The participating companies all had a common interest in the outcome.

MITI's role was to ensure that the major players cooperated in this effort. This was no easy task as the participating firms had been rivals for decades and cooperation did not come easy. The government had a stick, however, as well as the power of moral suasion—it could deny them government funds.

VLSI was governed by a board of directors made up of the company presidents with the chairmanship rotating annually. Actual operations were headed by an executive director who was a widely respected former MITI official. The director was able to develop intense competition among the labs and among teams from the different companies.

When the association completed its four-year life span in 1980, its results shocked the world. It had not only perfected the 64K chip but it had developed the 256K RAM chip—a dramatic achievement over the 64K chip it started with. It had also applied for over 1,000 patents in VLSI processing technology.[22] In late 1981, in a long advertising article in *Scientific American*, Japan declared victory in the chip war.[23]

By the mid-1980s, the world's capacity to produce computer chips far exceed demand. The Japanese, in their quest for market dominance in the United States, began cutting prices—in effect dumping chips on the U.S. market. Overcapacity was so extreme that in one year alone prices fell by 80 percent. By 1985, the Commerce Department had evidence of massive dumping of both 64K and 256K RAMs—evidence obtained both from U.S. and Japanese sources. After protracted negotiations producing agreements on paper but no end to the dumping, President Reagan imposed tariffs of 300 percent on various Japanese products including laptop computers. MITI, recognizing that it had misread the U.S. resolve, imposed strict production and export controls.[24] The dumping stopped and the issue was quickly resolved.

The Machine Tool Industry

David Collis of the Harvard Business School, among others,[25] evaluated Japan's industrial policy with regards to the machine tool industry.[26] His approach was unique, however, in that he took a single worldwide industry as the unit of analysis and looked at how industrial policy affected the industry in different countries over time. The advantage of this comparative approach is that it tends to break down the researcher's potential ideological blinders.

It was back in the 1950s when Japan announced its designation of machine tools as a high-priority industry with the passage of the 1956 Extraordinary Measures Law for the Protection of the Machinery Industry. Specific programs included loans from the Japan Development Bank, a series of tax breaks, tariffs and import restrictions, and MITI control over licensing. Through an administrative guidance cartel, MITI also attempted to rationalize the industry by weeding out the small firms. This effort failed, however.

As the leading edge of the industry worldwide moved into numeri-

cal controls in the early 1970s, MITI set a goal for half of Japan's
output to be numerically controlled by the end of the decade. To
achieve this goal, MITI encouraged one company, Fujitsu FANUC, to
become the supplier of numerical control units for the entire machine
tool industry. The result was so successful that FANUC won 80–90
percent of the Japanese market and by the 1980s had 40–50 percent of
the worldwide market.

MITI also saw to it that the Japanese government provided a broad
10–15 percent R&D subsidy to the industry (largely from the proceeds
of the bicycle, motorbike, and powerboat racing funds). By the early
1980s, Japan had achieved dominance in the new microprocessor numerical control technology (CNC).

In 1976 Japan again changed its industrial policy strategy. MITI
funded a $60 million eight-year flexible manufacturing research proj-
ect. The goal was to develop basic standards for a Flexible Manufacturing System (FMS) to enhance the productivity of small- and
medium-sized firms. Participants included FANUC and nine machine
tool, four industrial machinery, and seven electronics firms. When the
project concluded in 1983, the Japanese government switched from
R&D assistance to low-interest loans to install the new systems. By
1985 Japan was the world leader in FMS installations.

Collis concludes, at least as far as the machine tool industry is
concerned, that Japan's industrial policy was successful. It was flexible
in that different government policies followed different stages of the
industry's evolution. It was coherent in that the specific programs
acted directly on market imperfections. In sum:

> At each stage in the industry's evolution Japanese industrial policy
> assisted firms in successfully performing along the key strategic dimen-
> sions. This successful and efficient approach to implementation helped
> establish Japan's machine tool industry as the dominant world producer
> of standard low-cost NC machine tools.[27]

Politics and Industrial Policy

If we in the United States think about Japanese industrial policy at all,
it is typically about manufactured goods. But industrial policy, not just
in Japan but everywhere, covers services like banking and other financial services, agriculture, construction, and retailing. It is no accident

that Japan's rapid transformation into the global financial hegemon it has become is dazzling. By the early 1990s Japan had become the world's financial superpower. It had the world's 8 largest banks, 16 of the top 25, and 23 of the top 50. It is no wonder that, at that time, it held well over one-third of the total international bank assets (compared to less than 15 percent for U.S. banks).[28]

But the history of Japanese industrial policy toward some of the other service industries—like construction—is more interesting. In large part, political money lies behind the industrial policies of some segments of Japanese industry.

No matter which country in the world one is in, the candidates and the parties with the most money generally win the elections. Japan is no exception. Conservative parties ruled Japan for all but nine months between 1945 and 1993. And while the LDP "lost" its majority in 1993 and had to form a coalition government, that coalition and those following it have also been traditionally conservative.

As will be seen, this is no accident. About 90 percent of all Japanese now live in urban areas—that is, in cities with populations of 50,000 or more. And about half of these urban dwellers are either directly or indirectly involved in the distribution system or the construction industry. Furthermore, because of gerrymandering, rural electoral districts, until very recently, had been politically weighted as much as three times greater than urban areas, making the farmers an important LDP voting block (about 70 percent of farmers generally vote LDP). As long as these construction workers, retailers, distributors, and farmers supported the LDP and now the conservative coalition—and support means contributing massive amounts of funds through their industrial associations—conservative factions of whatever label were and are likely to remain in power. Obviously, these groups support conservative government because it protects their sectors from international competition and gives them huge subsidies and tax advantages.[29]

Agriculture

Given farm support for the LDP, the farming sector is probably the most heavily protected industry in Japan. And it is the Japanese consumers who take the hit. In many cases, food goods on the store shelves in Japan cost five or six times the world market prices. But consumers do not seem to mind (much).

The iron triangle of agricultural industrial policy is composed of the Ministry of Agriculture, Forestry, and Fisheries (MAFF), the National Federation of Farmers (Zenno), and the LDP Farm Policy Research Committee. They are supported by a range of other groups of which the LDP Farm Policy Group (zoku) is among the most influential.

Farm industrial policy has a number of components, among which agricultural subsidies play a significant role. Agricultural price supports account for about one-fourth of MAFF's annual budget with about 60 to 70 percent of all agricultural products receiving price supports. For the individual farmers these price supports have been an extraordinary blessing. Largely through income received from the supports, farm income has risen from about 70 percent of nonfarm income in 1950, to 90 percent in 1970, 100 percent in 1975, and is about 115 percent today.

A second component of Japanese agriculture policy has been a move toward Japanese total food self-sufficiency. Attempts have been made to both improve farm productivity and diversify the different farm products produced. While both policies have been somewhat successful in and of themselves, self-sufficiency has not been achieved. Japan's total food self-sufficiency is only about 65 percent, and Japanese agriculture is extraordinarily inefficient by world standards.[30]

As with other industries, protectionism has been a major part of Japan's agricultural industrial policy. Nowhere is this more obvious than with rice. The rice market is monopolized by the *nokyo,* which sell about 95 percent of the crop at fixed price—a price about five times the international market level. Rice is heavily protected by both tariffs and import quotes. And while the United States has pushed for trade liberalization in some agricultural areas, it has not done so with rice. This is mainly because one of the justifications for protecting rice is that it is a central aspect of Japanese national culture. Overall, political scientist William Nester concludes that

> By neoclassical economic measures, Tokyo's farm policies have been an immense failure since protection annually adds $65 billion to Japan's food bill. . . . By neomercantilist measures they have been highly successful. The political trade-off of protectionism for votes has allowed the LDP to remain in office and continue the industrial policies that helped transform Japan from a developing country into the world's manufacturing, financial, and technological powerhouse.[31]

Distribution

Japan's distribution system is equally as inefficient as its agricultural system and for many of the same reasons—politics and industrial policy. In the United States there is one retail store for about every 120 people. In Japan there is one for every 68 people. Over 60 percent of Japan's retail stores are little mom-and-pop operations employing two people or less. In the United States, a product passes through two middlemen from producer to consumer, in Japan, the figure is seven. Thus Japan's 25 million wholesalers and retailers employ over 10 million people—a substantial voting block.

The LDP and MITI (which manages the distribution system) have "protected" these workers from the "excess competition" of the free market. And, again, the consumer pays. The average price of consumer goods in Japan is almost 50 percent higher than in the United States.

To ensure that the "super-store" craze or anything like it never hits Japan, MITI is responsible for approving new stores and the expansion of old ones larger than 1,500 square meters (3,000 square meters in the top eleven cities). (It takes up to seven years to receive MITI approval for a new outlet.) Not only that, but local small stores have veto power over the opening of any larger stores.

This means that stores are squeezed for space. Because the goods travel through such an inefficient distribution network, the retailer must choose between handling Japanese goods (with a known market) in his limited space or take a chance on an exorbitantly priced foreign product. Thus, even if foreign goods manage to get through Japan's tariff barriers, quotas, arbitrary standards, and red tape, there is still no room on the retailers' shelves for foreign products.

As if these aren't barriers enough, the government's monopolistic sale-agent law forces foreign producers to sell through only one designated import agent who has exclusive marketing rights over the specific product. The only problem is that most of these agents also sell Japanese products, which compete directly with the foreign good. The Japanese products already have large sales and are thus already profitable to the agent. Guess which products get pushed?

Japan's cartel system extends to the distribution system. In the consumer electronics market, for example, the distribution system is monopolized by the keiretsu. About 70 percent of the sales of each of the twelve top electronics manufacturers are through their own networks.

Matsushita and Toshiba each have systems of 41,000 wholesalers and retailers.[32]

Is this marketing system likely to change? Perhaps, but only slowly.[33] Even if it does become simpler and more rational, author William Nester does not believe American products will sell. "MITI is still singing the same tired old refrain that Japan's markets are completely open and foreign firms do not sell more because their products are inferior and they do not try hard enough."[34]

Construction

The construction trades have historically been the LDP's most lucrative sources of funds. Japan's construction market is the world's largest and about 80 percent of LDP Diet members have close ties to the industry. More than half a million construction firms employ over 5 million workers, thus supporting about 25 million people when families are included. American firms have virtually no presence in this market.

Bids on government construction projects are thoroughly rigged (*dango*) to keep industry employment at inflated levels. Policymaking in the industry is led by the Ministry of Construction, which coordinates the rigged bidding system, and also by MITI through its Small and Medium Enterprise Agency, and the Ministry of Transportation on projects like airports and highways. The government manages the construction market so that only certain firms are eligible to bid on given projects. The private sector rotates bidding. Winning bids are always rotated so that all firms have at least enough work to stay in business.

The industry is, of course, protected from "excessive competition." Rationalization of the construction industry might cost a half a million jobs and cause defection from the LDP. It will never happen.[35]

MITI Is Not Always Right

These examples, of course, are of Japanese industrial policy "successes." But the Japanese bureaucracy is hardly immune from mistakes, as is illustrated by MITI's history of relationships with the auto industry. In the early 1950s, a motor vehicle industry barely existed in Japan. It is estimated that car production was at least twenty years behind Europe and the United States. Policies and guidelines issued by

MITI in 1952 restricted "unnecessary" imports and encouraged "desirable" ones—especially those required for mass production. The auto companies thus rushed to make agreements for joint ventures with foreign firms to establish manufacturing facilities in Japan. Some ten such proposals were developed and submitted to MITI for approval, but only three were approved as MITI did not want the limited Japanese market to become overcrowded.

In 1955, MITI proposed a National Car Development Program based on a model with a speed of 60 miles per hour, a price of 150,000 yen ($420), and a production of 2,000 per month. Under the competition, MITI would select the best car from prototypes submitted by the auto manufacturers and would arrange for bank loans and direct support from the Treasury. However, the manufacturers successfully resisted this discrimination in favor of one company.

MITI again tried to concentrate the industry into an oligopoly by drafting a new law recommending restraints on new entries, control of new models, priorities in allocating Treasury loans, and a reorganization of the industry. The law was never enacted, however, largely because of the strong opposition by the keiretsu groups.

In 1965, in spite of MITI's wishes, there were eleven carmakers in Japan's small market (600,000 cars per year). MITI had still not given up on its desire to "rationalize" automobile production. It therefore brokered a merger between Nissan and Prince. Nissan was strong financially but weak technically and Prince was strong technically but weak financially. The merger improved the quality of Nissan's product and moved it into direct competition with the industry leader—Toyota—creating the "Big Two" in the industry. This somewhat satisfied MITI's desire for an oligopolistic auto industry, but MITI was in for a big shock. In 1969 the vice president of Mitsubishi Heavy Industries (a keiretsu with huge financial resources) announced an agreement with Chrysler to form a new automobile company. The chief of MITI's Heavy Industry Bureau said that "the announcement hit him like water poured into his ear while he was sleeping."[36] By 1970, Chrysler began selling Mitsubishi cars in the United States as the Dodge Colt. It soon became Japan's third-largest automaker.

MITI was humiliated. It was finally forced to concede that its plans to reorganize the auto industry were in a shambles. So, while MITI is an important player in industrial policy, it does not always get its way.[37]

Again, not too many years ago (in the late 1970s), MITI's image received a blow from which it never fully recovered. The Toshiba Machine Company, a member of the Mitsui keiretsu, was caught violating regulations of the Coordinating Committee for Multilateral Export Controls (COCOM) by selling eight computer-guided milling machines to the Soviet Union. The Toshiba incident infuriated the United States as these advanced machine tools would allow the Soviets to produce silent propellers for their submarines. One Pentagon official writing in *Foreign Affairs* estimated that it would cost $30 billion for the United States to develop a device to defeat the quiet-running Soviet subs.[38]

MITI was implicated in this scandal when it was found that the Ministry had advised Japanese corporations how to get around the COCOM rules. And, while the Japanese public made little of the Toshiba event, MITI lost a great deal of its mystique in the eyes of the world.

Japanese Industrial Policy—How Successful?

There has been a standing debate in the United States about the effectiveness of Japanese industrial policy. However, it was only in the 1980s that the Japanese themselves began to examine the effectiveness of their own industrial policy. One such effort was conducted at the Tokyo Center for Economic Research by some of Japan's leading economists.[39] One should note at the outset that many of Japan's economists received their economic training in the United States, and many of those educated in Japan were trained by economists who were educated in the United States. Thus, the conservative bias against industrial policy common to U.S. economists can also be found in Japanese economists—at least in those contributing to the Tokyo Center study.

Economist Ryutaro Komiya of the prestigious University of Tokyo indicates that Japan has actually experienced three subperiods of industrial policy.[40] Immediately following the Second World War, the two main tasks of industrial policy were reconstruction and achieving economic independence. During this period industrial policy consisted of a system of more or less direct government controls. The system showed the influence of the Soviet Gosplan, the wartime economic model adopted by Japan. Industries considered "basic" or "important" to Japan's future were provided with subsidies, low-interest loans, and were given priority in import allocations. The authority of the responsible government department in controlling industries was considerable.

The second period, that of high economic growth, saw an industrial policy in Japan aimed at developing industries that government officials—with the backing of the public—believed Japan *should have*. Komiya believes that these industries were those that involved an element of national prestige. They tended to be industries, symbolic of industrial might, that were common to industrial nations or those that attracted attention; they had "news value" both domestically and internationally. During this period the leverage of government disappeared little by little. The reality of industrial policy declined in importance and the power of the market became more central.

The third period, beginning in the 1970s, saw more and more industries turning to the government for adjustment assistance. Here, support developed for rationalizing and/or supporting declining industries.

Komiya believes that the guiding principle behind the formulation of Japanese industrial policy in all eras has been the prevention of "excess competition." In Japan, excess competition "has been used in conjunction with demand, for the lessening of competition in all sorts of industries, not only in unconcentrated industries. Such industries include competitive oligopolies, concentrated tight oligopolies, industries in which market prices are unregulated, and publicly regulated industries, which in addition are virtual monopolies (such as domestic scheduled passenger airline service)."[41]

The Genkyoku System

In Japan, ministries of the government provide supervision of virtually every significant industry. This *genkyoku*, or ministerial bureau, division, or section under whose jurisdiction a given industry falls, wants its industries to be orderly and organized. The bureaucrat sees excess competition tied to the Confucian concept of appropriate elder/younger relations. Thus government officials see the ideal industrial situation as one in which an industry is composed of only a few firms with stable market shares whose size, earnings, and profits are essentially unchanging. Any time large firms go bankrupt, the industry becomes unprofitable, the work force shrinks, or foreign competition makes inroads into market share, the bureaucrats must clean up the mess. This means that they may face questions from members of the Diet or the press. Thus government officials do not want to see excessive competition, or competition in any form, arise in their areas. From their perspective, a stability should be maintained that allows all firms to make a reasonable profit—a system "in which 'junior' firms respect their 'elders.' Thus officials have tried to see to it that, whenever possible, measures are instituted that assure that none of their firms get into trouble, that their firms remain profitable, and that their industry is not faced with the specter of import competition or the entry of foreign firms."[42]

Their preference for Confucian order and a xenophobic tendency to exclude foreigners cause officials in the genkyoku for an industry to see it desirable to consolidate firms or reorganize industries—a procedure called rationalizing. Genkyoku officials think nothing of restricting imports, implementing price agreements, organizing cartels, restricting output, and the like; all in the name of rationalization.

Overall, MITI is the single most important genkyoku ministry with five genkyoku bureaus—the Heavy Industries Bureau, the Chemical Industries Bureau, the Textile and Light Industries Bureau, the Coal and Mining Bureau, and the Public Utilities Bureau. Bureaus are divided into divisions and then further subdivided into sections.[43] But MITI is not the only genkyoku ministry. The Ministry of Agriculture, Forestry, and Fisheries; the Ministry of Health and Welfare; the Ministry of Transport; and the Ministry of Finance all perform genkyoku functions.

The genkyoku bureaus are typically organized vertically along industry lines, but within MITI there are also four horizontal bureaus that cut across industries. They are the International Trade Bureau, the Trade Promotion Bureau, the Enterprise Bureau, and the Safety and Environmental Protection Bureau.

Each genkyoku is responsible for drawing up policies relating to its industry(ies). These policies are passed by the Diet and become industry laws—like the Electronics Industry Law (1957).

Industry Associations and Shingikai

There are two industrial counterparts to the genkyoku—industry associations and policy councils (shingikai). There are literally hundreds of industry associations, like the Japan Automobile Manufacturers Association. The main purpose of these associations is to work with the genkyoku to see that the government adopts policies favorable to their industries.

Shingikai are used on major policy matters. The members of each shingikai are formally nominated by the minister and typically consist of industry corporate executives, industry leaders, and former bureaucrats, with a very small number of academics and/or journalists. The shingikai are consultative bodies whose opinions are solicited in the process of policy formulation. Given that they are nominated by the minister, if anything, they are captives of the ministry. *But*, they perform an extremely important function. These forums have been important sources of information and have served to obtain consensus on policy matters.

High-Technology Industries

Science and technology policy is typically a component of national industrial policy, and this certainly is the case with Japan. Industrial policy considerations were clearly reflected for the first time in the so-called "large-scale projects" sponsored by MITI's Agency of Industrial Science and Technology. The system was developed to compete directly with the West. The government provided the full amount of funds needed for the development of the technology—funds that MITI doubted would be provided by the private sector. Numerous large-scale projects were funded—some successful and some not.

Information industry projects produced results beyond all expectations. Led by the computer industry, the information industries form the core of Japanese high-technology industries and thus the focus of industrial policy efforts. This is clearly illustrated by the various legislation passed by the Diet supporting the development of the information industry: the Law on Temporary Measures for the Promotion of Electronics Industry (1957), the Law on Temporary Measures for the Promotion of Specified Machinery Industries (1971), and the Law on Temporary Measures for the Promotion of Specified Machinery and Information Industries (1978).

However, Japanese high-technology industry policy does not stop with supply-side measures like VLSI, but is also supplemented by demand-side policies. MITI fiercely promoted the introduction of computers into government offices to generate demand. It also made sure that the computers purchased were Japanese.

Ken'ichi Imai of the Hitotsubashi University Institute of Business Research believes that one reason why Japan's technology industrial policy is successful is its consensual nature—he calls it "soft" industrial policy. With a soft industrial policy, consensus is developed through a close exchange of information among related firms using industry associations, or *shigikai*. Once consensus is obtained and the direction an industry should take with the relevant firms is established, the ideas are diffused far and wide throughout the society.

The first step is to select strategic areas with high innovation potential—areas where Japan already has a knowledge base. The *genkyoku* then assemble experts from the chosen industries, and firms are mobilized to draw up detailed scenarios for the future. The results are published in the reports of deliberation councils. Based on the understandings reached in these councils, assistance is provided to induce technological development.[44]

Conclusion

It is unquestionably true that Japan, with her world-class industries and rapid rise as an economic power, is a clear demonstration of successful industrial policy based on a strong relationship between government and industry. It is also true that the activities of one of the government bureaucracies, the Ministry of International Trade and Industry, contributed to this development. But the cases of successful government intervention in economic sectors are now somewhat dated. Has industrial policy in Japan lost its clout? Or, is an industrial strategy an appropriate vehicle for a developing nation but not a developed nation? As Japan has matured economically, perhaps it no longer needs an industrial policy.

Three points need to be made. First, Japanese industrial policy is far from dead. Second, industrial policy *appears* to be relatively dormant because the power of the bureaucracy in Japan has declined—and this is particularly true of MITI. Finally, the prominence of industrial policy on the Japanese agenda has in fact declined and has been replaced by other policy concerns.

But this does not mean that Japan has relinquished or even loosened its protectionist trade policies. The most visible example in recent years has been the conflict between the United States and Japan regarding autos and auto parts. During much of 1994 and early 1995, the

Clinton administration had been working to open up the Japanese auto market to U.S. products. The discussions have centered on getting Japan to deregulate its after-market auto parts, measures to increase the number of dealers marketing U.S.-made cars, and to take steps to increase the use of U.S.-manufactured parts in Japanese automakers' assembly plants in Japan (Chapter 4).

While the auto dispute may be the most visible example of U.S. frustration with Japan's protectionist policies, it is hardly the only such dispute between the two. The United States is at odds with Japan over landing rights for Federal Express. But, this said, on the other side of the coin is the fact that the heart of Japan's industrial policymaking apparatus—the bureaucracy—has lost policymaking influence in recent years. And this came at a time when MITI's power in and of itself was on the downswing.

Masami Tanaka, director of the Division of Ceramic and Building Materials of MITI, points out that over the past decade industrial policy has become less important in overall government economic policy. This is because business has become strong and independent and because MITI policy options are more restricted than they once were.

In addition, one of the dilemmas of bureaucratic dominance in modern Japan is that the recent emphasis on high technology has changed the nature of industrial policy. Japan's traditional approach to economic success has been the adoption and improvement of foreign technologies. The recent emphasis, however, is on establishing a firm base of scientific research. In addition, "new" industries do not "automatically" fall under MITI's jurisdiction. Biotechnology is an example of such a "new" industry.[45]

Political events have also contributed to the current policy lull. Up until 1993, the Liberal Democratic Party had ruled Japan, dominating both houses of the legislature since the end of World War II (and thus the executive branch as well, because the legislature appoints the chief executive officer, the Prime Minister). Opposition was provided by a Socialist Party of moderate strength, a weak Communist Party, and several other minor parties. Given this domination, it was hardly surprising that the bureaucrats staffing ministries like MITI were solidly Liberal Democrats. This is part of the reason why the ministries worked in such close harmony with the elected government.

However, in 1993 much of that changed. The LDP, while the dominant party, had really never been a monolithic organization but was always a conglomeration of five or six factions, much like the nation-states of nineteenth-century Europe. The factions have been subject to constant realignment, as illustrated by the events of the summer of 1993 when the LDP lost its hold on the Diet to a group of "reformers" consisting of former LDP Diet members, with Morihiro Hosokawa assuming the position of Prime Minister in a new coalition government.

But with the enormous political support the LDP was once able to assemble, what happened to the system? In a word, corruption. Over the years, the LDP had enormous strength. From its founding in 1955 until its dominant faction, Takeshita, split in late 1992, it had totally prevented the Japanese Socialists and Communists from ever coming to power. The problem was that during this entire period the bureaucracy really ruled the country. And what happened over these years was an increasingly successful effort of the party to corrupt the bureaucracy.

During the "reforms" of 1993 and 1994, Japanese analysts continued to stress that the fundamental problem of the country was to democratize the bureaucracy. This, in fact, was one of Prime Minister Hosokawa's "reform" themes and one that political strongman Ichirō Ozawa tried to implement. But the bureaucracy, and especially MITI, seems to have survived.[46] Chalmers Johnson cites Japanese professor Jirōs Yamaguchi, who believes that real "reform" "would actually require a combination of the French Revolution and the Allied Occupation in order to make much difference in the ways Japanese conduct their public affairs."[47]

This has indeed been the case. Real reform never arrived. Japan briefly toyed with an ineffective Socialist prime minister in Tomiichi Murayama, who lasted only eighteen months in office. In January 1996 he was replaced by Ryutaro Hashimoto, president of the still-powerful Liberal Democratic Party. Hashimoto's background is mainstream bureaucracy. He is a career politician who served as minister of three of Tokyo's bureaucracies—transportation, finance, and trade—before his election as party president in August 1995. He has been called more bureaucratic than the bureaucrats.[48]

Finally, there has been an acknowledged change in public priorities in Japan. For many years following World War II, economic growth, and later international competitiveness, were the main national goals. But as the nation became wealthy, social goals emerged in importance—quality of life seems to have replaced economic growth as the main priority. Japan is struggling now to deal with serious social problems such as an aging population, long working hours, high consumer prices, poor housing, and an unhealthy concentration of the population in the Tokyo area.

As a consequence, industrial policy is becoming more of a shared responsibility between the national government and the prefectures. Kangawa University economist Koji Sato reports:

> Industrial policy is no longer the product of a monolithic central government engaged primarily in target[ing] industries for growth. Rather, policymaking influence has devolved onto local governments and it takes many more forms and affects a wider array of institutions. What was happening with Japan's industrial policy and regional economic development strategy during the 1980's can be viewed as the localization of national-level issues, similar to the local and state activism in promoting economic development in the United States during the 1980's.[49]

One of these efforts was MITI's "Technopolis" development policy for regional high-technology development. Back in 1980 and supported by the passage of the Technopolis Law in 1983, MITI attempted to stimulate the building of a Japanese technostate of research cities dispersed throughout the country. These centers are based on the U.S. Silicon Valley experience as well as on the development of Tsukuba Science City in Japan.

The technopolis centers are extremely popular with prefecture and local officials because they are the center of action. MITI's role has been to stimulate the concept and to provide some funding plus eligibility for national tax incentives and special depreciation allowances.[50]

The technopolis concept was a completely new one for MITI as it relied almost totally on local initiative. The Kanagawa Science Park (KSP) in Kawasaki is typical of the development under the program. It was initiated under Kanagawa Prefecture's industrial policy virtually independent of the national government policy. The prefecture's Comprehensive Industrial Policy was adopted in 1982 with a goal of diversifying Kanagawa's industrial structure to include knowledge-intensive and technology-intensive industries. The KSP was completed in late 1989 at a cost of Y465 billion, of which only Y40.2 billion came from the national government. There are 117 firms in the KSP with 4,000 employees—80 percent of whom are scientists and engineers.[51]

The mere fact that Japanese politics are less stable than in the past and that the relationships between politics, the bureaucracy, and industry are slowly changing, should not suggest that industrial policy has become a dinosaur and is moving toward extinction—it is not. The auto negotiations detailed in Chapter 4 makes this perfectly clear; but then so do numerous other Japanese government activities—particularly in the high-tech arena.

Take the issue of flat panel displays for example, (U.S. activities in this area are covered in Chapter 6). The Japanese government's interest in high-resolution displays is not new. It extends back to a time when they were trying to develop screens upon which legible *kanji* and *kana* characters could be displayed. This was the Pattern Information Processing System (PIPS) program, ran from 1971 to 1981. Most of the work was carried out at the Electro-Technical Laboratory run by MITI's Agency of Industrial Science and Technology. Over the years, Japanese development of displays, in particular liquid crystal displays, has been enormously successful, with the Japanese maintaining a very strong lead over both the United States and Europe. But this has not deterred the Japanese government from continuing support to the industry. While the agencies are not expending large sums of money, they have been stimulating firms to develop larger displays—presumably to make it easier to sell products associated with high-definition television. Several programs have been directly aimed at advanced displays. These include a seven-year $100 million collaborative program to build a one-meter, diagonal, color flat-panel display for HDTV. The project is co-funded by MITI, the Ministry of Posts and Telecommunications (MPT), and private firms. Government funding came from the sale of NTT shares, tobacco taxes, and motorboat racing fees.[52]

U.S. experts, largely academic scholars, saw the payoff from this exercise as being years away. For example: "True high-definition LCD projectors are still several years away from introduction to the market; large area AM-LCD flat panels are probably seven to ten years away from introduction."[53] Very comforting for a while. But only a year later, while sitting in a hotel room in Tokyo, the author came across a small news item buried in a corner of a back page in the *Japan Times*:

"Plasmatron" set developed by Sony

Sony Corp. has developed flat-panel display technology for large screens and will incorporate it in wall-hanging television sets to be marketed in fall 1996, the company said Monday.

Developed jointly with U.S. based Tektronix Inc., plasmatron is a flat-panel display using plasma addressed liquid crystal technology, which utilizes plasma instead of a transistor as an electronics switch, Sony officials said.

The simple manufacturing process allows for lower production costs of fine resolution flat-panel displays, they said. . . .

The company plans to initially introduce a 25-inch set that is 10 cm wide, to be followed by a 40-inch set, the officials said, adding that prices have not been decided.[54]

Is the flat-panel display battle over before it even begins? Has the United States lost a multibillion dollar industry before it became seriously involved?

One must not forget that MITI still has an enormous amount of authority. No industrial facility is built anywhere in Japan without MITI's approval. The ministry establishes industrial standards. It directs investment by the Japan Development Bank. It has the power to suspend antitrust laws and form cartels. It approves most licensing of technology. And, of course, it drafts the laws that provide the guidance for industries.[55] Japan is still a communitarian society and it still rejects Western economic practices. And although Japan in the recent past toyed with reform, government operations and policy have changed little and are unlikely to change in the near future.

Notes

Notes for Chapter 1

1. *Economic Report of the President 1992*, p. 3.
2. *Economic Report of the President 1995*, p. 19.
3. Ibid., pp. 21, 29, 40, 64–66, 118, 193.
4. Otis L. Graham, Jr., *Losing Time*, p. 6.
5. A term coined by John Chamberlain, *The American Stakes*.
6. Otis L. Graham, Jr., *Losing Time*, p. 280.
7. Ibid., p. 3.
8. Ibid., p. 52.
9. Ibid., p. 156.
10. Ibid., p. 157.
11. Ibid., p. 49.
12. Ibid., p. 63.
13. Ibid., p. 66.
14. Ibid., p. 3.
15. David W. Pearce (ed.), *The MIT Dictionary of Modern Economics*.
16. Douglas Greenwald (ed.), *The McGraw-Hill Encyclopedia of Economics*.
17. David R. Henderson, *The Fortune Encyclopedia of Economics*.
18. William G. Sheperd, *Public Policies Toward Business*, p. 5.
19. Productivity is the "value of the output produced by a unit of labor or capital." Michael E. Porter, *The Competitive Advantage of Nations*, p. 6.
20. Ibid.
21. Laura D'Andrea Tyson, *Who's Bashing Whom? Trade Conflict in High-Technology Industries*, p. 12.
22. Charles L. Schultze, "Industrial Policy: A Dissent."
23. James C. Miller III, *The Economist as Reformer: Revamping the FTC, 1981–1985*, pp. 71–88.

24. Otis L. Graham, Jr., *Losing Time,* pp. 26–27.
25. Ibid., pp. 26–35.
26. Ibid., pp. 37–42.
27. Ibid., p. 44.
28. Ibid., pp. 52–53.
29. Pat Choate and Gail Garfield Schwartz, *Being Number One.*
30. Lester Thurow, *The Zero-Sum Society.*
31. *Business Week,* "The Reindustrialization of America."
32. R.D. Norton, "Industrial Policy and American Renewal."
33. *Business Week,* "America's Restructured Economy."
34. Felix Rohatyn, *The Twenty-Year Century.*
35. Amitai Etzioni, *An Immodest Agenda.*
36. Robert Reich, *The Next American Frontier.*
37. Paul R. Krugman, "Targeted Industrial Policies: Theory and Evidence."
38. Robert Z. Lawrence, *Can America Compete?*
39. Richard B. McKenzie, *Competing Visions.*
40. Ibid.
41. Otis L. Graham, Jr., *Losing Time,* p. 109.
42. Ibid., pp. 111–112.
43. Ibid., pp. 159–165.
44. Ibid., pp. 165–166.
45. Ibid., pp. 167–169.
46. Ibid., pp. 207–239.
47. Laura D'Andrea Tyson, *Who's Bashing Whom?* p. 1.
48. Dieter Ernst and David O'Connor, *Competing in the Electronics Industry,* p. 27.
49. Michael E. Porter, *The Competitive Advantage of Nations,* p. 12.
50. Ibid., p. 13.
51. Ibid., p. xiii.
52. Ibid., pp. 126–128.
53. Laura D'Andrea Tyson, *Who's Bashing Whom?* p. 133.
54. Robert B. Reich, *The Work of Nations.*
55. George C. Lodge, *Perestroika for America,* pp. 15–17.
56. Peter Tasker, *The Japanese.*
57. George C. Lodge, *Perestroika for America.*

Notes for Chapter 2

1. Alexander Hamilton, "Report on the Subject of Manufacturers."
2. Ibid., p. 292.
3. Ibid., p. 290.
4. Ibid., p. 292.
5. Emmett S. Redford, *American Government and the Economy,* pp. 367–368.
6. Elmer E. Smead, *Government Promotion and Regulation of Business.*
7. Ann Roell Markusen, *Profit Cycles, Oligopoly and Regional Development,* pp. 83–84.

8. Ann Markusen, Peter Hall, Scott Campbell, and Sabrina Deitrick, *The Rise of the Gunbelt: The Military Remapping of Industrial America,* pp. 31–32.

9. That is, where regulation has moved beyond the scope of making occasional decisions for industries to decisions on many matters, and where regulation is continuous rather than occasional or intermittent. Regulation of the medical profession, for example, is intermittent, while regulation of airlines was, for many years, comprehensive. Defined in Emmet S. Redford, *American Government and the Economy,* p. 569.

10. Ibid., pp. 361–367.

11. *Nebbia v. New York,* 291 U.S. 502 (1934).

12. Louis Galambos and Joseph Pratt, *The Rise of the Corporate Commonwealth,* p. 43.

13. Ibid., pp. 43–70.

14. Emmett S. Redford, *American Government and the Economy,* pp. 371–394.

15. Ibid., p. 390.

16. Ibid., pp. 395–404.

17. 49 Stat. at L. 1985 (1936).

18. Elmer S. Smead, *Government Promotion and Regulation of Business,* pp. 228–251.

19. Ibid., pp. 273–274.

20. Emmett S. Redford, *American Government and the Economy,* pp. 411–413.

21. Ibid., p. 511.

22. Ibid., pp. 510–526.

23. Ibid., p. 516.

24. Guy Gugliotta, "Hill Conferees Clear Major Farm Changes"; Guy Gugliotta, "Congress Passes Bill Dropping Agriculture Subsidies"; "Clinton Signs Farm Measure Ending Subsidies."

25. *Barnard v. Monongahela Natural Gas Co.,* 216 Pa. 362, 365, G5A71.801, 803 (1907). Quoted in Emmett S. Redford, *American Government and the Economy,* p. 476.

26. *Sterling v. Constantine,* 287 U.S. 378 (1932).

27. Emmett S. Redford, *American Government and the Economy,* pp. 274–298. Also see E. Anthony Copp, *Regulating Competition in Oil,* pp. 109–139.

28. William Greider, *Secrets of the Temple,* pp. 310–314.

29. Ibid., p. 311.

30. The "Blue Eagle" symbol of the NRA indicated a company's willingness to participate in the government's recovery program, which meant, among other things, subscribing to wage and hour guidelines. Many of the nation's major industrial sectors ended up joining the program.

31. The CCC was eventually transferred to the Department of Agriculture.

32. James S. Olson, *Saving Capitalism: The Reconstruction Finance Corporation and the New Deal, 1933–1940.*

33. Ibid., p. 227.

34. Louis Galambos and Joseph Pratt, *The Rise of the Corporate Commonwealth,* pp. 143–144.

35. Ibid., p. 144–151.

36. Kenan Patrick Jarboe, "A Reader's Guide to the Industrial Policy Debate."

Notes for Chapter 3

1. Kenan Patrick Jarboe, "A Reader's Guide to the Industrial Policy Debate," pp. 200–203.

2. Robert B. Reich and John D. Donahue, *New Deals: The Chrysler Revival and the American System*, p. 3.

3. Ibid., pp. 61–68.

4. Ibid., pp. 87–159.

5. Ibid., p. 185.

6. Ibid., p. 231.

7. Ibid., pp. 206–337.

8. Ibid., pp. 238–263.

9. William Greider, *Secrets of the Temple*, pp. 624–633; see also Jack W. Aber, "Continental Illinois Corporation."

10. L. William Seidman, *Full Faith and Credit: The Great S&L Debacle and Other Washington Sagas*, p. 76.

11. William Greider, *Secrets of the Temple*, p. 629.

12. L. William Seidman, *Full Faith and Credit*, p. 112.

13. James R. Barth, *The Great Savings and Loan Debacle*, pp. 14–64.

14. National Commission on Financial Institution Reform, Recovery, and Enforcement, *Origins and Causes of the S&L Debacle: A Blueprint for Reform*, p. 34.

15. Ibid., p. 33.

16. Ibid., p. 30.

17. Ibid., p. 34.

18. Ibid., p. 40.

19. Ibid., pp. 35–55.

20. Ibid., p. 44.

21. James R. Barth, *The Great Savings and Loan Debacle*, pp. 14–64.

22. Kathleen Day, *S&L Hell: The People and the Politics Behind the $1 Trillion Savings and Loan Scandal*.

23. L. William Seidman, *Full Faith and Credit*, p. 195.

24. One of the provisions of FIRREA was to eliminate the "goodwill" gimmick that allowed some thrifts to appear healthy when they were not. The elimination of the goodwill gimmick caused a number of shaky thrifts to go belly-up. In the summer of 1996 the Supreme Court ruled that Congress acted illegally when it changed the rules, throwing many S&Ls into bankruptcy. Lawsuits against the government by the damaged savings institutions could add as much as $20 billion to the bailout costs. Jerry Knight and Joan Biskupic, "High Court Ruling May Add Billions to S&L Cleanup Cost"; Rudolph A. Pyatt, Jr., "What-ifs Still Haunt the History of the S&L Crisis."

25. L. William Seidman, *Full Faith and Credit*, p. 195.

26. Ibid.

27. In July 1991 the RTC was reorganized along private sector lines. A separate CEO position was created, the Oversight Board's functions were reduced to oversight, and the FDIC was removed from the picture, losing its RTC responsibilities.

28. L. William Seidman, *Full Faith and Credit*, pp. 208–209.

29. Ibid., pp. 224–226.

30. Federal Deposit Insurance Corporation, *Final Report on the FDIC/RTC Transition,* p. 2.

31. Susan Schmidt, "RTC Issues Additional Questions to Hillary Clinton in S&L Probe."

32. L. William Seidman, *Full Faith and Credit,* pp. 196–197.

33. Robert B. Reich and John D. Donahue, *New Deals,* p. 116.

34. Ibid., p. 245.

35. Ibid. Economists have traditionally opposed VERs. They are clearly protectionist in design and intent. They restrict competition and ultimately have counterproductive effects on the domestic producers they are designed to benefit.

Notes for Chapter 4

1. Jagdish Bhagwati, "Aggressive Unilateralism: An Overview."

2. Thomas O. Bayard and Kimberly Ann Elliott, *Reciprocity and Retaliation in U.S. Trade,* p. 1.

3. Jagdish Bhagwati, "Aggressive Unilateralism: An Overview," p. 46.

4. Laura D'Andrea Tyson, *Who's Bashing Whom?*

5. Ibid., p. 10.

6. I.M. Destler, *American Trade Politics,* p. 20.

7. Ibid., pp. 3–22.

8. Ibid., pp. 309–319. Used with permission from the Institute for International Economics

9. Thomas O. Bayard and Kimberly Ann Elliott, *Reciprocity and Retaliation in U.S. Trade Policy,* p. 19.

10. Ibid., pp. 33–34.

11. Ibid., p. 39.

12. Ibid., pp. 42–45.

13. Laura D'Andrea Tyson, *Who's Bashing Whom?* pp. 66–71.

14. Thomas O. Bayard and Kimberly Ann Elliott, *Reciprocity and Retaliation in U.S. Trade Policy,* p. 137.

15. Ibid., pp. 141–142.

16. Ibid., pp. 134–148.

17. José A. Mendez, "The Development of the Colombian Cut Flower Industry: A Textbook Example of How a Market Economy Works."

18. David E. Sanger, "U.S. Trade Panel Seeks Stiff Tariffs on Japan."

19. "U.S. Delays Details, But Turns Up Heat on Japan in Trade."

20. "Luxury-auto Inventories Drop."

21. "Japan, U.S. Reach Accord on Car Trade."

22. "No Targets in Car Deal, Hashimoto Promises."

23. "Japan, U.S. Reach Accord on Car Trade," p. 16.

24. "Text of Japanese-U.S. Announcement on Bilateral Car Accord," p. 4.

25. John Tagliabue, "How Europe Manages Car Trade," p. 19.

26. "Carmakers Will Boost Overseas Output," p. 1.

27. "What Will Carmakers Do? Head Abroad and Expand."

28. "Japan, U.S. Reach Accord on Car Trade."

29. I.M. Destler, *American Trade Politics,* pp. 166–169, 240–241.

30. Thomas O. Bayard and Kimberly Ann Elliott, *Reciprocity and Retaliation in U.S. Trade Policy,* p. 86.

31. Gary Clyde Hufbauer and Jeffrey J. Schott, *NAFTA: An Assessment,* p. 1.

32. Gary Clyde Hufbauer and Jeffrey J. Schott, *NAFTA: An Assessment.*

33. Peter Behr, "In the NAFTAmath, Some Texas-Sized Gains."

34. Jeffrey J. Schott and Johanna W. Buurman, *The Uruguay Round: An Assessment.*

35. Ibid., pp. 19–20.

36. "Text of the State of the Union Address," p. A14.

37. Kevin Sullivan, " 'Feeling Good,' and the Trade Talks Are Easy," p. A27.

38. Don Phillips and Sandra Sugawara, "U.S., Japan Settle Air Cargo Dispute"; Paul Blustein, "Weaker Computer Chip Agreement Called The Beginning of 'New Era' for U.S., Japan."

39. Paul Blustein, "Clinton Claims on Auto Trade Disputed.

40. Kevin Sullivan, " 'Feeling Good,' and the Trade Talks Are Easy"; Sandra Sugawara, "Land of the Rising Sum."

Notes for Chapter 5

1. Joel Garreau, *Edge City: Life on the New Frontier,* p. 5.

2. Max O. Stephenson, Jr., "The Policy and Premises of Urban Development Action Grant Program Implementation: A Comprehensive Analysis of the Carter and Reagan Presidencies," p. 19.

3. Large cities that did not meet the distress criteria could still apply for UDAG under the "pockets of poverty" provision.

4. Paul Gatons and Michael Brintnall, "Competitive Grants: The UDAG Approach," pp. 116–120.

5. U.S. General Accounting Office, *Urban Action Grants: A Review of Two San Antonio, Texas, Development Projects.*

6. Michael J. Rich, "UDAG, Economic Development, and the Death and Life of American Cities," p. 151.

7. U.S. Department of Housing and Urban Development, Office of Policy Development and Research, *An Impact Evaluation of the Urban Development Action Grant Program.*

8. Michael J. Rich, "UDAG, Economic Development, and the Death and Life of American Cities."

9. United States Joint Committee on Taxation, *General Explanation of the Economic Recovery Tax Act of 1981.*

10. Irving L. Blackman, *The New Depreciation Rules . . . A Tax Gold Mine,* p. c.

11. Ibid., pp. 1–2.

12. This was changed to 18 years in 1984 and 19 years in 1985.

13. The option of straight-line recovery was permitted. Recovery periods available were 15, 35, or 45 years.

14. Irving L. Blackman, *The New Depreciation Rules . . . A Tax Gold Mine,* pp. 1–25.

15. Gailen L. Hite and Raymond J. Krasniewski, "The 1981 Tax Act: Cost Recovery Choices for Real Property," p. 204.

16. Ibid.

17. Robert Veres, "The Sunset Hour," pp. 62–63.

18. California Department of Real Estate, *The Impacts of Tax Reform on Real Estate Investment in California*, p. 19.

19. Donald R. Epley, *Highlights of the 1986 Tax Reform Act and Its Impact on Real Estate*.

20. James R. Barth, *The Great Savings and Loan Debacle*; L. William Seidman, *Full Faith and Credit*.

21. National Commission on Financial Institution Reform, Recovery, and Enforcement, *Origins and Causes of the S&L Debacle: A Blueprint for Reform*, pp. 40–41.

22. James M. Poterba, "Taxation and Housing Markets: Preliminary Evidence of the Effects of Recent Tax Reforms," pp. 147–153.

Notes for Chapter 6

1. Jacques S. Gansler, *The Defense Industry*.

2. George C. Lodge, review of *The Ethical Basis of Economic Freedom*, quoted in Jacques S. Gansler, *The Defense Industry*, p. 29.

3. John Mintz, "Aircraft Firms Go Wing to Wing in a $750 Billion Dogfight."

4. Glenn R. Pascall and Robert D. Lamson, *Beyond Guns and Butter: Recapturing America's Economic Momentum after a Military Decade*, pp. 65–73.

5. Ian McIntyre, *Dogfight: The Transatlantic Battle over Airbus*, pp. 117–126.

6. Glenn R. Pascall and Robert D. Lamson, *Beyond Guns and Butter*, pp. 71–77.

7. Ibid.

8. Defense Science Board, Final Report of the 1988 Summer Study, *The Defense Industry and Technology Base*, p. 47.

9. Ibid., p. 55.

10. Lester Thurow, *The Zero-Sum Solution: Building a World-Class American Economy*, p. 268.

11. Glenn R. Pascall and Robert D. Lamson, *Beyond Guns and Butter*, pp. 87–89.

12. Ibid., p. 102.

13. Thomas G. Donlan, "Redoubtable DARPA: It Shapes the Future of U.S. Technology."

14. Kristin Knauth, "Rethinking America's Technology Policy."

15. Breck W. Henderson, "DARPA Invests $4 Million as Venture Capital in High-Technology Companies."

16. But as President Bush was slapping down ARPA with one hand, he was increasing the technological commitment to Commerce with the other. Thanks to George Bush, Commerce now has an Advanced Technology Program that provides seed money for path-breaking innovations. And his nascent Technology Administration increased its efforts to commercialize research performed in federal labs. Kristin Knauth, "Rethinking America's Technology Policy."

17. "Uncle Sam's Helping Hand."

18. David P. Angel, *Restructuring for Innovation: The Remaking of the U.S. Semiconductor Industry,* pp. 65–76.

19. Ibid., p. 157.

20. Ibid.

21. Peter Grindley, David C. Mowery, and Brian Silverman, "SEMATECH and Collaborative Research: Lessons in the Design of High-Technology Consortia," p. 729.

22. Michael J. Kelly, Telephone interview.

23. Ibid.

24. Ibid., 729–730.

25. David P. Angel, *Restructuring for Innovation,* p. 169.

26. Ibid., pp. 169–173.

27. Peter Grindley, David C. Mowery, and Brian Silverman, "SEMATECH and Collaborative Research," p. 731.

28. Ibid., pp. 732–734.

29. David P. Angel, *Restructuring for Innovation,* p. 173.

30. James E. Gover, "Analysis of U.S. Semiconductor Collaboration," p. 111.

31. Peter Grindley, David C. Mowery, and Brian Silverman, "SEMATECH and Collaborative Research."

32. Vic Comello, "Is Sematech a Model for Global Competitiveness?" p. 28.

33. Craig I. Fields, "Statement Before the House Science, Space, and Technology Committee; Science Research and Technology Subcommittee," p. 96.

34. Ibid., pp. 94–104.

35. Dale Cripps, "The Next Generation of Television."

36. Jeffrey A. Hart, "The Politics of HDTV in the United States."

37. U.S. Congress, Office of Technology Assessment, *Assessing the Potential for Civil-Military Integration: Selected Case Studies,* p. 2.

38. Ibid., pp. 10–14.

39. U.S. Congress, Office of Technology Assessment, *Flat Panel Displays in Perspective,* p. 10.

40. Flat Panel Display Task Force, *Building U.S. Capabilities in Flat Panel Displays,* p. I-6.

41. U.S. Congress, Office of Technology Assessment, *Flat Panel Displays in Perspective,* pp. 50–59.

42. U.S. Congress, Office of Technology Assessment, *The Big Picture: HDTV and High Resolution Systems.*

43. Michael J. Kelly, Telephone interview.

44. James Fallows, "Flat Growth," p. 137.

45. Jeffrey A. Hart, "Policies of the Clinton Administration Toward the Advanced Display Industry: A Precedent-Setting Decision for U.S. Industrial Policy," p. 6.

46. U.S. Congress, Office of Technology Assessment, *Flat Panel Displays in Perspective,* pp. 75–79.

47. Ibid., p. 2.

48. Jeffrey A. Hart, "Policies of the Clinton Administration Toward the Advanced Display Industry: A Precedent-Setting Decision for U.S. Industrial Policy," pp. 7–8.

49. Ibid., p. 9.

50. James Fallows, "Flat Growth," p. 139.

51. George C. Lodge and Sharon Novak, "The Flat Panel Display Initiative."

52. Gary Chapman, "Push Comes to Shove on Technology Policy," p. 44.

53. Gary Chapman, "Push Comes to Shove on Technology Policy."

54. George C. Lodge and Sharon Novak, "The Flat Panel Display Initiative," p. 14.

Notes for Chapter 7

1. Bob Davis, "White House and Auto Makers Prepare Joint Effort to Triple Fuel Efficiency."

2. William J. Clinton and Albert Gore, Jr., "Technology for America's Economic Growth, A New Direction to Build Economic Strength," p. 33.

3. Partnership for a New Generation of Vehicles, *Program Plan, 1994*, p. 2.

4. Partnership for a New Generation of Vehicles, *Program Plan, 1995*, p. 5–2.

5. Ibid., p. 5–3.

6. "USCAR Consortia: Stepping Stones to PNGV."

7. Statement of John F. Williams in *Electric Vehicles and Advanced Battery R&D*, p. 60.

8. U.S. House of Representatives, Hearings Before the Subcommittee on Science, Space, and Technology, *Electric Vehicles and Advanced Battery R&D*.

9. Statement of John F. Williams in *Electric Vehicles and Advanced Battery R&D*.

10. Cary Gravatt, Personal interview.

11. Partnership for a New Generation of Vehicles, *Program Plan, 1994*.

12. Cary Gravatt, Personal interview.

13. Ibid.

14. Partnership for a New Generation of Vehicles, *Program Plan*, 1994, p. 27.

15. Cary Gravatt, Personal interview.

16. Partnership for a New Generation of Vehicles, *Inventions Needed for PNGV*.

17. Yam provides a useful cost and performance comparison: Liquid helium costs about $4 per liter and undergoes rapid boil-off. Liquid nitrogen costs about 10 cents per liter ("cheaper than Kool-Aid") and lasts nearly 60 times as long as liquid helium at the same heat load. Philip Yam, "Current Events: Trends in Superconductivity."

18. U.S. Office of Technology Assessment, *High-Temperature Superconductivity in Perspective*; Richard E. Morrison, *Superconductivity Research and Development Activities in U.S. Industry: 1987 and 1988*; Gerald Hane, *Research and Development Consortia and Cooperative Relationship in Japan's Superconductivity Industry*.

19. U.S. Office of Technology Assessment, *High-Temperature Superconductivity in Perspective*; *Ceramic Bulletin* "High-Temperature Superconductivity: Who Will Win?"; CSAC, "A National Program for U.S. Market Leadership in Superconducting Energy Systems."

20. Electric Power Research Institute, *A National Program for the Superconducting Electric Power System of the Future*.

21. ISIS, "Towards Wider Commercialization of Superconductivity."

22. White House Office of Science and Technology Policy, *Federal Research Program in Superconductivity.*

23. American Superconductor considers Sumitomo its main competitor.

24. Clement Tisdell, *Science and Technology Policies: Priorities of Governments*; Harvy Averch, *A Strategic Analysis of Science and Technology Policy.*

25. Daniel Okimoto, *Between MITI and the Market: Japanese Industrial Policy for High Technology.*

26. Paul Stoneman, *The Economic Analysis of Technology Policy.*

Notes for Chapter 8

1. Otis L. Graham, Jr., *Losing Time,* p. 6.

2. Kenan Patrick Jarboe, "A Reader's Guide to the Industrial Policy Debate," pp. 200–203.

3. Clyde V. Prestowitz, Jr., *Trading Places,* p. 65.

4. Glenn R. Pascall and Robert D. Lamson, *Beyond Guns and Butter,* p. 102.

5. Ibid., pp. 71–77.

6. Jeffrey A. Hart, "Policies of the Clinton Administration Toward the Advanced Display Industry: A Precedent-Setting Decision for U.S. Industrial Policy," pp. 7–8.

7. Laura D'Andrea Tyson, *Who's Bashing Whom?* pp. 2–3.

8. Robert McGough, "Sweet Charity."

9. Kevin Sullivan, " 'Feeling Good,' and the Trade Talks Are Easy," p. A27.

10. Clyde V. Prestowitz, Jr., *Trading Places,* p. 230.

11. Ibid., pp. 233–235.

12. Ibid., p. 235.

13. Michael E. Porter, *The Competitive Advantage of Nations.*

14. Ibid., pp. 12–13.

15. Ibid., pp. 617–682.

16. Paul Krugman, *Peddling Prosperity: Economic Sense and Nonsense in the Age of Diminished Expectations.*

17. Paul Krugman, *Pop Internationalism.*

18. Paul Krugman, *Peddling Prosperity,* pp. 250–267.

19. Paul Krugman, *Pop Internationalism,* p. 5.

20. Ibid.

21. Ibid., p. 9.

22. Ibid., pp. 3–23.

23. Ibid., p. 30.

24. Ibid., p. 31.

25. Ibid., p. 94.

26. Ibid., p. 98.

27. James Brander and Barbara Spencer, "Export Subsidies and International Market Share Rivalry."

28. Paul Krugman, *Pop Internationalism,* p. 110.

29. Ibid., p. 113.

30. Murray Weidenbaum, "Sponsoring Research and Development," p. 46.

31. David Birch, *Job Creation in America: How Our Smallest Companies Put the Most People to Work,* p. 18.

32. George C. Lodge and Sharon Novak, "The Flat Panel Display Initiative," pp. 9–12.

33. Emmett S. Redford, *American Government and the Economy,* pp. 371–394.

34. Clyde V. Prestowitz, Jr., *Trading Places,* pp. 235–236.

Notes to the Appendix

The author wishes to thank Professor Koji Sato of Kanagawa University for comments on this appendix. Errors, of course, are the author's alone. Note: Japanese names are presented in the Western manner with the given name first and the surname last.

1. Clyde V. Prestowitz, Jr., *Trading Places,* p. 34.

2. Eugene Kaplan, *Japan.*

3. Hugh Patrick and Henry Rosovsky (eds.), *Asia's New Giant.*

4. William R. Nester, *Japanese Industrial Targeting,* pp. 4–5.

5. Takashi Inoguchi and Tomoaki Iwai, *"Zoku Giin" No Kenkyu* in William R. Nester, *Japanese Industrial Targeting,* p. 27.

6. Seizaburo Sato and Matsuzaki Tetsuhisa, *Jiminto Seiken* in William R. Nester, *Japanese Industrial Targeting,* p. 27.

7. William R. Nester, *Japanese Industrial Targeting,* p. 29.

8. Ibid., pp. 31–32.

9. David Bobrow and Stephen Chan, "Assets, Liabilities, and Strategic Conduct," p. 51.

10. George C. Lodge, *Perestroika for America,* p. 31.

11. Chalmers Johnson, *MITI and the Japanese Miracle,* pp. 52–53.

12. Ibid., pp. 58–59.

13. Ibid., pp. 63–71.

14. "Few objections are possible when administrative guidance is couched in terms of the national interest." Ibid., p. 266.

15. Ibid.

16. Industrial rationalization means state intrusion into the detailed operations of individual firms in the industry being justified as an attempt to improve the firms' operations (or even to abolish the enterprises). Ibid., p. 27.

17. Kent E. Calder, *Crisis and Compensation.*

18. David Friedman, *The Misunderstood Miracle.*

19. Richard J. Samuels, *The Business of the Japanese State.*

20. Clyde V. Prestowitz, Jr., *Trading Places,* p. 33.

21. Ibid., pp. 33–36.

22. George C. Lodge, *Perestroika for America,* pp. 76–78.

23. Gene A. Gregory and Akio Etori, "Japanese Technology Today."

24. Clyde V. Prestowitz, Jr., *Trading Places,* pp. 40–55.

25. For example, David Freidman, *The Misunderstood Miracle.*

26. David J. Collis, "The Machine Tool Industry and Industrial Policy, 1955–82."

27. Ibid., p. 102.
28. William Nester, *Japanese Industrial Targeting*, p. 207.
29. Ibid., p. 44.
30. Ibid., p. 45–62.
31. Ibid., p. 62.
32. Ibid., pp. 62–69.
33. Mark Schreiber, "Imports Start to Shake Japan's Consumer Markets."
34. William R. Nester, *Japanese Industrial Targeting*, p. 66.
35. Ibid., pp. 69–76.
36. Chalmers Johnson, *MITI and the Japanese Miracle*, p. 287.
37. Ibid., pp. 287–288.
38. George R. Packard, "The Coming U.S.-Japan Crisis."
39. Ryutaro Komiya, Masahiro Okuno, and Kotaro Suzumura (eds.), *Industrial Policy of Japan*.
40. Ryutaro Komiya, "Introduction," in Ibid., pp. 1–22.
41. Ibid., p. 11.
42. Ibid., p. 12.
43. The hierarchy is much like the two, three, and four digits of the Standard Industrial Code (SIC) of the United States.
44. Ken'ichi Imai, "Industrial Policy and Technological Innovation," in Ryutaro Komiya, Mashairo Okuno, and Kotaro Suzumura (eds.), *Industrial Policy of Japan*.
45. Masami Tanaka, "Government Policy and Biotechnology in Japan," in Stephen Wilks and Maurice Wright (eds.), *The Promotion and Regulation of Industry in Japan*.
46. Chalmers Johnson, *Japan: Who Governs?* pp. 183–231.
47. Ibid., p. 231.
48. Kevin Sullivan, "Assertive New Face on Japan's Future."
49. Koji Sato, "Regional Industrial Policy and the Role of Prefectural Government in Japan Supporting Knowledge-Intensive and Technology-Intensive Industries," p. 34.
50. Sheridan Tatsuno, "Building a Japanese Technostate," in Raymond W. Smilor, George Kozmetsky, and David V. Gibson (eds.), *Creating the Technopolis*.
51. Takao Kubo, Personal interview.
52. Michael Borrus and Jeffrey Hart, "Display's the Thing."
53. Ibid., p. 43.
54. " 'Plasmatron' Set Developed by Sony," p. 10.
55. Clyde V. Prestowitz, Jr., *Trading Places*, pp. 115–121.

Bibliography

Aber, Jack W., "Continental Illinois Corporation" (Boston, MA: Boston University School of Management, 1985).

Angel, David P., *Restructuring for Innovation: The Remaking of the U.S. Semiconductor Industry* (New York: Guilford Press, 1994).

Averch, Harvey, *A Strategic Analysis of Science and Technology Policy* (Baltimore, MD: The Johns Hopkins University Press, 1985).

Barth, James R., *The Great Savings and Loan Debacle* (Washington, DC: AEI Press, 1991).

Bayard, Thomas O., and Kimberly Ann Elliott, *Reciprocity and Retaliation in U.S. Trade Policy* (Washington, DC: Institute for International Economics, 1994).

Behr, Peter, "In the NAFTAmath, Some Texas-Sized Gains," *Washington Post National Weekly Edition* (August 29–September 4, 1994), p. 19.

Bhagwati, Jagdish, "Aggressive Unilateralism: An Overview," in Jagdish Bhagwati and Hugh T. Patrick (eds.), *Aggressive Unilateralism: America's 301 Trade Policy and the World Trading System* (Ann Arbor, MI: University of Michigan Press, 1990).

Bingham, Richard D., and John P. Blair (eds.), *Urban Economic Development* (Beverly Hills, CA: Sage, 1984).

Birch, David, *Job Creation in America: How Our Smallest Companies Put the Most People to Work* (New York: Free Press, 1987).

Blackman, Irving L., *The New Depreciation Rules . . . A Tax Gold Mine* (Chicago: Blackman, Kallick, 1984).

Blustein, Paul, "Clinton Claims on Auto Trade Disputed," *Washington Post* (April 12, 1996), pp. F1, F8.

———, "Weaker Computer Chip Agreement Called the Beginning of 'New Era' for U.S., Japan," *Washington Post* (August 3, 1996), pp. F1, F7.

Bobrow, David, and Stephen Chan, "Assets, Liabilities, and Strategic Conduct:

Status Management by Japan, Taiwan, and South Korea," *Pacific Focus* 1 (January 1986), pp. 23–55.

Borrus, Michael, and Jeffrey A. Hart, "Display's the Thing: The Real Stakes in the Conflict over High-Resolution Displays," *Journal of Policy Analysis and Management* 13 (Spring 1994), pp. 21–54.

Bowman, Lee, "Budget-cutting Theories Come in Many Flavors," (Cleveland) *Plain Dealer* (March 31, 1995), p. 4–A.

Braga, Carlos Alberto Primo, and Simão Davi Silber, "Brazilian Frozen Concentrated Orange Juice: The Folly of Unfair Trade Cases," in J. Michael Finger and Nellie T. Artis (eds.), *Antidumping: How It Works and Who Gets Hurt* (Ann Arbor, MI: University of Michigan Press, 1993), pp. 83–101.

Brander, James A., and Barbara J. Spencer, "Export Subsidies and International Market Share Rivalry," *Journal of International Economics* 18 (February 1985), pp. 83–100.

Brownstein, Ronald, "Clinton Drawing Visionary Blueprint of Global Economy," *Los Angeles Times* (December 5, 1994).

Business Week, "America's Restructure Economy," *Special Issue* (June 1, 1981), pp. 55–100.

———, "The Reindustrialization of America (New York: McGraw-Hill, 1992). Based on a special issue of *Business Week* (June 30, 1980), pp. 55–146.

Calder, Kent E., *Crisis and Compensation: Public Policy and Political Stability in Japan 1949–1986* (Princeton, NJ: Princeton University Press, 1988).

California Department of Real Estate, *The Impacts of Tax Reform on Real Estate Investment in California* (Sacramento, CA: California Department of Real Estate, December 1991).

"Carmakers Will Boost Overseas Output," *Japan Times* (June 30, 1995), pp. 1, 16.

Ceramic Bulletin, "High-Temperature Superconductivity: Who Will Win?" vol. 69 (July 1990), pp. 1110–12.

Chamberlain, John, *The American Stakes* (New York: Carrick and Evans, 1941).

Chapman, Gary, "Push Comes to Shove on Technology Policy," *Technology Review* 95 (November–December 1992), pp. 43–49.

Choate, Pat, and Garfield Schwartz, *Being Number One* (Lexington, MA: Lexington Books, 1980).

Clinton, William J., and Albert Gore, Jr., "Technology for America's Economic Growth, A New Direction to Build Economic Strength" (February 22, 1993).

"Clinton Signs Farm Measure Ending Subsidies," *Washington Post* (April 5, 1996), p. A15.

Collis, David J., "The Machine Tool Industry and Industrial Policy, 1955–82," in A. Michael Spence and Heather A. Hazard (eds.), *International Competitiveness* (Cambridge, MA: Ballinger, 1988), pp. 75–114.

Comello, Vic, "Is Sematech a Model for Global Competitiveness?" *R&D Magazine* (October 25, 1993), pp. 25–26, 28.

Copp, E. Anthony, *Regulating Competition in Oil: Government Intervention in the U.S. Refining Industry, 1948–1975* (College Station, TX: Texas A&M University Press, 1976).

Council on Superconductivity for American Competitiveness (CSAC), "A National Program for U.S. Market Leadership in Superconducting Energy Systems Addressing: Industrial Competitiveness (Washington, DC: Council on Superconductivity for American Competitiveness, 1994).

Cripps, Dale, "The Next Generation of Television," *HDTV Newsletter,* obtained on May 1, 1997, http://www.fedele.com/website.hdtv.

Davis, Bob, "White House and Auto Makers Prepare Joint Effort to Triple Fuel Efficiency," *Wall Street Journal* (September 29, 1993), p. 1.

Day, Kathleen, *S&L Hell: The People and the Politics Behind the $1 Trillion Savings and Loan Scandal* (New York: Norton, 1993).

"Decontrol in Works for Car Inspections," *Japan Times* (June 10, 1995), p. 16.

Defense Science Board, Final Report of the 1988 Summer Study, *The Defense Industry and Technology Base* (Washington, DC: Office of the Undersecretary of Defense for Acquisition, October 1988).

Destler, I.M., *American Trade Politics,* 3rd ed. (Washington, DC: Institute for International Economics, 1995).

Donlan, Thomas G., "Redoubtable DARPA: It Shapes the Future of U.S. Technology," *Barron's* (April 3, 1989), pp. 14–15, 18, 20, 22.

Economic Report of the President: Transmitted to the Congress February, 1995 (Washington, DC: Government Printing Office, 1995).

Economic Report of the President: Transmitted to the Congress February, 1992 (Washington, DC: Government Printing Office, 1992).

Electric Power Research Institute, *A National Program for the Superconducting Electric Power System of the Future* (Palo Alto, CA: Electric Power Research Institute, 1991).

Electric Power Research Institute (EPRI), *A National Program for the Superconducting Electric Power System of the Future,* prepared by the Ad Hoc Industry Working Group on Power Applications of High-Temperature Superconductors (Palo Alto, CA: Electric Power Research Institute, 1991).

Epley, Donald R., *Highlights of the 1986 Tax Reform Act and Its Impact on Real Estate* (Chicago, IL: Society of Real Estate Appraisers, 1987).

Ernst, Dieter, and David O'Connor, *Competing in the Electronics Industry: The Experience of Newly Industrializing Economies* (London: Pinter, 1992).

Etzioni, Amitai, *An Immodest Agenda: Rebuilding America Before the Twenty-First Century* (New York: New Press, 1983).

Fallows, James, "Flat Growth," *Atlantic Monthly* 274 (November 1994), pp. 134–139.

Federal Deposit Insurance Corporation (FDIC), *Final Report on the FDIC/RTC Transition* (Washington, DC: Federal Deposit Insurance Corporation, December 29, 1995).

Fields, Craig I., "Statement Before the House Science, Space, and Technology Committee; Science Research and Technology Subcommittee," in U.S. Congress, House, *High Definition Television,* Hearing Before the Committee on Science, Space, and Technology, One Hundred and First Congress, First Session, March 22, 1989 (Washington, DC: Government Printing Office, 1989), pp. 94–104.

Finger, J. Michael, "Reform," in J. Michael Finger and Nellie T. Artis (eds.), *Antidumping: How It Works and Who Gets Hurt* (Ann Arbor, MI: University of Michigan Press, 1993), pp. 57–79.

Finger, J. Michael, and Nellie T. Artis (eds.), *Antidumping: How It Works and Who Gets Hurt* (Ann Arbor, MI: University of Michigan Press, 1993).

Flat Panel Display Task Force, *Building U.S. Capabilities in Flat Panel Displays* (Washington, DC: U.S. Department of Defense, September 30, 1994).

Freidman, David, *The Misunderstood Miracle: Industrial Development and Political Change in Japan* (Ithaca, NY: Cornell University Press, 1988).

Galambos, Louis, and Joseph Pratt, *The Rise of the Corporate Commonwealth: U.S. Business and Public Policy in the Twentieth Century* (New York: Basic Books, 1988).

Gansler, Jacques S., *The Defense Industry* (Cambridge, MA: MIT Press, 1980).

Garreau, Joel, *Edge City: Life on the New Frontier* (New York: Doubleday, 1991).

Gatons, Paul, and Michael Brintnall, "Competitive Grants: The UDAG Approach," in Richard D. Bingham and John P. Blair (eds.), *Urban Economic Development* (Beverly Hills, CA: Sage, 1984), pp. 115–140.

Gover, James E., "Analysis of U.S. Semiconductor Collaboration," *IEEE Transactions in Engineering Management* 40 (May 1993), pp. 104–112.

Graham, Otis L., Jr., *Losing Time: The Industrial Policy Debate* (Cambridge, MA: Harvard University Press, 1992).

Gravatt, Cary, Assistant to the Director, National Institute of Standards and Technology, U.S. Department of Commerce. Former Executive Secretary, Partnership for a New Generation of Vehicles, Office of the Under Secretary for Technology, U.S. Department of Commerce. Personal interview. June 25, 1996. Atlanta, GA.

Greenwald, Douglas (ed.), *The McGraw-Hill Encyclopedia of Economics,* 2nd ed. (New York: McGraw-Hill, 1996).

Gregory, Gene A., and Akio Etori, "Japanese Technology Today," *Scientific American* (October 1981), pp. 15–46.

Greider, William, *Secrets of the Temple* (New York: Simon & Schuster, 1987).

Grindley, Peter, David C. Mowery, and Brian Silverman, "SEMATECH and Collaborative Research: Lessons in the Design of High-Technology Consortia," *Journal of Policy Analysis and Management* 13 (Fall 1994), pp. 723–758.

Gugliotta, Guy, "Congress Passes Bill Dropping Agriculture Subsidies," *Washington Post* (March 29, 1996), p. A15.

———, "Hill Conferees Clear Major Farm Changes," *Washington Post* (March 22, 1996), pp. A1, A10.

Hamilton, Alexander, "Report on the Subject of Manufactures," in Arthur Harrison Cole (ed.), *Industrial and Commercial Correspondence of Alexander Hamilton* (New York: Augustus M. Kelley, 1968), pp. 247–320.

Hane, Gerald, *Research and Development Consortia and Cooperative Relationship in Japan's Superconductivity Industry* (Tokyo: National Institute of Science and Technology Policy, First Theory-Oriented Research Group, 1991).

Hart, Jeffrey A., "Policies of the Clinton Administration Toward the Advanced Display Industry: A Precedent-Setting Decision for U.S. Industrial Policy." A paper presented at the 16th Annual Meeting of the Association for Public Policy Analysis and Management, Chicago, IL, October 27–29, 1994.

———, "The Politics of HDTV in the United States," *Policy Studies Journal* 22 (Summer 1994), pp. 213–228.

Henderson, Breck W., "DARPA Invests $4 Million as Venture Capital in High-Technology Companies," *Aviation Week and Space Technology* 132 (April 30, 1990), p. 25.

Henderson, David R. *The Fortune Encyclopedia of Economics* (New York: Warner Books, 1993).

Hite, Gailen L., and Raymond J. Krasniewski, "The 1981 Tax Act: Cost Recovery Choices for Real Property," *Journal of the American Real Estate and Urban Economics Association* 10 (Summer 1982), pp. 200–208.

Hufbauer, Gary Clyde, and Jeffrey J. Schott, *NAFTA: An Assessment*, rev. ed. (Washington, DC: Institute for International Economics, 1993).

Imai, Ken'ichi, "Industrial Policy and Technological Innovation," in Komiya, Okuno, and Suzumora (eds.), *Industrial Policy of Japan*, pp. 205–229.

Inoguchi, Takashi, and Tomoaki Iwai, *"Zoku Giin"* (Tokyo: Nihon Keiza, Shinbuasha, 1987).

International Superconductivity Industry Summit (ISIS), "Towards Wider Commercialization of Superconductivity," Joint Communiqué of the 2nd International Superconductivity Industry Summit, May 1993.

"Japan, U.S. Reach Accord on Car Trade," *Japan Times* (June 30, 1995), pp. 1, 16.

Jarboe, Kenan Patrick, "A Reader's Guide to the Industrial Policy Debate," *California Management Review* 27 (Summer 1985), pp. 198–219.

Johnson, Chalmers, *Japan Who Governs? The Rise of the Developmental State* (New York: Norton, 1995).

——, *MITI and the Japanese Miracle: The Growth of Industrial Policy, 1925–1975* (Stanford, CA: Stanford University Press, 1982).

"Kantor and Hashimoto Pleased with 'Significant' Agreement," *Japan Times* (June 30, 1995), p. 4.

Kaplan, Eugene, *Japan: The Government-Business Relationship* (Washington, DC: Government Printing Office, 1972).

Kelly, Michael J., Northrup-Grumann Chair of Manufacturing and Design, California State University at Los Angeles; former Director of the Defense Manufacturing Office of the Defense Advanced Research Projects Agency. Telephone interview. August 16, 1996.

Knauth, Kristin, "Rethinking America's Technology Policy," *Business Tokyo* 6 (April 1992), pp. 20–23.

Knight, Jerry, and Joan Biskupic, "High Court Ruling May Add Billions to S&L Cleanup Cost," *Washington Post* (July 2, 1996), pp. A1, A9.

Komiya, Ryutaro, "Introduction," in Komiya, Okuno, and Suzumura (eds.), *Industrial Policy of Japan*, pp. 1–22.

Komiya, Ryutaro, Masahiro Okuno, and Kotaro Suzumura (eds.), *Industrial Policy of Japan* (Tokyo: Academic Press Japan, 1988).

Krugman, Paul, *Peddling Prosperity: Economic Sense and Nonsense in the Age of Diminished Expectations* (New York: Norton, 1994).

——, *Pop Internationalism* (Cambridge, MA: MIT Press, 1996).

——, "Targeted Industrial Policies: Theory and Evidence," Federal Reserve Bank of Kansas City, *Industrial Change and Public Policy: A Symposium Sponsored by the Federal Reserve Bank of Kansas City* (Kansas City: Federal Reserve Bank, 1983), pp. 123–155.

Kubo, Takao, President, Kanagawa Science Park, Kawashaki, Japan. Personal interview. June 15, 1995.

"Last-Minute Deal Averts a U.S.-Japan Trade War," *International Herald Tribune* (June 29, 1995), pp. 1, 12.

Lawrence, Robert Z., *Can America Compete?* (Washington, DC: Brookings, 1984).

Lodge, George C., *Perestroika for America: Restructuring U.S. Business–Government Relations for Competitiveness in the World Economy* (Boston, MA: Harvard Business School Press, 1990).

————, Review of *The Ethical Basis of Economic Freedom* (ed. by Ivan Hill), *New York Times* (October 24, 1976).

Lodge, George C., and Sharon Novak, "The Flat Panel Display Initiative," (Boston, MA: Harvard Business School, April 27, 1995).

Lustig, Nora, Barry P. Bosworth, and Robert Z. Lawrence (eds.), *North American Free Trade: Assessing the Impact* (Washington, DC: Brookings, 1992).

"Luxury-auto Inventories Drop," *Japan Times* (June 27, 1995), p. 10.

Markusen, Ann Roell, *Profit Cycles, Oligopoly, and Regional Development* (Cambridge, MA: MIT Press, 1985).

Markusen, Ann, Peter Hall, Scott Campbell, and Sabina Deitrick, *The Rise of the Gunbelt: The Military Remapping of Industrial America* (New York: Oxford, 1991).

McGough, Robert, "Sweet Charity," *Financial World* (April 4, 1989), pp. 26–27.

McIntyre, Ian, *Dogfight: The Transatlantic Battle over Airbus* (Westport, CT: Praeger, 1992).

McKenzie, Richard B., *Competing Visions: The Political Conflict over America's Economic Future* (Washington, DC: Cato Institute, 1985).

Mayer, Martin, *The Greatest-Ever Bank Robbery: The Collapse of the Savings and Loan Industry* (New York: Scribner's Sons, 1990).

Mendez, José A., "The Development of the Colombian Cut Flower Industry: A Textbook Example of How a Market Economy Works," in J. Michael Finger and Nellie T. Artis (eds.), *Antidumping: How It Works and Who Gets Hurt* (Ann Arbor, MI: University of Michigan Press, 1993), pp. 103–120.

Miller, James C., III, *The Economist as Reformer: Revamping the FTC, 1981–1985* (Washington, DC: American Enterprise Institute, 1989).

Mintz, John, "Aircraft Firms Go Wing to Wing in a $750 Billion Dogfight," *Washington Post* (February 27, 1996), pp. C1, C4.

Morrison, Richard E., *Superconductivity Research and Development Activities in US Industry: 1987 and 1988* (Washington, DC: National Science Foundation, Division of Science Resources Studies, 1990).

"NAFTA Aids Exports for 3 Countries," (Cleveland) *Plain Dealer* (August 19, 1994), p. 1–C.

"NAFTA: So Far, So Good," *Wall Street Journal* (October 28, 1994), p. R1.

National Commission on Financial Institution Reform, Recovery and Enforcement, *Origins and Causes of the S&L Debacle: A Blueprint for Reform* (Washington, DC: Government Printing Office, July 1993).

Nebbia v. New York, 291 U.S. 502 (1934).

Nester, William R., *Japanese Industrial Targeting: The Neomercantilist Path to Economic Superpower* (New York: St. Martin's Press, 1991).

"No Targets in Car Deal, Hashimoto Promises," *Japan Times* (July 1, 1995), p. 7.

Norton, R.D., "Industrial Policy and American Renewal," *Journal of Economic Literature* 24 (March 1986), pp. 1–40.

Nusser, Nancy, "U.S. Job Losses under NAFTA Haven't Turned Up," (Cleveland) *Plain Dealer* (November 25, 1994), p. 18–A.

Olson, James S., *Saving Capitalism: The Reconstruction Finance Corporation and the New Deal, 1933–1940* (Princeton, NJ: Princeton University Press, 1988).

Okimoto, Daniel, *Between MITI and the Market: Japanese Industrial Policy for High Technology* (Stanford, CA: Stanford University Press, 1989).

Packard, George R., "The Coming U.S.-Japan Crisis," *Foreign Affairs* (Winter 1987/88).

Partnership for a New Generation of Vehicles, *Program Plan* (Washington, DC: Department of Commerce, July 1994).

————, *Program Plan* (Washington, DC: Department of Commerce, November 29, 1995).

————, *Inventions Needed for PNGV* (Washington, DC: Government Printing Office, March 1995).

Pascall, Glean R., and Robert D. Lamson, *Beyond Guns and Butter: Recapturing America's Economic Momentum after a Military Decade* (Washington, DC: Brassey's, 1991).

Patrick, Hugh, and Henry Rosovsky (eds.), *Asia's New Giant: How the Japanese Economy Works* (Washington, DC: Brookings, 1976).

Pearce, David W. (ed), *The MIT Dictionary of Modern Economics,* 3rd ed. (Cambridge, MA: MIT Press, 1986).

Phillips, Don, and Sandra Sugawara, "U.S., Japan Settle Air Cargo Dispute," *Washington Post* (March 28, 1996), pp. D1, D12.

" 'Plasmatron' Set Developed by Sony," *Japan Times* (June 27, 1995), p.10.

Porter, Michael E., *The Competitive Advantage of Nations* (New York: Free Press, 1990).

Poterba, James M., "Taxation and Housing Markets: Preliminary Evidence of the Effects of Recent Tax Reforms," in Slemrod (ed.), *Do Taxes Matter? The Impact of the Tax Reform Act of 1986.*

Prestowitz, Clyde V., Jr., *Trading Places: How We Allowed Japan to Take the Lead* (New York: Basic Books, 1988).

Przeworski, Adam, and Henry Teune, *The Logic of Comparative Social Inquiry* (New York: Wiley, 1970; reprinted by Krieger Publishing, Malabar, FL 1985).

Pyatt, Rudolph A., "What-ifs Still Haunt the History of the S&L Crisis," *Washington Post (Washington Business)* (July 15, 1996).

Rayport, Jeffrey F., and George C. Lodge, "DARPA" (Boston, MA: Harvard Business School, February 14, 1990).

Redford, Emmett S., *American Government and the Economy* (New York: Macmillan, 1965).

Reed, Ingred W., "The Life and Death of UDAG: An Assessment Based on Eight Projects in Five New Jersey Cities," *Publius* 19 (Summer 1989), pp. 93–109.

Reich, Robert B., *The Next American Frontier* (New York: Penguin Books, 1983).

————, *The Work of Nations* (New York: Vintage Books, 1992).

Reich, Robert B., and John D. Donahue, *New Deals: The Chrysler Revival and the American System* (New York: Times Books, 1985).

Rich, Michael J., "UDAG, Economic Development, and the Death and Life of American Cities," *Economic Development Quarterly* 6 (May 1992), pp. 150–172.

Rohatyn, Felix, *The Twenty-Year Century: Essays on Economics and Public Finance* (New York: Random House, 1983).

Samuels, Richard J., *The Business of the Japanese State* (Ithaca, NY: Cornell University Press, 1987).

Sanger, David E., "U.S. Trade Panel Seeks Stiff Tariffs on Japan," (Cleveland) *Plain Dealer* (May 7, 1995), pp. 1–A, 17–A.

Sato, Koji, "Regional Industrial Policy and the Role of Prefectural Government in Japan Supporting Knowledge-Intensive and Technology-Intensive Industries," *Economic Review* 2 (Kanagawa University, Yokohama, Japan) (October 1994), pp. 33–55.

Sato, Seizaburo, and Matsuzaki Tetsuhisa, *Jiminto Seiken* (Tokyo: Chuo Koronsha, 1986).

Schmidt, Susan, "RTC Issues Additional Questions to Hillary Clinton in S&L Probe," *Washington Post* (January 3, 1996), p. A12.

Schott, Jeffrey J., and Johanna W. Buurman, *The Uruguay Round: An Assessment* (Washington, DC: Institute for International Economics, 1994).

Schreiber, Mark, "Imports Start to Shake Japan's Consumer Markets," *Japan Quarterly* (January–March 1995), pp. 33–43.

Schultze, Charles L., "Industrial Policy: A Dissent," *Brookings Review* (Fall 1983), pp. 3–12.

Schwab, Susan C., *Trade-Offs: Negotiating the Omnibus Trade and Competitiveness Act* (Boston, MA: Harvard Business School Press, 1994).

Seidman, L. William, *Full Faith and Credit: The Great S&L Debacle and Other Washington Sagas* (New York: Times Books, 1993).

Shepherd, William G., *Public Policies Toward Business,* 7th ed. (Homewood, IL: Richard D. Irwin, 1985).

Slemrod, Joel (ed.), *Do Taxes Matter? The Impact of the Tax Reform Act of 1986* (Cambridge, MA: MIT Press, 1990).

Smead, Elmer E., *Government Promotion and Regulation of Business* (New York: Appleton-Century-Crofts, 1969).

Smilor, Raymond W., George Kozmetsky, and David V. Gibson (eds.), *Creating the Technopolis: Linking Technology Commercialization and Economic Development* (Cambridge, MA: Ballinger, 1988).

"Statement by Larry Lynn, Director, Defense Advanced Research Projects Agency, Before the Subcommittee on Acquisitions and Technology, Senate Armed Services Committee," March 20, 1996

"Statement by Larry Lynn, Acting Director, Advanced Research Projects Agency, Before the Subcommittee on National Security, House Appropriations Committee," March 23, 1995.

Stephenson, Max O., Jr., "The Policy and Premises of Urban Development Action Grant Program Implementation: A Comprehensive Analysis of the Carter and Reagan Presidencies," *Journal of Urban Affairs* 9 (Winter 1987), pp. 19–35.

Sterling v. Constantine, 287 U.S. 378 (1932).

Stoneman, Paul, *The Economic Analysis of Technology Policy* (Oxford: Clarendon Press, 1987).

Storper, Michael, "Competitiveness Policy Options: The Technology-Regions Connection," *Growth and Change* 26 (Spring 1995), pp. 285–308.

Sugawara, Sandra, "Land of the Rising Sum," *Washington Post* (September 5, 1996), pp. D10, D12.

Sullivan, Kevin, "Assertive New Face on Japan's Future," *Washington Post* (January 12, 1996), pp. A17, A20.

————, " 'Feeling Good,' and the Trade Talks Are Easy," *Washington Post* (April 19, 1996), pp. A27–A28.

Tagliabue, John, "How Europe Manages Car Trade," *International Herald Tribune* (June 29, 1995), p.19.

Tasker, Peter, *The Japanese: A Major Exploration of Modern Japan* (New York: Dutton, 1987).

"Text of Japanese-U.S. Announcement on Bilateral Car Accord," *Japan Times* (June 30, 1995), p. 4.

"Text of the State of the Union Address," *Washington Post* (January 24, 1996), pp. A13–A14.

Thurow, Lester, *The Zero-Sum Society* (New York: Basic Books, 1980).

————, *The Zero-Sum Solution: Building a World-Class American Economy* (New York: Simon & Schuster, 1985).

————, *The Future of Capitalism: How Today's Economic Forces Shape Tomorrow's World* (New York: Morrow, 1996).

Tisdell, Clement, *Science and Technology Policies: Priorities of Governments* (London: Chapman and Hall Ltd., 1981).

Tyson, Laura D'Andrea, *Who's Bashing Whom? Trade Conflict in High-Technology Industries* (Washington, DC: Institute for International Economics, 1993).

"Uncle Sam's Helping Hand," *The Economist* 331 (April 2–8, 1994), pp. 77–79.

USCAR Consortia: Stepping Stones to PNGV," *Concerning Cars & Trucks* 7 (December 1994), p. 8.

U.S. Congress, Office of Technology Assessment, *Assessing the Potential for Civil-Military Integration: Selected Case Studies,* OTA-BP-ISS-158 (Washington, DC: Government Printing Office, September 1995).

————, *High-Temperature Superconductivity in Perspective* (Washington, DC: Government Printing Office, 1990).

————, *The Big Picture: HDTV and High Resolution Systems,* OTA-BP-CIT-64 (Washington, DC: Government Printing Office, June 1990).

————, *Flat Panel Displays in Perspective,* OTA-ITC-631 (Washington, DC: Government Printing Office, September 1995).

"U.S. Delays Details, but Turns Up Heat on Japan in Trade," (Cleveland) *Plain Dealer* (May 11, 1995), p. 1–C.

U.S. Department of Defense, *SMES: Superconducting Magnetic Energy Storage,* prepared by Office of Technology Applications, Ballistic Missile Defense Organization (Washington, DC: U.S. Department of Defense, 1993).

U.S. Department of Energy, *Superconductivity Program for Electric Power System: FY 1994–1998 Multi-year Plan* (Washington, DC: Department of Energy, Office of Utility Technologies, 1994).

U.S. Department of Housing and Urban Development, Office of Policy Development and Research, *An Impact Evaluation of the Urban Development Action Grant Program* (Washington, DC: U.S. Department of Housing and Urban Development, January 1982).

U.S. General Accounting Office (GAO), *Urban Action Grants: An Analysis of Eligibility and Selection Criteria and Program Results* (Washington, DC: GAO, July 1989).

————, *Urban Action Grants: A Review of Two San Antonio, Texas, Development Projects* (Washington, DC: GAO, 1986).

U.S. Joint Committee on Taxation, *General Explanation of the Economic Recovery Tax Act of 1981* (December 29, 1981).

————, *General Explanation of the Tax Reform Act of 1986* (May 4, 1987).

U.S. House of Representatives, Hearings Before the Subcommittee on Energy of the Committee on Science, Space, and Technology, U.S. House of Representatives, One Hundred Third Congress, Second Session, June 30, 1994, *Electric Vehicles and Advanced Battery R&D* (Washington, DC: Government Printing Office, 1995).

Veres, Robert, "The Sunset Hour," *Financial Planning* 15 (July 1986), pp. 56–65.

Webman, Jerry A., "UDAG: Targeting Urban Economic Development," *Political Science Quarterly* 96 (Summer 1981), pp. 189–207.

Weidenbaum, Murray, "Sponsoring Research and Development," *Society* 29 (July–August 1992), pp. 39–47.

"What Will Carmakers Do? Head Abroad and Expand," *International Herald Tribune* (June 29, 1995), pp. 1, 12.

White House Office of Science and Technology Policy, *Federal Research Program in Superconductivity,* prepared by the Materials Technology Subcommittee, Communication Group on Superconductivity (Washington, DC: White House Office of Science and Technology Policy, 1994).

Wilks, Stephen, and Maurice Wright (eds.), *The Promotion and Regulation of Industry in Japan* (New York: St. Martin's Press, 1991).

Yam, Philip, "Current Events: Trends in Superconductivity," *Scientific American* vol. 269 (December 1993).

Index

Richard D. Bingham teaches economic development at the Levin College of Urban Affairs, Cleveland State University, where he is also the Senior Research Scholar of the Urban Center. He has written widely in the fields of economic development and urban studies. His latest books include *Dilemmas of Urban Economic Development,* edited with Rob Mier, and *Global Perspectives on Economic Development,* edited with Edward Hill. He is founding editor of the journal *Economic Development Quarterly,* and is president of the Urban Politics section of the American Political Science Association.